VISIONS OF HARMONY

ANNE TAYLOR

VISIONS OF HARMONY

A Study in Nineteenth-Century
Millenarianism

CLARENDON PRESS · OXFORD

1987

Oxford University Press, Walton Street, Oxford OX2 6DP

Oxford New York Toronto
Delhi Bombay Calcutta Madras Karachi
Petaling Jaya Singapore Hong Kong Tokyo
Nairobi Dar es Salaam Cape Town
Melbourne Auckland

and associated companies in
Beirut Berlin Ibadan Nicosia

Oxford is a trade mark of Oxford University Press

Published in the United States
by Oxford University Press, New York

British Library Cataloguing in Publication Data
Taylor, Anne
Visions of harmony: a study of nineteenth-
century millenarianism.
1. Millenarianism–United States–
History–18th century   2. Millenarianism
–United States–History–19th century
236'.3'0973   BR525
ISBN 0-19-211793-9

Library of Congress Cataloging in Publication Data
Taylor, Anne.
Visions of harmony.
Bibliography: p.   Includes index.
1. New Harmony (Ind.)–History–19th century.
2. Owen, Robert, 1771-1858.   3. Millennialism–Indiana–
New Harmony–19th century. I. Title.
HX656.N5T39   1986   335'.9772'34   86-16436
ISBN 0-19-211793-9

Typeset by Joshua Associates Limited, Oxford
Printed in Great Britain by
The Alden Press, Oxford

FOR NANCY GREENWAY

ACKNOWLEDGEMENTS

As a newcomer to the continuing history of New Harmony I am indebted to those more expert than I who gave me their unstinted advice. In particular Professor Karl J. R. Arndt was generous in his consent that I should draw upon his work for the purposes of this book. His knowledge of the Harmony Society is unrivalled and his enthusiasm for their way of life infectious.

A vast amount of material is to be found on both sides of the Atlantic. I have to thank the Trustees of the New Harmony Workingmen's Institute for permission to quote from the remarkable collection of papers there. The Librarian, Mrs Aline Cook, greatly eased my task of reading them, and I had the benefit of Mrs Josephine M. Elliott's comprehensive knowledge. I am most grateful for the hospitality at New Harmony of Mrs Jane Blaffer Owen and of Mrs William Glasford.

The Indiana Historical Society kindly gave me permission to quote from its numerous publications. I am grateful to John Hoffman, Librarian of the Illinois Historical Survey for copies of microfilm held at the University of Illinois at Urbana-Champaign. I must thank Mrs Katharine Haramundanis for permission to quote from the Garnett-Pertz Collection in the Houghton Library, Harvard. Miss Carol M. Spawn of the Academy of Natural Sciences of Philadelphia gave me a great deal of help. Quotations from the letters of Charles Lucien Buonaparte and of S. G. Morton appear by permission of the American Philosophical Society in the same city. I must also thank Professor Donald E. Pitzer of the Center for Communal Studies, University of Southern Indiana, Evansville; D. A. Hopple; and Ian MacPhail, Librarian of the Morton Arboretum at Lisle, Illinois.

Extracts from the Sidmouth Papers appear by permission of the Devon County Record Office. I am grateful to the Librarian of Newtown Public Library, of the Co-operative Union in Manchester, of the Signet Library, Edinburgh and of Nuffield College, Oxford. I have also to thank Professor J. F. C. Harrison; Mr Peter Barber; and Miss Angela White-legge of the Goldsmiths' Library, University of London. Finally this book is the product not only of its author's long and often despairing travail, but of the care of its editor, Peter Sutcliffe, whose faith in it prevailed.

CONTENTS

LIST OF ILLUSTRATIONS

PART I

THE PROPHET OF IPTINGEN

IMAGINARY TOWNS, REAL PLACES

O F all the qualities that went to the making of the American West imagination was supreme. Courage and patience might sustain the early settlers in the face of extreme physical hardship, but imagination was the spark to their energy and nourished their endurance. While the common dream was of prosperity in a new country, there were wilder ones that might more properly be called illusions. It was the extraordinary fate of the town of Harmony on the Wabash River in the State of Indiana to be the place where not one, but successive illusions were confronted by reality.

To fly at night over the country now is to be reminded of how it all began. A pattern of rectangular light stretches as far as the eye can see. It is made by the highways that follow imaginary lines drawn on a map 200 years ago. Lands taken from the Indians for sale and settlement by whites were marked out into square sections; the discipline was observed no matter how many parts each section yielded.

Some dreams failed to materialize. Towns sprang up and quickly disappeared. Those that survived owed their growth to intangible factors in a greater degree than was the case of the old established world. The west was so vast, so splendidly endowed with natural features, that purely geographical causes for the distribution of population counted for less on the frontier. When 100 shallow river crossings led to the sprawling Congress lands, it was often luck and a special enterprise that determined which huddle of log cabins at what landing would grow into a town.

At the beginning of the nineteenth century the land seemed limitless and so was relatively cheap. It was the people who gave it value. Wherever they appeared in any number the price of land rose. The vanguard of the western movement had been composed of white hunters who lived almost as simply as the Indians they displaced, and followed them back into the woods at the least threat of neighbours. Their desire to be left alone was respected but their isolation was acknowledged to be the reason why they would remain so miserably poor. Wherever people moved in with the intention of improving upon their old standard of life, it was quickly seen that the greater the number gathered together the more easily they would prosper. In this the family as a working group played an obvious and a crucial role; the question was what other means might be found to promote the desired result.

As subsistence farming did not content the majority of settlers for very long, they cast about for ways of improving their lot, but in the absence of capital and markets the choice was limited. Far too many chose to keep a store; their profit was precarious. Others put up travellers in varying degrees of dirt and discomfort. There were more lawyers than cases to be heard, 'agents' and land speculators galore. Anyone seen to be making money was certain to attract the undivided attention of his neighbours, and their respect, for they knew only too well how difficult making money was.

So in 1814, when a group of Swabian immigrants began to build the town of Harmony (or *Harmonie* as it was called at first) on the Wabash River in the Territory of Indiana, it became at once an object of curiosity. Its inhabitants were evidently prosperous, a consequence of their system of organization in which capital was associated with labour—a rare phenomenon anywhere then. To many people on both sides of the Allegheny Mountains and in Europe once they came to know of it, this system promised much, even a way of ending the exploitation of working people, the seemingly inevitable accompaniment to the Industrial Revolution. But what the onlookers did not at first understand—and there were some who never understood, with what consequences will be seen—the system was only a means to a remarkable end. *Harmonie* was very strange: an imaginary town in a real place, a mirage created by the group's leader, George Rapp, for only one purpose. It was to be a place in which to await the Second Coming of the Lord.

CHAPTER I

A PLACE PREPARED BY GOD

EXTREME religious fervour was to bring nearly 1,000 people to the tremendous and frightening course of abandoning their homeland, Württemberg, for Indiana at a time when it was a wilderness, far beyond the limit of the known world. They hoped that in so doing they would cheat man's common destiny, turn aside the wrath of God, and escape the consequences of original sin. They came from a part of Europe which for hundreds of years had been regularly shaken by such fantasies, some of which had given rise to the bloodiest of conflicts. The appearance of Separatist groups such as the Harmony Society, as this one was called, always posed a threat to the established order, and nowhere more than in the small states beside the Rhine in the old province of Swabia.

There discontent arising from social causes was peculiarly apt to find expression in forms of religion, which among the Southern Germans was by instinct and tradition warm, intense, emotional. In Württemberg where nearly all the members of the Harmony Society were born, religion lay like lees in wine, always ready to come up; whenever that occurred a threat was posed not only to the tranquillity of the Lutheran Church but also to the State, for both were united in the person of the Duke.

The particular emotion which gave rise to the exodus was as old as heresy itself. Sometimes its force was such as to propel its adherents out of the body of the Church altogether; sometimes the leaders of the Church were strong enough and sufficiently wise to contain the dissenters and reconcile them; at others the offence was deemed so great as to bring down excommunication and even death upon them. Whatever the effect, it proceeded from the same cause: an irresistible longing on the part of the individual for direct spiritual communication with Jesus Christ, without intervention of clergy, or interpolation of ritual.

Most European countries experienced this phenomenon, treating it with varying degrees of forbearance. In England its chief exponents, the Society of Friends, the Quakers, suffered harsh persecution before the principle of toleration was extended to them. In Germany it could be fanatical and bizarre, but by the mid-seventeenth century its manifestation was markedly restrained and its adherents received the name of Pietists. They remained a considerable affront to the Lutheran Church, nevertheless, and at the beginning of the eighteenth century a law was passed in Württemberg the intention of which was to deal gently with the dissidents in the hope of reconciling them to the established order. Outright condemnation was reserved for those preachers who offered to convert the people. The local clergy were to keep close watch on them; if they did not desist and recant they were to be exiled. The punishment was severe—Swabians were notoriously attached to their homeland. But it was intended to remove the source of disaffection from a people highly vulnerable to all kinds of enthusiasm. Anything more drastic would create martyrs, and that was something the authorities greatly feared.

George Rapp had been born in 1757 in the village of Iptingen, which was like all the other villages in the rolling country bordering on the Rhine. Low hills bore carefully tended vines and tidy orchards; there was scarcely room for pasture and none at all for waste ground. In the village half-timbered houses clustered together and round the church; there were no outlying dwellings. Strangers were rarely seen except perhaps the pastor coming to a new cure. George Rapp's father was a farmer, not prosperous, for whom his son worked in the fields in summer, learning to weave in the winter. It was the custom for the villagers to turn their hands to various trades, so that they were largely independent of the outside world. It was also a practice among young men—and Rapp was no exception—to wander for some years as a journeyman in their trade. A familiar blight lay on the Duchy. There were far too many people, no work, and insufficient land to feed them all. Even the most prosperous class of farmer, the vine-growers, needed extra arable land to support themselves in the years when the vintage was poor. They survived only by being far-sighted people, very hard working and frugal, and accustomed to putting by.

When Rapp was a young man they bore an extra burden in the person of their Duke who ruled for fifty years. Karl Eugen was a despot and revelled in the role. 'I am the nation and the image of God on earth', he declared. In his youth a libertine he was commonly said to have fathered enough illegitimate sons to found a regiment. He built preposterous gilded palaces in imitation of Versailles. One of his passions was for hunting and to this end he kept vast forests in which the game could roam freely but no peasant might go. His acquaintance, Casanova, said that his greatest pleasure was making people afraid of him. There is a scathing denunciation of Karl Eugen's court in Friedrich Schiller's play, *Kabale und Liebe*, in which the Duke is condemned for selling his subjects into military service under foreign rulers, a practice Karl Eugen adopted to raise money for his extravagances.

In such a climate patronage was the sole means of advancement, and corruption flourished even in the Church, a charge which, when his time came, Rapp did not hesitate to bring against its ministers. They could not bridge the chasm between the Duke and the more passionately devout of his subjects, and so it was that Separatist religious groups increased. One of these, at Tübingen, was led by a former butcher, Michael Hahn, whose acquaintance Rapp made during his journeyman years and who helped to awaken the force within him. Preachers like Hahn were invited to hold clandestine meetings in the farmers' houses; as one historian put it, belief fled from the cold church with its arid practices into the country parlour.

When he was in his twenties Rapp returned to Iptingen, married, and had two children, Johannes and Rosina. But as he told the church authorities at his first examination, as early as 1780 he was visited by a secret unrest, a desire to renounce the good things of life, dearly though he loved them. For some time he fought the temptation alone, receiving the compassion of Christ in the struggle, evidence of grace which deeply moved him. In 1785, in great agony of mind he went to Tübingen where he fell ill. It was then that Michael Hahn came to him and assured him that though he would go through many trials he would find Christ in the end. And said Rapp, 'I surrendered my will to God so that my will became His will, and His will my will.'

It was due to the vigilance of the Pastor of Iptingen that in April 1785 the 28-year-old journeyman weaver and his wife were brought before the ecclesiastical court. George and Christina Rapp were charged with absenting themselves from Holy Communion. It was a serious offence but not the gravest fault in Pastor Genter's eyes. He was convinced that Rapp intended a direct challenge to his own authority. Genter warned his superiors of the possibility of a new Separatist movement in the area, directed by Rapp. It was the beginning of a contest between the weaver and the Church leaders that lasted nearly twenty years and ended only when Rapp sought the wilderness in America.

Rapp's evidence was given not in a spirit of defence but as a ringing declaration of the revelation that had been vouchsafed to him. Genter used all the resources of his position and a superior education to under-mine Rapp, as many others were to do during his long life. But Rapp's knowledge of the Bible was profound, his use of its authority devastating, and his demeanour was so composed and confident that his opponents were quite outfaced. He told the court that after a time of doubt and trial he had experienced a spiritual rebirth. Christ had entered into him and would always be with him. Rapp had no more need of the intercession of the Church and so he had absented himself from Holy Communion. Christina stoutly supported her husband. That was why he stayed away from church, because there he found the power within him was diminished. Its ways were not strict enough for him.

The authorities took no action against him in 1785. Perhaps they hoped that left alone he would conduct his inner life quietly and in private as the Pietists did; if so they were mistaken. Two years later further charges were laid against him. He had caused dissension in the village by calling loyal church members hypocrites; he had abused the sacraments, saying the Lord's Supper was blasphemous, and called Sunday a Jewish Feast which need not be observed as a day of rest. He declared that everything in the Bible was a testimony of the Word that no one but he and his followers (now about a dozen) understood. He sneered at Pastor Genter and his fellow clergy as scholars who, having studied theology at great expense had altered by their scholarship the very nature of the church.

There was truth in this last charge. By then the spirit of the Enlightenment had so penetrated the Lutheran Church that some clergy preached a form of rationalism their congregations found uncongenial. According to one of the historians of the Harmony Society, at the time of Rapp's schism the Church presented a deplorable aspect. 'Philosophy had come, with its high sounding terminology and invaded the hallowed precincts of scriptural truth the pulpit became the rostrum whence the shepherdless masses were entertained with vague essays on such general themes as righteousness, human dignity, light, prayer, truth and right.' In their zeal for the new learning which admitted natural science to an equal place beside philosophy, some clerics delivered regular if laboured instructions to their congregation—farmers all—on how to raise cattle, bees, and fruit. But Rapp's attitude to the clergy was so offensive as to suggest a more personal reason for his hostility. As subsequent events were to show, his passion for knowledge was as great as his contempt for academic learning, and with it went a capacity to use this knowledge in practical affairs.

In 1787 Rapp was once again examined by the church authorities. On this occasion Genter accused him of wishing to form a church within a church and—most dangerously—a state within a state. There was substance in these charges for Rapp had deliberately set about taking sheep from Genter's flock. He visited the sick during the time of service, held meetings at his house, and in a little storehouse among the vines, on Sundays and in the evenings, when people were free to attend. Then he began to preach. Tall, straight, and vigorous, he made a striking figure in his black clothes and long black beard. People from the neighbouring villages walked over to Iptingen to hear him. He was fluent and commanding and spoke of stirring things; of repentance; of the inspiration of the Holy Ghost; of the corrupted spirit of the times and the coming ruin of the Church. 'Of all the preachers they heard there was none whose words had power to touch their hearts like those of Mr Rapp,' said one of his hearers. Genter's authority was further undermined when Rapp stressed the right of all men to celebrate Christ themselves in baptism, confirmation, and communion. Only he insisted that those who took part must have a clearer understanding of the meaning of such ceremonies than he thought they gained from Genter. He and some of his followers began to keep their children from school, saying that their 'simplicity' would be contaminated by other children. The fact that they baptized their new-born babies themselves was a civil misdemeanour of some importance, since no one could be confirmed who had not been lawfully baptized, and a certificate of confirmation was essential for legal marriage in Württemberg.

The Church authorities who examined him in 1787 found themselves in a dilemma, for many of the ideas that were disturbing Rapp's neighbours could not be dismissed as alien to the Church. Some were identical to those that Martin Luther preached, especially the doctrine of the priesthood of all believers and the longing for spiritual union with Christ. Rapp's answers on this occasion were marked by arrogance and by contempt for those who disagreed with him. He said he professed no particular religion, recognized no ecclesiastical law, and would swear no oath, though he would obey the civil government. Christ would save him and his followers; all others were doomed, even Michael Hahn for he would not denounce the 'Babel' that was the established church. Considering his arrogance and the threat of trouble he represented, the authorities dealt gently with him (far more so than, for instance, the English government did with the Quaker, George Fox). They warned him that if he persisted in his course, he and his followers would be exiled from Württemberg. To mark their disapproval of his offensive remarks they also decreed that Rapp must be imprisoned for two days. It was tantamount to putting him in the stocks, and it was a mistake, for it gave him a splendid opportunity to rally support. When he objected to the sentence, the official reading it bade him be silent, remarking that the prisoner was not called to be a prophet. On the contrary, Rapp replied, 'I am a prophet and am called to be one.'

After his brief imprisonment Rapp was left in peace for some years and the local clergy advised to ignore him. During that time his followers grew in number and cohesion and, in the quiet countryside, became conspicuous as a group, particularly after Rapp ordered the men to grow long flowing beards, an unusual sight at the time. They crowded into the small villages to hold love feasts—the *agape*—and to celebrate their own communion. Loyal members of the Church were disturbed by reports that they sang unusual songs, interpreted the Bible according to their own inspiration, and read mysterious books.

These books were not so much mysterious as mystical since they included works by the seventeenth-century writer, Jacob Boehme, whose inspiration touched, among others, the English Quakers; by the Pietists, Francke and Spener; and by Jung Stilling, in whose naïve and visionary pages the time of the Second Coming was precisely calculated. This event lay at the heart of George Rapp's belief and dominated his preaching. It was a symbol of what he most desired—grace to preserve himself and his disciples from the fate which, as a consequence of Adam's Fall, must engulf all but the chosen few. Rapp with his pride, his bursting energy, his love of life, and his awareness of unusual ability could not endure the thought that he, like others, must come to the miserable end fore-shadowed by the doctrine of original sin in which he firmly believed. As countless others did he sought a special dispensation.

He thought he saw a means of achieving this in Boehme's book which described Adam's state in the Garden of Eden before the Fall. Rapp understood that his task was to persuade his followers to shape their lives according to this ideal state. The process was complex, arduous, and took place over a considerable number of years. It called for the highest standard of conduct among its adherents, complete obedience to their leader's will (which, after all, was God's will), perfect love one to another, order in all their affairs, however trivial—in short an all pervading harmony. Since the Garden of Eden knew no kind of conflict the Rappites were forbidden to bear arms. And since, before Eve appeared, Adam contained within himself both male and female elements, the act of procreation was unknown. Hence the special respect given to those among Rapp's followers who abstained from the sexual act. In fact those who were most committed to him had no desire to bear children since they knew that the millennium would shortly commence.

Something that never failed to move Rapp's audience was the fact that he knew of a tremendous event that was about to happen in the world. This was his prophet's sceptre as the Bible was his orb, which he interpreted according to his need.

The hope of the millennium was part of Swabian folklore; in times of stress it was almost their only recourse. Baden, Württemberg, Konstanz, the countries of the Upper Rhine which made up the province of Swabia were so crowded as to be vulnerable to all kinds of disaster. Famine, pestilence and invading armies oppressed their people. So urgent was their need for refuge that, at different times, numbers of them set out for Palestine in the belief that it must afford them an actual place of salvation. That kind of faith lived by portents, of which death, disease, and war were the most convincing. The outbreak of the Revolution which swept away the existing order in France appeared the clearest indication of an approaching cataclysm. Hope that the Last Days had come revived all over Europe, but it swept like flames through Württemberg.

Now the terrifying language of the Book of Revelation thundered in Rapp's sermons; he grew in authority and compelled belief. The church officials spoke apprehensively of Munster and the Peasants' War when such ideas had brought disaster. While their backs were turned, they now realized, the Separatists round Iptingen had grown into a church and Rapp was their Bishop as he had always intended. Would he lead his congregation out of the enlightened eighteenth century back into the dark times of the sixteenth?

Matters came to a head in the first years of the new century when bitter complaints were renewed by loyal members of the church, affronted by *der Räpple*, the crazy one, the 'great seducer', whose relentless proselytizing set husbands against their wives and divided children from their parents. At the same time Rapp came into new conflict with the civil authorities. He refused to sanction military service by his followers. The question was once more a burning issue in Württemberg. Though Karl Eugen was long since dead the memory of his selling his subjects into foreign armies festered on. The present ruler, the Elector, wished to be made King. The title was at the disposal of the dictator of Europe, Napoleon Buonaparte, who thought to bestow it on the Elector in return for Württembergers to fight the enemies of France. There was much distaste for this old bad bargain to which the Rappites were furiously opposed.

Rapp's refusal to sanction military service was dangerous, and coincided with moves by his opponents in religion to appeal directly to the Elector for redress. In February 1803 the church authorities were obliged to act. Rapp was warned not to preach outside his village while the consistory set in motion a far-reaching investigation of the Separatists. In December the result of this was known; the recommendations were once again remarkable for their moderation. If their neighbours agreed the Separatists were to be excused military service on payment of a fine. They must send their children to school and have them baptized in church. No Separatist might hold public office. But long before this compromise was published Rapp had solved the problem it would have posed to his authority by disappearing.

In the summer of 1803 he and three others, including his son Johannes who was now grown up, made their way to America in search of a place to settle. As always the Bible was the authority for this decisive step. Rev. 12: 1 reads, 'And there appeared a great wonder in heaven, a woman clothed with the sun and the moon under her feet and upon her head a crown of twelve stars.' As all millennialists knew, this woman would bring forth a man child who would rule the world. But first she must sojourn in the wilderness, 'where she hath a place prepared by God.' According to Professor K. J. R. Arndt who has made a lifelong study of the Harmony Society, George Rapp took the symbol of the woman clothed with the sun to mean his congregation. The course was clear; he and his followers must seek the wilderness; they must leave Württemberg.

It was a bold and drastic step whose effect would be felt in the country round Iptingen for more than a generation. In the eighteen years since Rapp had announced his revelation his followers had come to be numbered in thousands. Ambition and determination, allied to a restlessly enquiring mind, and fused by a rare energy made him a natural leader. Within the group his conduct was marked by an embracing warmth which in spite of his relative youth—he was 46—inspired the Rappites to call him Father. During those years he had found time to pursue his studies; besides philosophy these included alchemy.

Though Rapp was accused of growing rich from the contributions of his followers, there is nothing to suggest that this was so. He was certainly more prosperous than his father had been but he ascribed this to hard work and fortunate harvests. Though each member of the group contributed as he was able to the expense of their meetings, and a common purse was maintained for the poor among them, there was no move to pool their resources further before they departed to America.

Before he sailed Father committed his disciples to the care of his adopted son, the 29-year-old Frederick Rapp. He was the second most remarkable person in the Harmony Society, wielding the temporal power on George Rapp's behalf, nearly always standing between him and the outside world. It was he who conducted all the Society's business once they had settled down, from the pinched early years to the time when it was well on the way to assembling a fortune in land, in goods, in silver specie. His sense and probity earned him respect among the merchants with whom he dealt; he was, besides, endowed with great practical ability. Yet this outward strength went with a religious emotion so profound that it sometimes bordered on hysteria. Little is known of his origin except that he was born Friedrich Reichert in 1775, and became a stonemason. Though he was not related to George Rapp he came to Iptingen in 1798 to live in his house and take his name. He had relations of his own but henceforth his whole existence centred on Rapp's family. It is in the letters that passed between George and Frederick Rapp that we learn so much about the fortunes of the Harmony Society in America.

Many years later, at Economy in Pennsylvania, the third town that he built, Father Rapp told a traveller how he came to choose the place of sanctuary. In 1802, he said, he wrote to Napoleon Buonaparte asking for permission to settle in that part of Louisiana on the lower Mississippi ruled by France. The First Consul, as he then was, occupied a special place in the Rappite pantheon, as he did among other millennialists. His activities on the battlefields of Europe enhanced their sense of time expired. Some saw him as the Beast itself while others hailed him as the warrior Christ descended to earth.

In 1800 that part of Louisiana which Spain occupied, including New Orleans, was retroceded to France. Two years later, according to George Rapp, Napoleon was only too pleased to grant him permission to settle there, but the Württemberg authorities put so many obstacles in his way that his plans were overtaken by the Louisiana Purchase. Why the transfer to American sovereignty caused him to change his mind is not known, but he went instead to Pennsylvania.

Landing at Baltimore in July 1803 Rapp spent a year riding over the State of Pennsylvania looking at land offered for sale. He was comforted in his wandering by the many Germans who still spoke and dressed and lived as his own people did. Many of them practised a similar belief, being descended from the religious dissidents who had come to the State in the seventeenth century at the special invitation of its English Quaker founder, William Penn. But they could not help Rapp to find land at a price he could afford east of the Allegheny Mountains. In those days its long barrier marked the division between the settled part of the United States and its largely empty interior. Rapp needed a sufficient acreage to grow food for nearly a thousand people, and he had to have a care for its climate and aspect since they proposed to earn their living by making wine, the skill they knew best.

The obstacles he encountered were described in a letter to Frederick Rapp, written in October 1803. Various parcels of land had been offered to him but most were too dear and all were widely scattered. Riding to see them was hard on him, he complained. The journey to America had also been hard, dangerous, and horribly long. Do not persuade anyone who is not already anxious to come, he warned Frederick. Yet some things found favour with him. The country people were polite, and kind to one another. Whoever was willing to work might become rich. There was religious freedom, and to be excused from military service cost $1 a year. Cattle and horses were larger than those in Württemberg, and women rode astride. To shoot the birds, which were wonderfully large, was to be able to eat, for game belonged to everyone.

Six months later he had to confess to Frederick that he did not yet know where God had prepared the place for them. The people in the newly-cultivated clearings where he went in search of land he could afford welcomed him, invited him to preach, and some times pressed him to stay. But he was very homesick; the year he set aside for his reconnaissance seemed to him interminable. He was tired, even frightened by the difficulties God had neglected to reveal to him before he set out.

The absence of his followers diminished him. As one who knew him in Württemberg said, he was a man of great daring and broad knowledge. Yet he was also immensely vain, requiring constant adulation to sustain him. Thus fortified he was steadfast, obstinate, obsessed, able to accomplish remarkable things by reason of his concentrated energy. Without it he was weak, nervous, a vulnerable stranger in a hostile land. This first unhappy experience far from home seems to have strengthened his determination to build a sure fortress for his religion that he would never willingly leave.

He went into Ohio to seek advice from John Heckewelder, a member of the *Unitas Fratrum*, the Moravian Brethren, whose entire life had been spent as a missionary among the Indians and who was probably better acquainted with the territory west of the Alleghenies than anyone else alive. Like Rapp, Heckewelder's life had been shaped by a peculiar religious discipline that owed something to German Pietism, but more to the enthusiasm of one individual; in his case the Saxon nobleman and religious fanatic, Count Zinzendorf. Heckewelder's parents had been among those Protestants forced to flee from Bohemia and Moravia in 1727 and who had found shelter at Herrnhut on the Count's estate. There, in due course, he formed the exiles into an order whose missionary zeal to convert savage peoples was as consuming as that of the Jesuits. In fact, the belief and attitudes taught to boys like Heckewelder at the Brethren's great teaching centre at Bethlehem in Pennsylvania, with its emphasis on a childlike innocence, sacrifice, and absolute subjugation to Almighty God, was rather similar to that which Rapp desired to instil in his followers. As such it accorded more nearly with the primitive beliefs and practices of the Indians than did the intellectual rigour of the Society of Jesus.

When George Rapp got to know them, the Moravian Brethren had abandoned some of the strict rules they had found it necessary to observe while building in the wilderness. During that time, for instance, they held all things in common, an arrangement they referred to as the 'divine Economy'. It did not survive long once they became prosperous. Like the Quakers, the Moravian Brethren became good businessmen while remaining loyal and pious members of their order. Several befriended George Rapp and sympathized with him in his dilemma.

With Heckewelder's advice Rapp found 40,000 acres of suitable land in Ohio. In July 1804 he travelled back to Washington where he called on Thomas Jefferson to ask for special terms to enable him to buy. Jefferson was obliged to point out that, even as President of the United States, he could not dispose of government land as if he were Elector of Württemberg. That was something only Congress could do. But he received George Rapp most kindly and wrote on his behalf to his Secretary of the Treasury, Albert Gallatin. If the Rappites went and sat down on the land of Ohio, the usual thing would happen, Jefferson said; speculators would come in and bid up the price. Could Treasury officials somehow prevent this until Congress had time to consider the matter? No, Gallatin replied, his officials would have nothing to do with it; he seemed embarrassed by Jefferson's request.

Rapp was now in a dreadful dilemma. Three weeks before Jefferson wrote to Gallatin 300 of his followers had arrived at Baltimore; in September two ships landed many more at Philadelphia, bringing the total to some 1,400. With them was Frederick Rapp.

He found the task of organizing the mass emigration agonizing. His letters to his adopted father were full of frantic images, jumbled prophecies of war, disease and death, the doom which he and his companions believed would soon fall on Württemberg. A kind of terror, a dreadful urgency accompanied Frederick's preparations to lead the people to America. He had an additional burden to bear, of being stigmatized as an instrument that broke up families. For in the ancient villages round Iptingen this is what the journey to America implied; above all in those households where husband and wife could not agree about Father Rapp. There was great commotion not only among the Separatists, but also among their friends and relatives, when Frederick announced the date of departure; the strain on him was immense. 'With all my strength I wrestled to know the will of God', he wrote to George Rapp, 'my anxieties in the end accumulated to such a degree that the marrow of my bones was affected and I became ill. ... Everyone was leaning on me.' And they continued to do so.

The journey to America from Amsterdam took eighty days. The Rappites were spared the ultimate indignity which afflicted so many of their countrymen, in that their passage was paid; they did not have to pledge their labour years ahead in the New World in order to get there. Trouble enough awaited them, however, when it was learned that their leader had nowhere for them to go. Some of the group pushed ahead into Ohio, towards the land that Rapp had seen but not bought; they were mostly lost to him. The others were obliged to camp for some months on land outside Philadelphia. Among the Germans who gave them charity at this time was a prosperous merchant, Godfrey Haga. He was a friend of John Heckewelder, and a member of the Moravian Brethren. He became the Harmony Society's agent in Philadelphia and its trusted counsellor.

Towards the end of 1804 Rapp, in desperation, contracted for 4,500 acres on the Connoquenessing creek, twenty-six miles from Pittsburgh in western Pennsylvania. The land needed clearing and was, he knew, unsuitable; as he said in a petition to Congress a year later, it was 'too small, too broken and too cold for to raise vine'. In the depths of winter they moved on to the site and built log cabins for shelter, they had little else. They had been obliged to sell their property in Germany for scarcely half its value; they had spent heavily on travel by land and sea. They paid cash for the land at $2\frac{1}{2}$ an acre and $2,000 more for cattle to stock it. Until crops began to yield they had to buy food for some 900 people. Their credit was not good; scarcely enough for a barrel of salt, scoffed one hostile observer. Food was limited.

These and other hardships caused some of Rapp's followers to desert him. Their demands, reinforced by the American courts, for the return of money they had advanced, caused Rapp acute embarrassment. It was to avoid a repetition of having to pay out sums of money when they could not afford it that, in February 1805, articles were drawn up which brought into being the Harmony Society.

Those who subscribed bound themselves to a contract which for some was to prove unbearably harsh. They pledged themselves and their wives and children to deliver all their property up to George Rapp and the Society 'in the town of *Harmonie*, Butler County, Pennsylvania'. They pledged obedience to the Society's superintendents and swore that they would make their children similarly obedient. If, for some reason, they found it necessary to withdraw, they swore never to demand any reward for work, or services rendered. For their part, Rapp and the Society agreed to admit them as members of the congregation, making available to them religious instruction and education. Lodging, drink, and clothing would be provided for them: if sick or unfit for work they would enjoy the same care and maintenance as before. Should they wish to depart they would receive back the money they had deposited without payment of interest. Their individual payments at the time of their first entry were recorded in writing. If they brought nothing into the congregation, on leaving they were promised a cash donation according to their conduct while there, or as their needs might require, which needs Father Rapp and the Society would determine.

Of course this contract, the basis for a system of communal living which, when the world perceived it, made the Society famous, rested upon Biblical authority. Acts 4: 32: 'And the multitude of them that believed were of one heart and of one soul: neither said any of them that ought of the things which he possessed was his own; and they had all things common.'

Such an agreement rested upon a foundation of trust and shared belief. But what of those members whose fervour waned? The contract immeasurably strengthened Rapp's hold over all his followers. What of those who, isolated in the wilderness, were refused the means to depart? What especially of the women who were even less able than the men to run away if they wanted to? There is evidence that, like others of its kind, the movement was not free from a sinister aspect, that a certain restraint, even coercion, was implied, if not openly invoked.

On 31 December 1805 a petition was laid before Congress asking for permission for the Harmony Society to buy land on favourable terms in the Indiana Territory where vast tracts taken from the tribes had just been made available. George Rapp, who went to Washington for the purpose, specified an area between the fork of the Mississippi and Ohio Rivers—in other words, the Wabash country. His interest in that region may have been promoted by John Heckewelder who was one of the few people to have been there already, having visited it in 1792 when he described it as lying far into Indian country. For all its remoteness Heckewelder praised the land as beautiful and fat, abounding in fruit trees, and the Wabash River full of fish. But Congress, visited by doubt as to the desirability of Germans making wine on US government land, turned Rapp's petition down by one vote. He and his followers were obliged to remain on the Connoquenessing.

Rapp tightened his grip in the years that followed, sometimes ruling with severity and increasing petulance. He spoke of outsiders with hatred; of newcomers to the Society with contempt for their unfitness; of his long-standing and loyal companions, slightingly. The warm affection that was so marked between the ordinary members of the Society was absent from his letters, except to Frederick, and when speaking of members of his family. His antagonism, together with new rules of conduct introduced in 1807 or 1808, drove more people away. When their experience was made known—and it lost little in the telling—it gave rise to hostile comment that descended to slander. Rapp forbade marriage between members of the Society and enjoined those already married to live in celibacy.

His enemies construed this instruction in the worst possible light. They said that his greed for profit was such that he begrudged the loss of labour by women who were pregnant. They accused him of wanting to take the whole wealth of the Society into his own hands. One other story lingered through the years—bizarre, unpleasant, widely circulated. The fact of its existence shows what danger to the Society lay in the ignorance of its neighbours and what ugly animosity that ignorance provoked. According to this rumour, George Rapp's son Johannes by his wife Christina, married in defiance of the order, and had a daughter, Gertrud. To punish him, Rapp had him castrated and so he bled to death. What facts are known are few. Johannes Rapp was indeed married and died in 1812—in an accident, according to one of the leading members of the Society. Though other members were anonymous in death, his grave, unusually, was marked with his name. His daughter, Gertrud, and her widowed mother lived with George Rapp for the rest of their lives.

The practice of celibacy was an extension of the belief to which the Rappites already subscribed; that as Boehme postulated, man before the Fall united male and female in his nature so that the act of procreation was unknown. In fact restraint was necessary, as it was in every isolated community, if it was to remain viable over the years. Moreover Rapp's influence would be all the greater if his followers had no rival claims upon their loyalty, while their work would be the more effective if there were no useless mouths to feed. The problem cannot have been strange to them, coming as they did from an overcrowded country where custom, if nothing else, may have imposed its own control on the population.

Much bitterness was felt against those people who departed from the Harmony Society. This was expressed by Frederick Rapp. 'And so the *Harmonie* will quickly cast out in all filth in order that the body may be cleansed and purified of all foreign substance. . . . Whoever has been in the *Harmonie* and has left it again be it for whatever cause it may, is not worthy of the Kingdom of God, and is a despiser of the suffering of Jesus.'

The positive side of this embattled attitude was expressed in a remarkable and famous achievement. The great majority of the people from Württemberg itself stayed loyal to Father Rapp whose incandescent presence so charged their labour that in a very few years a town was built, industries founded, and commerce begun on a scale to amaze the whole United States.

In 1812 a book was published which gave a vivid picture of their progress and condition. *Travels in the United States in the years 1806-11* circulated widely. It was written by a Scot, John Melish, who at the turn of the century was active in the Glasgow cotton industry. In 1806 he set up in business on his own, importing cotton from Georgia. His travels to America convinced him of the need for a guide to that country. With a taste for natural science, and liking maps, he decided to compile his own. His book was a huge and continuing success, going into many editions. Its description of the Harmony Society was by far the longest and most detailed of any single subject in the whole of Melish's itinerary, and appeared as an extract in many other publications. His picture of the town in western Pennsylvania was of a flourishing Utopia, prosperous, faithful to its name of *Harmonie*, full of contentment.

Melish spent some days in the town and was shown round by Frederick Rapp to whom, he was careful to remark, he submitted his account for approval before publication. Frederick gave Melish his version of the reasons why the Society left Württemberg; this inspired sympathy for the Rappites while being rather less than fair to the long forbearance shown by the ducal government. In 1785 when the movement began, Frederick explained, the Lutheran religion was predominant, but it had become authoritarian and 'in place of religion being made a principle to regenerate the mind, and regulate the life, it was connected with an engine of power to keep the people in check to the civil government.' The decline of the church was seen and felt by George Rapp who found himself compelled to bear testimony to the fundamental principles of the Christian religion. He and his followers were despised and persecuted so much that they 'groaned for deliverance'. God directed them to America, Frederick said.

Although in its petition to Congress of 1804 the Harmony Society described itself as consisting of 'tradesmen, farmers, and chiefly cultivators of the Vine', when Melish stayed at *Harmonie*, probably in 1810, among its workers were shepherds, tailors, shoemakers, hatters, all kinds of operatives in linen manufacture, potters, masons, brewers and distillers, brickmakers, ropemakers, a doctor, a storekeeper, and their assistants. By then the Society's manufactured goods were at a premium in the sparsely furnished frontier households; clothes, shoes, crockery, soap, candles, nails, barrels, beer, wine, and, above all, whisky. Each department of work was supervised by a master who trained apprentices. Frederick Rapp explained to John Melish when he was showing him round that the Society intended to concentrate its labour on manufacturing goods rather than on agriculture on which the profit was far less.

In his book Melish seized upon this point which was crucial to a wider debate. For many years statesmen and merchants alike had questioned what the future held for international trade when the population of the New World became substantial. Would the Americans content themselves with farming and buy manufactured goods from abroad? Or would they start to make their own, thus upsetting trade and threatening prosperity in Europe? The Harmonists appeared to herald change in this matter and one that many Americans already wished to see. Figures that Frederick Rapp must have supplied to Melish seemed to bear out the wisdom of this course; they were widely reproduced. Over the six or so years since the Rappites had arrived in the wilderness they had seen the land rise in value by $70,000, and with it the mills, machinery, and dwelling-houses. Sheep, cattle, hogs, manufactured goods, implements of husbandry, and maturing spirits went to make the total of their wealth which Frederick put at about $220,000.

What pleased Melish most was that he thought this impressive sum had not been amassed at the expense of people's well-being. He saw no poverty, no dirt, none of the brutal living conditions that went with manufacturing in towns like Glasgow. All was pleasant, open, ordered. The hills were terraced as in Württemberg so that vines could grow on the steepest part; apple orchards had begun to bear. Beehives were ranged in a shed open to the south and faced by flowering shrubs. Hops grew in at the window of the brewhouse. There were flowers everywhere, along the wooden bridge over the Connoquenessing, within the space enclosed round each house, between the hedges of the curious labyrinth. These hedges were disposed in such a manner 'as to puzzle people to get into the little temple, emblematical of Harmony in the middle'.

Walking through the town Melish found the people all activity and contentment. Girls sang melodious hymns at their spinning-jennies— music was the highest expression of the Harmonists' religious feeling, the art which they practised with great distinction. After church service Melish was honoured with a performance by the orchestra which consisted of three violins, a clarinet, a string bass, a flute, and two French horns. He was very moved by the service and enthused over the moral condition of the Harmonists. 'There is no vicious habit among them', he wrote. 'There is not an instance of swearing, or lying, or debauchery of any kind; and as to cheating so commonly practised in civilized society, they have no temptation to it whatever. As individuals they have no use for money—and they have no fear of want.' He did not comment on the practice of celibacy which had been introduced well before his visit; he may have been unaware of it.

At the service he attended George Rapp delivered the sermon with great animation, and the congregation listened with the most devout attention. But Melish made little of Rapp, remarking only that the 'old man's face beamed with intelligence, and he appeared to have a consciousness of having performed a good work.'

Melish's book was written according to a clear and systematic plan and gave its readers the impression of scientific exactitude in all his observations. This made his verdict on the moral uprightness and contentment of the Harmonists all the more convincing. Yet Melish's visit to *Harmonie* was brief. All that he saw was arranged by Frederick Rapp who was obviously concerned to make a good impression. To those who read his book it seemed that Melish had seen something wonderful made real.

That men could live together sharing everything was demonstrated by the early Christians. But the concept seemed to lie beyond the reach of ordinary men, though constantly attractive, and celebrated by writers of many different nationalities, among them Plato, Sir Thomas More, Condorcet, and Johann Christian Andreae. In the eighteenth century the example of the divine Economy of the Moravian Brethren and, a little later on, of the Shakers under Mother Ann Lee, appeared to suggest that the conditions of the New World were specially favourable to small groups of people living a communal life. (That it also happened to be celibate was by the way.) The Shakers in particular were known to have achieved a decent if somewhat frugal living by joining together in agriculture and commerce. The importance of the Harmony Society, as Melish presented it in his book, was that such an existence appeared not only viable, but with its manufacturing enterprises likely to be very profitable—in this context the statistics supplied by Frederick Rapp were highly significant. Many thoughtful people who flinched from the offensive and brutalizing sight of industrial towns in Scotland and the North of England devoutly wished that it might be so.

CHAPTER 2

WESTERN WATERS

As Pittsburgh advanced in industry and commerce *Harmonie* was no longer quite so isolated. But it was secure and secluded enough and accepted by its many German neighbours. It should have been among those towns destined to remain and flourish. But in 1814 a sudden and very surprising decision was taken to abandon it entirely for a distant, wild, and dangerous country, the Territory of Indiana. When pressed, as they often were, members of the Society defended the move as prompted by a need for more land, a warmer climate in which to cultivate the vine, and better access to river transport.

Their enemies charged George Rapp with using it as a device to prevent those of his disciples who were tired of his dictatorial rule and offended by his irascibility from running away. Though he never uttered a simple statement of fact Rapp was certainly aware of the effectiveness of building a new and more remote settlement in order to renew the commitment of his followers. Work was, in any case, a moral good to him, conferring spiritual benefit on those who performed it to the best of their ability. And obedience was the quality he prized above all.

The decision may have represented an act of imagination as well as faith for, according to Professor Arndt, the move may have been explained by the same passage from the Book of Revelation that brought the Rappites to America in the first place. In 1814 ten years had elapsed since the first arrival in the wilderness; perhaps the time had come to move on in the expectation of the Second Coming.

No doubt both religious and economic considerations played their part. References to spiritual preoccupations in the correspondence that passed between George and Frederick Rapp are too obscure for the uninitiated to understand, but their concern with practical matters is clear enough. Discussing the choice of new land they considered various essential items. Did the spring come early enough to favour the cultivation of the vine? Was there water that would serve to drive a mill? What kind of pasture was there for sheep? Was the river navigable at all seasons and easy of access? Necessity, and only that, dictated the development of the Connoquenessing land; it may be that once he had sufficient money in hand, Rapp reverted to his original purpose of settling some hundreds of miles to the west, on cheap government land where he believed vines would grow well and he would be in direct communication with the developing port at New Orleans.

In the spring of 1814 he and two others set out on horseback for the Ohio River and the country beyond. Like everyone else who passed through Kentucky, he was impressed by the great fertility of the land. And he was well received; as soon as the people heard they were from the Harmony Society they were treated with respect, he told Frederick; at all the inns they knew about it. But land was in demand, and dear, and the living was so easy the people would grow idle; that would not do for Father Rapp. In any case, he wrote from Limestone in Kentucky, his spirit would not rest until be had been to the Wabash; he had a premonition that it would be the place. So, at the end of April, Rapp and his companions crossed the Ohio and rode north-west through the Indiana Territory to Vincennes, a town on the east bank of the Wabash River, well beyond the furthest line of general settlement.

In the opinion of some very seasoned travellers, the 100-odd miles between the Ohio and the Wabash was the most difficult going in the whole United States, covered by thick undergrowth, blocked by trees felled by high winds, and infested with flies. There were no roads, only Indian paths, and scarcely any habitations. A great silence prevailed since the forest was so dense that no birds sang. The Wabash was a frontier in itself, roughly dividing forest land from the open prairies which stretched from its western bank to the Mississippi, and beyond. As yet they were quite unknown. Towards Vincennes the dark woods gave way to a succession of clearings covered with stunted oak, low shrubs, and grass. Trees were disposed about these clearings as if planted there by some deliberate art; some were huge, their trunks like towers.

In the middle of one such clearing lay Vincennes, surrounded by fields of tobacco, wheat, and Indian corn, a cluster of lime-washed houses whose whiteness relieved the eye after the forest gloom. In 1814 it was the site of a US Government land office where Rapp consulted maps. After having surveys made, in the second week of May he bought 7,000 acres lying on the east bank, fifty miles lower down the Wabash, towards its confluence with the Ohio. Part was public land, part belonged to settlers and there were squatters on it, each with a house and small clearing. All the rest was smothered in trees. The terms for government land were $2 an acre, 1 qr. down, the rest to pay in four years.

Rapp decided that he would build his town on a level plain above the river; it was full of fish that people came from miles around to catch in barrels when the water was low. There was a little hill about a quarter of a mile away on which vines could be planted. As it stood, this hill was worth more than the level land for there were stones for building on it, though none elsewhere. But the chief reason for his choice was that he thought it had access at all seasons of the year to New Orleans via the Wabash, Ohio, and Mississippi Rivers.

He was wrong. The Wabash is a savage river, untamed even today; subject to sudden raging floods that break its banks and cover all the bottom land. Its course is interrupted by shelving rocks and long spits of sand, so that when the water is low boats cannot get up it for weeks at a time. Nor was the climate much of an improvement upon that of Pennsylvania. As an early traveller noted, in summer, vapour rising copiously from the river and the immense forest produced storms that only served to aggravate the sultry heat. Rain descended in torrents, a momentary relief to parched soil, but leaving no trace. Only in the spring and autumn did a moderate and sustained flow of water make the Wabash easily navigable, as it was when Rapp first saw it.

One major drawback occupied his attention from the start, since it concerned the first essential for every new settlement, namely a mill to grind corn into flour. There was no suitable place for a water-driven mill in the town and much work would be required to construct one a mile away. This was begun forthwith. Grinding stones were ordered, for there were none to be had in Indiana. But Rapp had more ambitious plans for power; it will be your business to get a steam-engine for the factory, he warned Frederick. There was wood to drive it, and reports of a bank of coal further up the river which he would buy at the earliest opportunity.

By the first week of June Rapp was back at *Harmonie* in Pennsylvania, impatient to begin the removal of his people into Indiana and declaring himself bored by the various business transactions that had to be completed. On 20 June Frederick Rapp noted that the first group of people had left, taking with them $4,000 in cash and 40 wagon-loads of goods. They went by flat boat and their journey down the Ohio and up the Wabash would take roughly two weeks. Although at that time the war with England, which had begun in 1812, was not yet over, traffic on the Ohio was fast increasing.

Waiting to receive the people at the site of the new *Harmonie* was

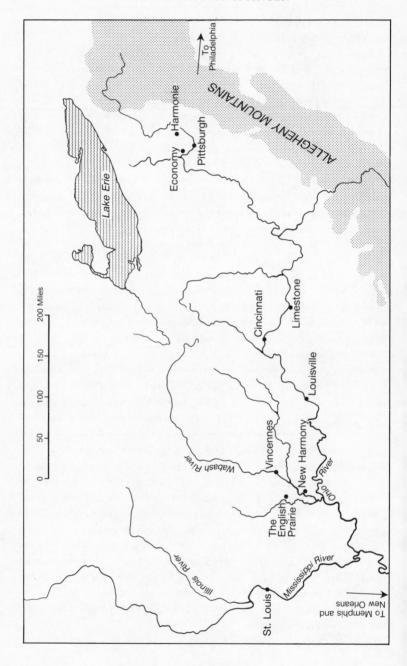

John L. Baker, a leading member of the Society and the one who, after Frederick Rapp, seems to have been sent most often out into the world, perhaps because he showed himself unmoved by its attractions. He hated being separated from his companions, finding it strange 'to have the torment of doing business with persons who are without order and stubborn and of the worst sort, who can hardly be induced by money and good words to perform a service, at which one is usually half defrauded'. Baker found it particularly hard to have to be absent from the regular meeting for worship at which Father Rapp presided, and from which they all drew strength.

He had many pressing tasks to perform at the new *Harmonie*. He had to consolidate the Society's holding of land around the site to protect it from the prying eyes of strangers, and that before speculators moved in. The Society's purchase had attracted much attention and people wanted to take up land near them. Baker was firm with owners who asked too high a price, threatening that the Society would move on if it did not get what it wanted. He had to arrange for the site to be surveyed and laid out, while building as fast as possible log cabins for the temporary accommodation of the workers on their way from Pennsylvania.

At the same time he was bombarded by letters from Frederick Rapp, full of admonition and enquiry. Baker must buy land on the opposite side of the river so that they would command the river. He must enquire for wool, and at what price, and whether it would be cheaper bought there or in Pennsylvania. He must look after the newly sown teasels (for raising the knap on cloth) and if it had not already been done, transplant them at once. Could he get salt (for curing meat) and at what price, asked Frederick. What did whisky cost in bulk? Would wine sell there? Could he get potatoes or should they be sent?

Baker's replies were calm and reassuring and full of useful information. He had found a good place for a ferry and secured both landings to the Society. Wheat and rye seed had been ordered in quantity, and 21 cows bought, each with its calf. Iron and iron goods (such as nails, tools, and other implements) were much in demand, Baker wrote, as were store goods. With difficulty, for it was quite overgrown with nettles, tropical cane, and other shrubs, he had explored the ground around the town. Great heaps of mussel shells lay uncovered by the river—a source of lime for making mortar, and he had also found potter's clay. 'In time one thing after another will be unfolded', he assured the Rapps.

But, as he looked about him, Baker must have needed all his faith and patience to keep up his spirits. The low flat land in the vicinity was smothered with dense undergrowth, in part consisting of grass so tall that man and beast hesitated to go through it. Trees shut in the river bank, and its muddy shore was piled with driftwood and decaying vegetation whose smell was rank. The river itself offered the only open prospect to the eye and that of a few hundred yards to the next of a hundred thousand bends; there was no horizon.

At the end of July Baker told George Rapp that he and his companions who now numbered well over a hundred, had suffered considerably when heavy rain penetrated their huts, and in the same week quite a few of them had been sick. But they had recovered and three more log houses had been built which would ease their very cramped living conditions. All is going well, Baker concluded, 'so far we are cheerful and busy in the brotherly service'. Then, on 8 August, he and two others put their signatures to a letter which told how things had changed.

Fever had taken hold of them and almost at once two of them died. The sickness assumed different forms; one man was seized by shivering fits and then became intensely hot; no means of cooling him had any effect, and he expired. Others felt no pain, only a slight affliction of the head, until the heat overpowered them and they fell into an endless sleep. 'We were rather frightened', the letter confessed, 'but if the Lord wishes to deal with us in this way then His Will be done.' They had no doctor, no one to nurse the sick, and no food suitable for invalids. There were no eggs—the nearest hens were fifteen miles away; milk from their few cows quickly turned sour in the hot and heavy air; there was hardly any flour, for the mill was not built and all they had was carried from Pennsylvania.

As the torrid summer wore on scarcely any of them escaped. The fever was recurring and terribly debilitating; some lay in bed unable to move, 'melancholy and confused'. Others endured a daily attack and after it bravely went about their ordinary tasks. John Baker's life hung in the balance for many weeks; his brother died in the same room. People in the neighbourhood with whom he had done business hastened to offer advice and help. In particular, Nathaniel Ewing, receiver of the Vincennes Land Office, expressed his concern that no doctor was called to visit the sick at *Harmonie*. 'What signifies the expence to saving the life of your friends', he wrote in some exasperation. Ewing advised the members of the Harmony Society not to neglect the fevers of the country. If caught in time they were easily overcome but if suffered to get a hold of the constitution 'they become verry obstinate and dangerous'.

The fever was a subject on which few people in the western country cared to dwell, a very serious problem for which a remedy long eluded them. In the summer of 1814 scarcely anyone escaped, and that was blamed upon the heat; it was the hottest summer for 15 years, the Society's neighbours told each other. In fact the sickness was the scourge of newly cleared land, especially on the damp and fertile river bottoms; it was, variously, malaria, or typhus. When Wabash fever nearly killed John Heckewelder, his friend Godfrey Haga told Frederick Rapp that he had been prescribed a kind of port made from grapes found in the area. The Harmonists had no port, only one barrel of currant wine which the sick drank laced with quinine. Apart from that they lived on soup, and quarrelled shakily among themselves as to whose turn it was to get out of bed to make it.

Thunderstorms broke the heat in the middle of September, but the sickness continued unabated. Then, on 1 October, to the joy and relief of his 'perplexed and helpless children', as they described themselves, Father Rapp appeared unexpectedly in the town. His first letters to Frederick Rapp describing the chaos that prevailed, convey a sense of shock that was obviously acute. Neglect had made the fever very bad, he observed and blamed it on the Society's doctor in Pennsylvania who had failed to dispatch sufficient medicine. Rapp now sent in haste for ipececuanha, an emetic, and more quinine. With care all might have escaped being ill, he declared, but the people in their 'sweet enthusiasm' used neither sense nor reason, and could not believe that God would not protect them from all harm. The building of the town would be delayed, he told Frederick—certain key workers such as carpenters having died. Others, being very weak, would take the winter to recover. He could not bear to write the names of those who died, he said; he did not want to know them; there were about thirteen.

In early November he wrote that though things still looked miserable enough, 'the eye of hope makes great and beautiful plans'. Soon his energy, and the faith his disciples placed in him, transformed his outlook. A sense of exhilaration pervaded his letters; wherever he went he saw advantages; whatever problems arose seemed capable of solution. But 'I must learn more than ever before in my life', he wrote. The land was healthy, he assured Frederick, but they had entered it at the wrong time of year when the weather was too hot. Where Baker had reported scant pasture for sheep—a serious drawback, for a major business of the Society was the manufacture of cloth from their wool—Rapp's optimistic eye discovered a wonderful abundance on high ground. Wolves were numerous, so the shepherds must have guns.

With obvious enjoyment, Rapp pondered how best to harness the water available in quantity on the land. He proposed to lead one little brook right through the centre of the town; the brickmaker, tanner, and whoever else needed it for his trade, could live along the stream. A sawmill might be built upon another which, he now perceived, could be made to have a fall of fifteen feet. Along the outer boundary of the town he found a pond fed by running water; this he devised as the place for stables for cattle and other beasts who liked to drink its salty tasting water. The plan of the town was clear in his head though one could scarcely walk there for the mess—logs already cut to size, branches, and the tops of felled trees that lay on the ground, filling the air with the buttery smell of newly-cut wood.

Criticism was directed, not at things, but at people whose imperfections vexed him. In spite of their demonstrable success in Pennsylvania he carped at what he considered his followers' ignorance of practical affairs. Settlers ought to be able to turn their hands to anything, he grumbled most unfairly to Frederick. A little later on he was outraged by a breakdown in his scheme of discipline which in his absence from old *Harmonie* permitted some of his followers to adapt a more elaborate style of dress, which they were still wearing when they arrived in Indiana; investigate this, he ordered Frederick. Lack of supervision had rendered the people quite wild, Rapp complained; it would take time to get them in order again.

To his mind those who had spent the summer in Indiana had no business falling ill. Because of it he had no one to send to Vincennes to lobby for the establishment of a post office at his town. This was something that Rapp had taken pains to promote in Pennsylvania since it enhanced the standing of a place and brought it trade, while keeping him in touch with the outside world where developments must be watched for signs of the millennium. In this context he was pleased to have a visit from Nathaniel Ewing in December, who brought him news of the Congress of Vienna and Napoleon's escape from Elba, both of which in his view bore out the message of Revelations. 'Christ's Return is soon to come', he wrote in a pastoral letter to those members of the Society left behind in Pennsylvania. Their temporary exile from his presence was necessary to advance the new arrangements in Indiana, he explained: 'the world must be paid in money'. All who served the general economy of the Society contributed to its happiness, Rapp assured his absent followers.

As there was no possibility of feeding so large a group on what was available locally, those in Pennsylvania acted as a commissariat, dispatching supplies of flour, lard, bacon, butter, eggs packed in flour, apples, and beer from *Harmonie* until the crops planted by the new community began to yield. They conducted an amazing operation whereby the movable property of the first town was brought in stages nearly 1,000 miles to the second. This began in the summer of 1814 and was pursued with the relentless efficiency of a colony of worker ants. Everything possible was packed in barrels—tools, seed, raw materials for the manufacture of goods, the goods themselves, plants, and personal belongings—and floated down the Ohio into the Wabash.

Soon the Society was producing manufactured goods again, this time with the help of a steam engine, an innovation watched apprehensively by Frederick. It was one of the first to be used in the West. Stores were opened at *Harmonie* on the Wabash and at Shawneetown on the Ohio River. The first customers, the local settlers, were impatient to buy; 'they walk about half naked and ask for all the articles', Rapp told Frederick. He thought whisky would sell very well; at one dollar a gallon 'they' liked to drink it neat. ('Their' habit was to put the bottle to their mouth and measure according to conscience.) Whisky was a means of barter in a region where cash was so scarce; what coin there was in circulation was silver, Spanish and English—a testimony to the exotic history of the West. To Father Rapp's disgust the local people saw very little of it. They paid with whatever they had to spare; skins of animals, or hides, or honeycombs, or even feathers which were plucked from live geese and poultry.

Among the articles sent for sale from old *Harmonie* were calendars, reams of paper, coffee, tobacco, spices, lengths of cloth—the coarse sold well but the fine did not for the Indiana people were so poor—hats, crockery, and medicine. This last was much in demand the following year when memories of the sickness of 1814 were still vivid. The settlers 'are all precautious [*sic*] now and want to provide themselves with the infallible preventative and Remedy for this disorder', Frederick noted. He laid in 50 lb. of Peruvian bark (quinine) and 16 lb. of brimstone, which he hoped would sell. One thousand fruit trees were sent to start an orchard, together with all the Lombardy poplars to be had in the neighbourhood of old *Harmonie*. Planted on both sides of the street in the new town it was hoped they would ward off fever.

Although Frederick Rapp was obliged to remain in Pennsylvania more than a year after the new settlement was begun, he made a flying visit to Indiana at Christmas 1814. His time was so precious that his journey down the Ohio was accomplished with reckless speed; instead of tying up every evening, the boats were pushed on through the dark, 50 or 60 miles at a time. The night concealed many dangers; currents, sandbanks, the so-called 'planters', large trees fast on the river bed, upright and immovable; 'sawyers', less firmly tethered but equally big, and moving up and down with the motion of the water; 'wooden islands' formed by driftwood piled against these, or other obstacles. Acutely conscious of his responsibility, and in spite of the presence of a pilot, Frederick stayed awake for several nights in succession, a lantern at his elbow, poring over a copy of the famous *Navigator* whose careful profile of the river thousands of emigrants had cause to thank. By the end of two weeks the boats on which they lived seemed narrow indeed, crowded with people, goods, and animals—in this case sheep. The difficulty in transporting the Society's prize flocks to Indiana was that there was very little pasture in the forest on the way and hardly room for fodder on board. Sometimes the sheep arrived already shorn, having eaten each other's wool on the voyage.

Frederick's arrival lightened the burden of affairs on George Rapp of which he frequently, and with relish, complained. One pressing matter they must have discussed during the short time they were together was the disposal of the town and land at old *Harmonie*. In the autumn of 1814 John Heckewelder interested himself in the sale on the part of a friend, but negotiations broke down partly, it seems, because Frederick Rapp asked for the money in silver. No further buyer appeared until the following spring when one, Abraham Ziegler, who came from the vicinity of the Moravian town at Bethlehem, agreed to pay $100,000. This was half the original asking price. Moreover the bargain was not in silver but in promises, for Frederick waived a down payment, relying on instalments to be paid by Ziegler, starting the following year.

Perhaps Ziegler's credit was enhanced by Frederick's impatience to be gone. He and the brethren at old *Harmonie* were ill at ease so long away from Father Rapp. As soon as the transaction was complete they gathered up their belongings, and with eight wagon-loads of goods, three riding horses and a cow, embarked for Indiana in four boats. As they left, even though it was the first week in May, a frost gripped old *Harmonie*. Frederick supposed the fruit blossom must be frozen, to say nothing of the vines. This is a miserable place, he wrote. Whatever he thought of the decision to move, it is clear he did not regret the change. Indiana was a better place to fulfil the spiritual duty he conceived was his: 'to make of a wild country fertile fields and gardens of pleasure'.

He found all things in order at the new town, for however 'wild' the people may have been in coming to the Wabash, they were docile enough by the time he arrived. With few children, *Harmonie* was a silent place and, after the 9 o'clock curfew, deserted, except for the watchmen on duty. Each morning a cart went round collecting milk; it carried a placard with special instructions about jobs to be done. Then, summoned by French horns, men, women, and children marched together to the fields, or to the various manufactories. They were dressed alike; the men in jackets and pantaloons recalling the Rhineland *tracht*, the women in grey dresses, their hair scraped up and under a cap. 'Of the personal attraction of females of this masculine species of labor', one visitor wrote sadly, 'it is not necessary to speak.' Later the Harmonists' movements were controlled by a bell on the steeple of the church, a thing of great wonder on the frontier. Ordering it from a Liverpool firm, Frederick Rapp explained that it was intended to reach members of the Society in distant parts of the settlement. 'The Sound should therefore not only be Solemn but *loud*', he requested.

By the early summer of 1815 the orchard was finished and vines set out on the hill. Land was being cleared for Indian corn, wheat had been sown in early March, and flax was to follow. The sawmill was under construction, as was a dam. In spite of their difficult voyage the sheep had cast lambs, and there was already 9,000 lb. of pork in the smokehouse, waiting to be sold. Frederick set about ordering more goods for the store, which had sold out, and raw materials for the newly-built factory. He engaged agents at New Orleans to receive the cargoes of flour, pork, and cloth the Society would soon dispatch down-river. As for Father Rapp, he celebrated the first spring in Indiana with a song of praise; the woods were green, the herbs were growing, everything was coming to a new birth, he wrote: 'it is surely a joy to live here'.

The first few years in Indiana appear to have been happy ones. In spite of the grievous number of deaths from fever (the 1820 census showed that more than half its households had suffered at least one death), the creation of *Harmonie* on the Wabash was a source of satisfaction and pride. The Society's huge archive contains much evidence to show how closely its members held to their leader's ideas. Letters written by those few who were obliged to travel on the Society's behalf demonstrate their piety, humility, and loyalty, and the extent to which they were attached to their companions and their home. Essays, poems, notes on subjects like the colour of flowers, and the meaning of their names, collected under the title *Feurige Kohlen* [burning coals], reveal the lighter aspect of the Rappites' culture, while the numerous songs and hymns they composed demonstrate that as well as sustaining the drudgery of work in the fields they were people capable of expressing their belief with grace and deep emotion.

The best expression of George Rapp's singular philosophy was in the town itself, a symbol of ordered decorum. Its outward form was visible in the stoutly built log cabins, soon to be replaced by frame and brick buildings which lined the regularly laid out streets. Well-cultivated fields, orchards, and rows of vines surrounded the dwellings and the whole was defended from the outside world by a thick belt of trees—oak, wild cherry, ash, walnut, and cypress. Strangers coming unexpectedly upon the town rubbed their eyes in amazement, so little did it resemble any other place on the frontier, where order and cleanliness were rare luxuries.

There was a fine frame church with a belfry, and a mansion for Father Rapp with a promenade upon its roof rather like a captain's walk. Several large buildings were built in brick; no one is quite sure today what their purpose was; possibly they served as dormitories for the unmarried, but it has been suggested that those who had lost relations or friends through fever came together there for greater comfort. In any case the dwellings were large, airy, well-proportioned—something in the pitch of the roof recalling Iptingen. Small brick houses for individual families were designed to an identical pattern and provided with a form of insulation, each component part was numbered and spares were held in a central store. Their design broke with American tradition in that there was no entrance directly from the street and no welcoming porch. Instead one went through a gate in a fence and in through a door at the side. According to one later resident, the blank faces these houses presented to the street gave *Harmonie* an ancient and mysterious air.

The lives of its inhabitants were the expression of Rapp's belief that Christ might be expected sooner where harmony prevailed. Moderation, simplicity, and obedience had to govern their behaviour which was closely controlled. At work each person was assigned to a particular department under the direction of a supervisor who alone gave orders, handled money, and drew supplies. At home each household was given into the charge of one person responsible for the spiritual well being of its members. Regular confession was the custom; those who were perplexed, or had offended, found themselves before Father Rapp to receive advice and exhortation. Punishment was to be held up to general disapproval, or in extreme cases, to be ostracized.

The great majority of the members of the Society never left the

confines of the village. A handful of men were required to man the flatboats taking produce down to New Orleans and one or two others ran the
store at Shawneetown. All other business was in the hands of Frederick
Rapp who drew up contracts and signed all documents on the Society's
behalf.

Such a peculiar and strict way of life naturally did not appeal to all
members equally; their commitment varied, especially where the practice
of celibacy was concerned. Rapp did not altogether prohibit marriage;
there is evidence that he performed several such ceremonies during the
Wabash years. Some couples even produced children during that time
but these were transgressions of the general rule. The greatest bitterness
was felt by those who, wishing to depart, were dismissed with what they
considered less than a fair payment (it might be as little as $ 25), and those
who failed to persuade their nearest and dearest to leave with them.

For instance in 1816 a savage denunciation of the Society and its leader
found its way to Württemberg. Now that peace had come in Europe, and
ships were moving, Jakob Schick could tell his parents and friends at
home of the maltreatment he had suffered at the hands of Rapp. For
seven years, he said he had worked for him but he had left the Society in
1812 with empty hands. It seems he sought some payment through the
American courts, but could prove no case against Rapp, who was
protected by the terms of the 1805 contract. Schick took his children by
force from the Society, but could not persuade his wife to leave, which
presumably explains the vehemence of his remarks. Error, superstition,
and religious mania had reached a high degree among a handful of
ignorant men, Schick wrote. Rapp allowed himself to be honoured as
divine, hearing confession, and pronouncing absolution. He moved to
the Wabash because he believed his hold over his followers was no longer
secure in Pennsylvania; many had run away. In Indiana many died for the
land was low and the water bad. The rest Schick called the poorest
creatures in the world because they submitted to rationed bread, compulsory work, and forced worship in a land where there was superabun-
dance and freedom. Rapp had it in mind to get more people from
Germany, Schick warned his relatives; the Württemberg government
(which had dismissed the first exodus as due to religious *schwärmerei*)
would do well to prevent such a move.

It seems that there was at least an element of truth in this. The leaders
of the Society had decided to replenish their work-force when the
factories in the newly built *Harmonie* were about to go into operation. In
July 1816 Frederick Rapp wrote to a vine grower near Iptingen ordering

hundreds of vine plants of different kinds and 100 plum trees. His letter contained a glowing account of the justice and freedom to be found in America and of the flourishing condition of *Harmonie*. There was room on the Society's lands for 100 German families to live happily without being bothered by lack of food or a visit from the beadle, Frederick wrote. As a result of this and other letters, the impression became widespread among those friends and relations who had stayed behind at the beginning of the century, that the Harmony Society was open to recruits, and that Godfrey Haga, its agent at Philadelphia, stood ready to redeem those who, unable to raise the money for their passage, bound themselves for the voyage.

These enticing letters were received at another time of great hardship in the history of the Swabian people. Once more they sought to relieve their material suffering by an act of faith in God. The year 1816 was the first of several when the vintage failed; the wine presses did not open that autumn for lack of grapes. Prices rose sharply and food was scarce and very dear. To make matters worse a new King of Württemberg imposed higher taxes. The consequence was a feeling of restlessness, a curious excitement which Rapp's sister, Barbara, writing from Iptingen, described to him. She said it was as if a wind had arisen to blow away all those people who had been awakened by religion; they had no roots in temporal things and wanted to emigrate.

This time the peculiar fervour of the Württembergers was encouraged and supported by that most curious and powerful man, Tsar Alexander I of Russia. He had recently come under the influence of the mystic, Madam von Krüdener, whose ideas about the millennium resembled those of Jung-Stilling. It was to promote a chiliastic dream that Alexander made available lands in the Caucasus where hundreds went in 1816, including some from Iptingen and its neighbourhood. Others set out for America, trusting in God and George Rapp.

By the summer of 1817 hundreds were arriving in Philadelphia destitute and often ill. They applied to Godfrey Haga to redeem them; until the money for their passage was paid the captain would not let them leave the ship. The alternative was to sell themselves, or, more easily, their children, into years of hard labour in order to release the rest of the family. Haga had not been given the money and wrote in sorrow and shame to Frederick Rapp asking for instructions. Many had set out in the firm belief that the Society would provide funds for their redemption and the journey to Indiana, he reminded Frederick: surely something must be done?

But Frederick was curiously reluctant to act, even though George Rapp himself urged him to help their fellow countrymen. Although he must have known many of the redemptioners personally, or by repute, he seems to have shrunk from them as from something evil. Eventually, he paid for about 150 to go free, some of whom, including apparently many children, went on to *Harmonie*. In this Frederick once again betrayed an odd, obsessive aspect of his nature; there would be difficulty in making the newcomers 'good people', he told Father Rapp; better for such persons to be bound to labour for some years in order to pay for their passage; the Americans could 'break them' better. As a result of this débâcle harsh things were said about the Rapps at Philadelphia. At the same time their Indiana neighbours discovered various reasons why the Society's presence in their midst was not the advantage they had first presumed.

When Indiana was admitted as a State in 1816 it had barely 70,000 inhabitants in its whole extent. The presence of a group of some 800 was a matter of great interest therefore. The Society was known to be possessed of capital—a thing as rare in Indiana at that time as it was vital to the development of the State—and to command a labour force huge in comparison to all others. Invitations to partake in local enterprise crowded in. Some were taken up; for instance, the Society held shares in the Vincennes Bank (which later failed), and at the State's request made a loan of 5,000 dollars to its treasury. But trading conditions were difficult, and Frederick Rapp's conduct of affairs reflected this. It was a time when banks proliferated, each issuing paper money that suffered a discount the further the notes strayed from home. Like other merchants Frederick looked for specie, or notes of the United States Bank, in every transaction. That was fair enough—and his fairness is apparent in the many letters dealing with debts owed to the Society. But once it was gathered in, the money was rarely put out again. According to Professor Arndt, it went to swell a secret hoard to make the Society proof against events in the outside world.

The Harmonists gained a reputation for meanness with their money and, something which did not sit well on a religious organization, lack of charity. Moreover, the monopoly in the production and sale of store goods which its access to capital and cheap labour, and its steam-engine, secured for it, was an affront to the many struggling merchants in the area. As for the farmers, in their task of clearing and cultivating land the odds against them were enormous. Even in this the Harmony Society was seen to be opulent. It was well known that whenever storms threatened

the harvest the whole town was summoned to assist; as many as 150
people were seen reaping a single field.

The local storekeepers complained of the Society for undercutting
prices. Their own goods had to reflect the distance they came and the
substantial profit they felt they deserved. At *Harmonie* goods were
manufactured on the spot with the help of machinery and no wages had
to be paid. Commerce languished because the Rappites had no particular
need to buy outside the town.

Far from recognizing their neighbours' difficulties, the Rappites
further provoked them by lack of cooperation, perhaps the greatest
offence in a frontier society. They had the best site on the Wabash for a
watermill, which the law obliged them to make available to all. People
came three days' journey to have their corn ground, only to be turned
away; the Rappites would not do it for them. The matter went to court,
where they were fined. Then, their conscientious objection to bearing
arms was unpopular in Indiana where the militia held an honoured place
as the community's only shield against marauding Indians. However
much their religious scruples were protected by law, those who held
aloof from such a service forfeited respect. As one of the Society's
neighbours remarked, 'military courage is here considered to be the
prince of all the virtues. Even quakers talk like soldiers.' Yet, instead of
quietly paying the fine which Federal law exacted from men of military
age who chose to be exempt, the Rappites tried to confuse the officers
sent to count heads, just to save a little money.

Most serious of all was the supposition that George Rapp's influence
over his followers was used to dictate how they should vote, in which
case his command of such a group could materially influence elections. In
1816, as the Indiana Legislative Assembly prepared the way for entry into
the Union, the rights and duties of all citizens was much in people's
minds. At Nathaniel Ewing's invitation, Frederick Rapp went along to
the Assembly and was duly elected a member, but his loyal service there
did not erase a suspicion that the Harmony Society as a whole paid less
than the proper attention to democracy.

It is not easy to understand what prompted George Rapp to this
unwise behaviour; the affront he offered to his neighbours bore comparison with that which he showed in Württemberg, with far less cause.
No doubt his arrogance got worse as he got older, his autocratic tenden-
cies too. But his overriding purpose was probably to keep his followers
aloof from the developing society surrounding them; he would trade
with the settlers but not associate with them for fear of diluting the

Swabian dream. Whenever they came to *Harmonie* their forlorn appearance would be enough to convince the unworldly members of his Society that, in terms of comfort and security, his system was better; their town the only place fit for the Lord to choose.

CHAPTER 3

A CALL TO CANCEL DOMESDAY BOOK

FATHER Rapp asked no more than that the town of *Harmonie* might prosper quietly until such time as Christ was ready to call him and his followers to their higher destiny; no other kind of notice was desired or sought by him. It was as a result of the description in John Melish's book of the contentment prevailing in the woods of Pennsylvania that the Harmony Society became the object of attention in England of men of philosophy and science. They looked to the great jurist, Jeremy Bentham, as their leader, and were alert to every new idea and process that seemed likely to promote the collective happiness of mankind.

In 1815 the *Philanthropist*, a journal of the utilitarians, reproduced in its entirety Melish's description of the first *Harmonie*. As an isolated manufacturing community placed under conditions favourable to development in whatever direction the managers of the establishment chose, *Harmonie* was bound to fascinate the members of the group, for they had recently become involved in something very similar; a new joint-stock company to run the huge cotton-spinning factory at New Lanark on the River Clyde. It was to be a laboratory for the proving of ideas directed at raising the condition of the manufacturing workers.

The *Philanthropist* was edited by James Mill, Bentham's principal literary interpreter at the time, and owned by William Allen, a Quaker chemist closely concerned in the leading humanitarian causes of the day. These included the abolition of slavery and the education of the poor. In whatever he did Allen relied on God's approval and James Mill's advice. The fourth person who kept an eye on New Lanark was Francis Place, a thoughtful and judicious man, self taught, who had made his way out of the most extreme poverty to become a master breeches-maker. Place, who became famous as 'the radical tailor of Charing Cross', was a natural politician, a brilliant organizer, and tactician. Though he liked to keep in the background, he was responsible for co-ordinating the efforts of those opponents of the Tory government whose greatest concentration of strength was in Westminster, where he had his shop and where Bentham lived. The two were close friends, and Bentham accompanied Place on foot as he delivered the finished garments to his customers, talking incessantly. Allen and Bentham, who were wealthy men, took shares in New Lanark; Place and Mill did not.

Melish's description of *Harmonie* in Pennsylvania was also of the greatest interest to the Manager of the New Lanark mills, and the largest shareholder, Robert Owen. He was a Welshman in his mid-forties who had come suddenly into the public's gaze in 1813 arrayed in the panoply of a reformer, whose manifesto was contained in the series of essays published as *A New View of Society*. When people spoke of Robert Owen the word they used most frequently was 'enthusiast'; they described him as one possessed. Owen was an enthusiast as defined by John Wesley— one believing things to be Miracles which are not. With two other partners Owen had bought the New Lanark mills in 1799 from the man who built them, David Dale, whose daughter he married in the same year. Dale's alleged neglect of the working population of New Lanark, their inherent faults, and Robert Owen's success in transforming them through kind and sensible management formed the pivot of the argument in *A New View of Society*.

In 1815 Owen was engaged in devising what he called 'a systematic plan for the gradual improvement of the British Empire' which, he maintained, he had been commissioned to produce by Ministers of Lord Liverpool's government. He had gained their confidence at his first visit to London in 1813, at the same time as he had become acquainted with their most effective opponents, Place and his colleagues. In particular, Owen was privately on the closest terms with the Home Secretary, Lord Sidmouth, and the Chancellor of the Exchequer, Nicholas Vansittart. From New Lanark he kept Sidmouth constantly informed of the progress of the scheme for reform upon which he was at work, believing himself to have been chosen and endowed for his colossal task by a supernatural force whose power was no less compelling than that to which George Rapp paid homage.

The mills and village at New Lanark provided the working model on which to try out his visionary ideas. The successful communitarian system described by Melish naturally fascinated him and he used it to support his argument in debate, at which he was adept. New Lanark was increasingly described, not as a mere factory, but as a 'community' or 'colony'. From 1815 onwards, as Owen engaged in strenuous propaganda, the name of *Harmonie* was often before the British public.

In 1818 a separate surge of interest in Rapp and his followers occurred as the result of yet another book. This attracted particular attention because it was the first to disclose their practice of celibacy. The author of the book, *Notes on a Journey from the Coast of Virginia to the Territory of Illinois*, was Morris Birkbeck, a Quaker farmer, a widower in his fifties, who in 1816 as a result of what he considered a demand for an unjustifiably large increase in rent for the land he worked in Kent, took a hasty decision, left all he had, and emigrated to the United States. There was no one to whom he could turn for advice, for he was one of the first Englishmen to consider settling in the West, where he had heard the climate and conditions were particularly favourable. In any case he was a self-assured man, confident of his skill as an agriculturist, possessing theoretical knowledge of new farming processes as well as practical experience.

He had been joined in this venture by a young man of 28, a friend of long standing called George Flower who, like Birkbeck, was a radical in politics and a Dissenter in religion, and found life under the repressive Liverpoool government far from congenial. He was without a settled purpose at the time, having painfully detached himself from an unendurably bad-tempered wife. Flower's home was at Hertford, north of London, so that he and Birkbeck were accustomed to an open rolling landscape, with orchards, and corn fields, and hop gardens; with green and distant views and high wide skies.

The obliterating blackness of the untouched forest which they encountered on the eastern side of the Alleghenies totally dismayed them. They shrank from the half light of the clearings in which the settlers had to live, encumbered by the rotting stumps of trees and the skeletons of those whose trunks had been girdled to make them die. They were however familiar with the description of the open grassy spaces in Gilbert Imlay's pioneering book about the west, and set out to find them as quickly as they could They had some difficulty, for the prairies were beyond the limit of settlement at the time, almost uninhabited, swept by great fires in the autumn, lit by Indians to promote the grazing; for lack of water, uncultivated. Their party which included Birkbeck's two daughters, two sons, and a young woman friend, remained in high spirits until it reached Vincennes, which they found to be the end of emigration; there were scarcely any people on the far bank of the Wabash. At Vincennes a sudden sense of isolation, of real fear at the vastness of the wilderness, sobered them. They were appalled at the discomfort, poverty, and what they regarded as squalor, in which the settlers they encountered lived, and how they looked, 'tall and pale like vegetables that grow in a vault, pining for light'. Sickness was rife.

In these circumstances, when they came across it, the security and order of *Harmonie* relieved and mightily impressed them. 'Concentration of capital and numbers is the only refuge from many privations and even suffering in these remote regions', Birkbeck concluded. His impression of *Harmonie* was not wholly favourable, however. He conceded that the Society was useful to the neighbourhood in furnishing articles that could not be got elsewhere, and he applauded the introduction of culinary plants and fruit trees. But he noticed that the reserve of its members and their inability to speak English made them despised as ignorant, so that their example of neatness and order was not likely to be imitated; 'men are not apt to imitate what they scorn'. Yet however ignorant, when contrasted with the slovenly habits of their neighbours, 'we see the good arising from mere association which advances these poor people a century, probably much more in the social scale beyond the solitary beings who build their huts in the wilderness'.

Birkbeck reserved his greatest disapproval for the practice of celibacy, describing it as 'slavish acquiescence under a disgusting superstition'; the reason why some people turned their backs on the Society in distaste. Birkbeck could not dismiss the suspicion from his mind that it was deliberate policy on the part of George Rapp to restrain the number of his followers who would otherwise become unmanageable. An act of policy to chain the multitude by means of superstition would indeed be base, he thought.

He and Flower took up far more Congress land than they needed—as much as they could afford—on the prairie 20 miles from *Harmonie*, across the Wabash in Illinois. While Flower returned to England to raise more money and publicize the place which their neighbours referred to as the English Prairie, Birkbeck proposed to erect a rudimentary village to house those agricultural workers they hoped to attract. These would be provided with cabins and provisions for a time in order that their labour might be available for the men of greater substance whom Birkbeck confidently expected to take up land near him.

In England emigration was seen as one means of escape from hardships arising out of the Napoleonic Wars, but it was by no means advocated or approved by all. When Birkbeck's book was published, he was hailed as its leading apologist. 'Unquestionably one of the most tempting points of view in which emigration has ever yet been represented to men of modest fortunes and industrious habits', commented the *Edinburgh Review.*

From the shelter of Long Island Birkbeck's plan was roundly denounced by a most rumbustious adversary, William Cobbett, who had been forced to quit England in 1816 when the Habeas Corpus Act had been suspended, for fear of imprisonment. Cobbett viewed emigration as desertion of the country he so passionately loved, and he could not see why Birkbeck advocated the western part of America in which to settle if he must. Better for men to go, if they had to go, to the East, within safe distances of cities like New York, or Philadelphia. Birkbeck and his friends riposted, and they fought it out, supported on either side by the two great antagonists, the *Edinburgh* and the *Quarterly Review*. As a result English Prairie was on everyone's lips and, in London, George Flower found himself besieged with hopeful applicants.

Cobbett, who received a first hand account of *Harmonie* from a friend, regarded the Rappites with robust distaste. He chastised them in his journal, the *Political Register*. 'Rapp, indeed, has done great things; but Rapp has the authority of Moses and that of Aaron united in his own person.' Rapp prospered as a result of celibacy, Cobbett charged, since there was 'first an absence of the expence [*sic*] attending the breeding and rearing of children, and, second, unremitting labour of women as well as men' . . . 'Where in all the world is the match of this to be found?' he asked.

Where else shall we look for a Society composed of persons willing and able to forego the gratification of the most powerful propensity of nature for the sake of getting money together? Where else shall we look for a band of men and women who love money better than their own bodies? . . . This Society which is a perfect prodigy and monster, ought to have the image of Mammon in their place of worship for that is the object of their devotion and not the God of nature.

Accounts of the Harmony Society, by Melish and Birkbeck, also came to the notice of Thomas Evans, a skilled artisan, variously described as a colourer of prints and a brace-maker. He was a political agitator of long standing. In 1818 he emerged from Cold Bath Fields prison to which he had been sent without trial two years before by Lord Sidmouth, who considered the society founded by him, called the Spencean Philanthropists, treasonable and dangerous. Evans's mentor, a schoolmaster called Thomas Spence who had died in 1814, had advocated the public ownership of land as the only solution to the economic distress which had England in its grip. Evans therefore rejoiced to hear of the Rappites' success; it put him in mind of schemes like those of Sir Thomas More, James Harrington, and Spence himself. 'The Utopian and visionary theories so long the objects of incessant ridicule as being utterly impractical are [at *Harmonie*] revealed in their utmost extent', he wrote, convinced that the Rappites were happy, moral, industrious, and pious. 'Now is the time to cancel Domesday Book and establish a partnership in the land; there is no other means to prevent the establishment of military discipline or the horrors of bloody revolution.'

By the time that Evans wrote his pamphlet, *Christian Policy in Full Practice among the People of Harmony*, the town had begun to attract a stream of curious visitors. In particular English travellers whose first destination was Birkbeck's settlement, did not fail to visit its celebrated neighbour. Their letters and journals provide a vivid glimpse of the loving care expended on the town.

In 1818 a manufacturer who had come out to English Prairie with a view to taking up some of Birkbeck's surplus, abandoned his intention after his first encounter with the Harmony Society so much impressed him. He was George Courtauld, head of the French Huguenot family who had started business in exile in London as goldsmiths, but turned their attention to throwing silk. George I, as this Courtauld is known to posterity, was a neighbour in Hertfordshire of Richard Flower who, in 1817, had followed his son, George, out to English Prairie. When a dispute with his partner freed him from the silk business, Courtauld headed for the Wabash country too. As a manufacturer, acquainted with the problems of supervising and educating a work-force, which in his case comprised girls from the London workhouses, Courtauld was in a position to appreciate Rapp's achievement. Himself a devout Unitarian with a strong inclination towards good works, he could not but admire the discipline displayed at *Harmonie*, the result apparently of religious principle and habit.

Courtauld hoped to be able to exploit the situation as the Harmony Society had done. He drew up plans for what he called an equitable association of people who would buy and work frontier land. This association was to resemble an ordinary joint stock company in that each person who contributed capital would receive a share of the annual profit and of the increase in value of the land which he expected to occur each year. But those who contributed only labour would also benefit in proportion. There was one proviso that Courtauld regarded as all important; 'as the peculiar suitableness of such associations arising from the scanty population, and uncultivated state of the country would be but temporary', he wrote, 'and as the equitable proportion of the profits from capital and labour, might vary considerably with the progress of the concern, the dissolution of the society at not very distant period should be provided for at the time of its foundation'. He suggested a limit of 7–10 years.

On the subject of celibacy as practised by the Harmonists, Courtauld rejected the charge made by, among others, William Cobbett. When land was abundant and needed only hands to work it, as on the Wabash, it would be folly indeed to discourage marriage on grounds of economy, he thought. He preferred the explanation put forward by his friend Richard Flower. He might be expected to know the truth for he had become friendly with the Rapps during the years he had spent at English Prairie—they shared an interest in the breeding of Spanish merino sheep. Flower, who was devout himself, was one of those who spoke of George Rapp as a true and effective religious leader. According to him the encumbrance created by families hindered spiritual development, and so the more dedicated of the Rappites forbore to marry. Courtauld wished that this explanation might be better known, and that the leaders of the Society would display more confidence in their neighbours. 'Reserve, especially in the interior of America frequently induces injurious suspicions or groundless surmises and should therefore be avoided by those who have no cause for concealment.'

Hurrying back to England, Courtauld wrote a pamphlet to publicize his equitable association, dedicated it to Frederick Rapp, and took it post haste to an acquaintance who was Manager of the only joint stock company in the textile trade, and whose interest in the Harmony Society was already a matter of record—Robert Owen of New Lanark.

By August 1819, when George Courtauld visited him, Owen's scheme for the transformation of society had taken a considerable leap forward, though much of the progress was only in his mind. The pledge to improve living and working conditions at New Lanark, embodied in the articles of partnership of the joint stock company formed at the beginning of 1814, had taken so long to be honoured that the other share-holders had remonstrated with Owen. By 1816 the main evidence of benevolent intentions was a building called by Owen the New Institution for the Formation of Character. This was designed to house a school, rooms for recreation and the instruction of adult workers after factory hours, a communal kitchen, and dining-rooms.

In the years since the formation of the new company, Owen had frequently been absent from New Lanark in pursuit of his larger vision of social reform. This now embraced the means of achieving an instant trans-formation of the whole human race, rather than the gradual improvement of the British Empire, and it had come to him in 1816 with the force of a revelation. The plan was based on the existing structure at New Lanark and would correct faults that could not otherwise be remedied. Moreover it offered a solution to the greatest problem facing England at the time—the thousands of destitute men and women wandering the country, surviving, if at all, as a charge upon the Poor Rate. Owen foresaw that the contribution that he and other property-owners were called upon to pay would shortly become an intolerable burden, while the vagrants themselves inspired in him the same fear of conspiracy and riot that haunted his good friend the Home Secretary.

Owen's plan, which he discussed with Francis Place shortly after he had conceived it, was to create self-contained villages whose inhabitants would feed themselves by cultivating the land around them—as those of New Lanark could not, there being no spare land available—while carrying on industry. As for the means of finance, Owen's original idea was to mortgage the Poor Rate to buy the land and then, as Francis Place recorded:

with another part of the money to build an oblong square ... and on each of its largest sides to build a row of huts, or houses, each containing two rooms ... in the space between these two rows a public kitchen, dining room, store houses, a school and a nursery ... from 800 to 1,000 paupers are to be put into them ... they are to cultivate the land and as they are for some time to be fed and clothed at the cheapest rate they are to produce at once much more than they consume and the surplus is to be sold to pay the interest of the money.

Eventually, when both interest and capital were paid off, the land would become the property of the community, though everything concerning it would be governed by strict regulations.

In a letter to James Mill, Place tried to convey the frenetic pace of Owen's thinking.

No objection can be taken, they (the paupers) are not to become as it were a rabbit warren, the population is to be regulated, there are to be no squabbles as to who the first occupiers shall be, they must be the paupers ... No objections from those now interested, none from prejudice or custom, no paupers to be made after first removal, no poverty, no crime, a true millennium, not for a thousand years but to eternity.

This was not to cancel Domesday Book, as Evans wanted, but to bind the prospective inhabitants as firmly and as closely to the land as any Anglo-Saxon serf. As Owen admitted later when under examination by a Parliamentary Select Committee, there would be heavy fines during the first five years, 'by way of punishment for any infringement of the rules'.

It also emerges from this that the very shape of the villages (which Owen never altered) was to play a crucial part. The Select Committee could not see why the villagers had to live in squares. Could not his measures be carried out with people remaining in separate habitations? No, said Owen, the arrangement was essential, 'to place the conduct of the people at all times before the eye of the community'. George Courtauld agreed with him as to the design; remarking that though *Harmonie* was handsomely laid out in wide, straight streets crossing each other at right angles, 'Mr Owen's plan for a village in the form of a square would be much more convenient and ornamental'.

Owen had Courtauld's account of *Harmonie* reprinted in at least one newspaper and included it in his latest piece of propaganda which he addressed to one of the leading political economists of the day, David Ricardo. Owen was in dispute with Ricardo and many of his colleagues over their *laissez-faire* attitude towards economic problems, and particularly with regard to the proposition that 'if you cause plenty and comfort to abound among the poor they will increase with such rapidity that the means of subsistence will no longer be found for them'. Owen contended that merely by erecting villages on his plan a means of subsistence for large numbers of people would immediately be provided. He seized upon *Harmonie* as an example. 'The Society at Indiana with greatly inferior machinery to that which may immediately be introduced into a British establishment is rapidly increasing in wealth (independent of the increased value of their land) and it is not found that individuals having once joined these establishments are returning to their former situation in society' he argued.

The fact that both John Melish and George Courtauld had praised the moral character, aptitude for work, and docile behaviour of the Rappites was of the greatest importance to Robert Owen, who valued these attributes above all others. In *Three Letters to David Ricardo* he therefore enlisted the example of the Harmony Society to bolster the weaker part of his thesis, but the one that obsessed him—that those people who were exposed to his system would not only acquire moral worth but instant happiness. 'No time should be lost in bringing this about. Already are the seeds of revolution sown in our country, and quickly must they produce a sanguinary harvest, unless the condition of the lower orders is greatly ameliorated.'

With regard to the economic aspect of his argument Owen's understanding was sound and his judgement shrewd. In fact his genius lay in the unremitting effort he made throughout his life to convince those in power in a developing industrial society of the urgent need to establish control over conditions of labour, the means of exchange, and the distribution of capital. In this he is rightly regarded as one of the forerunners of Socialism and as a predecessor of Karl Marx. But his purpose did not take justice into account, and his method of achieving control—through isolating groups of people in villages whose administration was, to say the least, paternalistic—was dismissed as hopelessly utopian by Marx, who held that change would come from within as soon as the working class realized its plight.

Though Owen's plan for Villages of Unity and Mutual Co-operation, as he called them, was cautiously welcomed as a useful experiment by many prominent people—politicians, churchmen and economists, David Ricardo included—it was immediately distasteful to the very people whose welfare it was designed to assist, as those who spoke for them did not fail to make clear.

Cobbett rumbled on, echoing his earlier strictures on the subject of the Harmony Society.

[Owen] is for establishing innumerable *communities* of paupers. Each is to be resident in an *inclosure*, somewhat resembling a barrack establishment, only more extensive. I do not clearly understand whether the sisterhoods and brotherhoods are to form distinct communities, like the nuns and friars, or whether they are to mix together promiscuously; but I perceive that they are all to be under a very *regular discipline*; and that wonderful peace, happiness, and national benefit are to be the result.

A leading article in the *Reformists' Register* edited by the political satirist, William Hone, was headed 'Let Us Alone, Mr Owen', and went on:

Robert Owen Esq., a benevolent cotton-spinner, and one of His Majesty's Justices of the Peace for the county of Lanark, having seen the world, and afterwards cast his eye over his very well regulated manufactory in the said county imagines he has taken a *New View of Society*, and conceives that all human beings are so many plants, which have been out of the earth for a few thousand years and require to be reset. He accordingly determines to dibble them in squares after a new fashion; and to make due provision for removing the offsets. I do not know a gentleman in England better satisfied with himself than Mr. Robert Owen. Everybody, I believe, is convinced of Mr. Owen's benevolence, and that he purposes to do us much good. I ask him to *let us alone*, lest he do us much mischief.

Owen's plan, Hone concluded, was aimed at turning the whole country into a workhouse.

Jonathan Wooler, Editor of the ultra radical paper, *Black Dwarf*, accused the government of secretly financing Owen's propaganda as a means of controlling the poor, and of stifling legitimate opposition. There may have been some truth in this, for Owen's friend, Vansittart, the Chancellor of the Exchequer, declared himself ready to ask Parliament for a grant of £20,000 of public money if funds from other sources were forthcoming to launch one such village scheme. Nothing came of it in the short term, nor did any significant amount of money come in from appeals to the public.

There were, however, other avenues to explore which Owen did not neglect. In the early years of the century while his father-in-law, David Dale, was still alive, he had observed him closely in his capacity as Joint Agent of the Royal Bank of Scotland. Under Dale's direction during nearly twenty years the Bank became the driving force behind Glasgow's spectacular advance in wealth and international trade. Owen was fascinated by the world of high finance and himself indulged in the discounting of bills and the buying and selling of shares. In September 1819 Francis Place, who kept a watching brief on all Owen's activities, told his friend, the economist Thomas Hodgskin, that Owen had put his proposals on quite a new ground, 'namely that the establishment of his villages would answer as a mere mercantile speculation, and if he could succeed in convincing the speculative men in the City that this was true, we should soon see Villages starting up'. In this context the detailed figures supplied by Frederick Rapp to John Melish demonstrating the commercial success of the first *Harmonie* must have been a valuable talking point.

George Courtauld returned to the United States in early 1820 and, with several members of his family, set up a company to develop land in Ohio. Not long after, however, he died while on a visit to Cincinnati. But by then a direct link had been established between *Harmonie* in Indiana and New Lanark in a letter written by Robert Owen, dated 4 August 1820.

The Rev. Mr. Rapp
MOST WORTHY SIR: Having heard much of your society, & feeling a peculiar interest respecting it I am induced to solicit a correspondence with you, in the expectation of procuring a correct account of your establishment.

My first attention was called to it by some travels published in America by a Mr Mellish [sic] who in 1811 visited the original settlement near Pittsburgh—and who gave many details which to me appeared to promise many future advantages. You have since had an opportunity of creating a second settlement under the full benefit of the experience derived from the first & the particulars of the result of these two experiments would be of real value to me in order to ascertain the practical inconveniences which arise from changes to society from a state of private to public property under the peculiar circumstances by which your colonies have been surrounded.

If you can furnish me with any authentic printed or manuscript, statement of the rise, progress & present state of Harmony, you would confer upon me a very particular obligation. The gentleman who conveys this letter will perhaps have the goodness to take the charge of them & bring them to England. Should this be inconvenient to him any parcel addressed for me to New Lanark, North Britain & forwarded to Mr Quincy Adams, the Secretary of State for the American Home Department, would I have no doubt come safe.

There is a colony here of about 2400 persons who I have already placed under new circumstances preparatory to a still more improved arrangement from which incalculable advantages to all classes may be expected. I am now in the midst of preparing a further development of the system I have in view & it will give me pleasure to send you a copy of it at the earliest opportunity after it shall be ready. In the meantime I send you copies of such works as I have already published & which I request you to accept.

I am sir yr most obt servt   Robt Owen

If an answer was returned to this it has not survived. Possibly it was, for several letters exist in which Frederick Rapp replied at length, and courteously, to enquiries about the nature of the Harmony Society from persons wishing to join. He always warned them that the rules were strict, and the life not suited to more than a very few. Whatever passed between the two 'colonies' it was sufficient to ensure that in 1824, when Father Rapp decided to abandon Indiana for an uncleared site on which to build from nothing a third and final town, Robert Owen was apprised of his intention to sell *Harmonie.*

No record exists, or has yet been found, in which the decision to move from Indiana back to Pennsylvania was clearly set down. Like the first it appears mysterious, a peremptory act of Father Rapp in response to a communication from on High which he and his followers had no choice but to obey. There is evidence that, more than thirty years after their beginning, the *Book of Revelation* still played an important part in the spiritual life of the Rappites; at *Harmonie* on the Wabash the great door of their second church which was still under construction in 1824, was carved with the apocalyptic symbol of the Golden Rose. Professor Arndt takes it to be significant that the move from Indiana took place exactly ten years after they arrived, as the move from Pennsylvania was ten years from their settling in the wilderness. Be that as it may, some clues exist as to why their departure might have been considered politic as well as fated. These are mostly, though not entirely, economic.

At the time Robert Owen wrote to George Rapp in 1820, things had begun to go seriously wrong. The boom that had promoted a mushroom growth of banks in the western country was ending; many banks failed and many who suffered were customers of the Harmony Society. It became difficult to sell the goods produced on the Wabash. Unlike their neighbours the Society could live on its own, as a closed religious order might have been expected to do. But George and Frederick Rapp were very uneasy at the decline in trade; lack of orders meant that the machines had to be stopped for a time, something that Father regarded as an affront to morality. One of his remedies was to put the men to work building a second church, a vast and beautiful edifice, with pillars of different kinds of wood—and on the door, the Golden Rose.

Then the Wabash River had proved a disappointing setback to their hopes of establishing a commercial centre serving markets throughout the West. Often it was in flood, threatening the buildings of the town, and dangerous to flatboats. Or it fell so low that no vessel could get up to *Harmonie* and heavy barrels of goods had to be manhandled to the nearest landing on the Ohio. Manpower was a problem; a great number of hands was needed to make full use of all the land they owned at *Harmonie*. By 1824 the original members of the Society had grown too old for much of the work; new blood was needed and it was hard to find.

In 1821 two emissaries were sent home to Iptingen to recruit, and to collect money due to the Society from the inheritances of its members. They were met without affection. Whatever the role played by George Rapp in the débâcle of 1816, the distress endured by those tempted to emigrate had been laid at his door, while tales of his greed and over-bearing behaviour freely circulated. As far as the Society's hold over its existing members went, it was true that this was tighter than ever. In 1818 the book that recorded what each person had brought to the common fund on joining was ceremonially burnt. From that time forward whoever wished to depart would receive back no more than the most humble member. When their Doomsday came the Rappites would truly stand as equals before the Lord.

As for their American neighbours in Indiana, the docility with which the Rappites accepted their circumscribed life was seen by them as a kind of servility, and they did not like it. The fact that women were employed in the fields offended the settlers; their own wives might struggle with a domestic burden beyond their strength but field work was for men. Prompted by runaways, sometimes young men and women who were moved to contravene the rule of celibacy, or indentured labourers, a legend grew up that Rapp was a tyrant who held people against their will while cheating them out of their rightful wage. Years of unspoken hostility eventually erupted into violence when settlers invaded the town in search of workers they imagined to be kept prisoner. The court case that followed the affray went against the Society. Frederick Rapp was moved by this to complain that they could not expect justice from a jury of local people.

All in all it made sense to seek a place adjacent to good water transport, healthier, and just as fertile, where they could be among people who understood them. In the spring of 1824 George Rapp began the search for a site back in Pennsylvania, not far from Pittsburgh and their first home.

In the prospectus for its sale drafted by Frederick Rapp, *Harmonie* in Indiana was described as 'a very Valuable property . . . well worthy of the attention of Capitalists'. Richard Flower who was about to visit England was commissioned to find a buyer on that side of the Atlantic. The minimum asking price was $150,000 on which Flower's commission was to be $5,000, plus 20 per cent of any advance on that sum; at the same time as they advised him of these terms, the Rapps warned Flower not to try to go much higher than the original figure. They were obviously anxious to avoid the kind of bargain they had struck over *Harmonie* in Pennsylvania whose new owner, Abraham Ziegler, had frequently to ask them for extra time in paying the instalments. Flower was also told that though they would advertise the town in American newspapers they would not sign any contract until 1 January 1825 in order to give him time to effect a sale in England—where the greatest number of 'Capitalists' might be supposed to reside—and to inform them of it.

As Frederick described it, *Harmonie* with 20,000 acres of first-rate land adjoining, was situated on the big Wabash 70 miles by water from its mouth, and only 15 miles by land from the Ohio River, 'the Wabash being navigable for many miles above *Harmonie* at all seasons for boats of 20 tons and a great part of the year for Steam boats of the Middle Class'. Among the many improvements on the property, the prospectus went on, were 2,000 acres of land in a high state of cultivation; 15 of which were in vineyards, 35 in orchards containing about 1,500 apple and pear trees, together with peaches [which grew virtually wild] and gardens of pleasure. There was a large 3-storey water-mill situated on a bayou of the Wabash; an extensive factory for cotton and woollen goods, with all the necessary outbuildings for dyeing and dressing broad cloth; 2 sawmills and 1 oil and hemp-mill; 1 large brick church, 'a frame ditto with steeples' and the famous bell. There were granaries, warehouses, barns, and stables; 2 large distilleries and a brewery with a malt-kiln. The dwellings consisted of 6 two-storey brick houses, about 60 feet square; 40 'convenient' two-storey brick and frame houses of various sizes, and '86 Log ditto'; all had kitchens, with stabling and well stocked gardens. The property was supplied with never-failing wells and springs of good water and a number of running streams. With the optimism that usually characterizes such productions, Frederick's prospectus concluded: 'The adjoining Country is now thickly Inhabited and there is a great demand for all kinds of Mechanics and for Manufactured Articles generally.'

Flower was armed with a list of prominent manufacturers to approach in England but it is likely that he went straight to Robert Owen who, given their mutual acquaintance with George Courtauld and his well-publicized interest in 'Villages', must have seemed the most promising contact. At any rate Flower arrived at New Lanark in July 1824.

Besides its master he found there Chester Harding, an American painter who left an account of the negotiations. He had become a friend of Owen after painting his portrait. Owen admired him both as an artist and for his backwoodsman's ability to turn his hand to anything. Harding had been brought up in the wilds of Kentucky and knew Indiana and Illinois well, having spent years wandering in the West in search of subjects, the most famous being the Indian scout, the legendary Daniel Boone. Knowing nothing of Flower's commission from the Rapps, Harding said he suspected him of talking up *Harmonie*, with a view to increasing the value of his land at English Prairie. When Owen jumped at the offer as a splendid opportunity to put his village scheme into operation, Harding was dismayed, and tried to persuade him to transfer his experiment somewhere nearer civilization—to Massachusetts, for example.

Harding was well aware of the heavy responsibility and expense awaiting the purchaser of *Harmonie*. The entire population was preparing to depart: soon they would abandon the flocks and herds and roving hogs to new masters, leaving the fields and gardens to be tilled by strangers, and handing on the old steam-engine to whoever could find a way to make it go.

Owen's enthusiasm made light of the difficulties. Flower's proposition was greeted so warmly by him that George Rapp was shortly able to tell Frederick of rumours to the effect that 'the famous Mr Owen' had already bought *Harmonie*; he only wished it were true, he said. In the opinion of most Americans and many English, Robert Owen was a very wealthy man, a most experienced industrialist, and a noted philanthropist, with access to persons in high places. His achievement was acknowledged to be the more striking in view of his manner, which was

renowned for its candour and simplicity. It was an impression Owen was
concerned to foster by every means he could, but it was not true. He was
not wealthy in the sense that most people understood, and he was not
simple. Beneath the surface was a quick and clever mind that betrayed
itself at times as boldly calculating. The effrontery he showed on these
occasions was such that those who became aware of it were at a loss to
reconcile it with the famous philanthropist and were driven to conclude
that Owen was unbalanced.

John Quincy Adams knew Robert Owen well over a long period. His
first encounter with him was in 1817 when he was US Minister in
London. Later, as Secretary of State and President, he was foremost
among the public figures whose support Owen tried to enlist for his
venture in America. Privately Adams thought that Owen was 'crafty
crazy'; 'a speculative, scheming, mischievous man'.

The contrast between the public aspect of Owen and his inner self was
due in part to the circumstances of his youth. He was born in 1771 at
Newtown in mid-Wales, the son of a saddler married to a farmer's
daughter. At the early age of ten he left Wales to be apprenticed to a
draper. England was a foreign country; he scarcely spoke the language.
What education he got came from observation rather than from books.
Soon he put on the manners and speech of his master's customers. In
those days drapers' establishments acted as country banks so that Robert
acquired a knowledge of finance as well as a feel for cloth. Both
contributed to his success when in Manchester in the early 1790s he
ventured into the cotton trade, then expanding rapidly. His first post as
Manager of a factory of some size was under Peter Drinkwater whose
reputation as an enlightened employer of work people has had to be
rescued from the aspersions a jealous Owen afterwards cast on it. In
about 1794 he set up on his own and, as countless others did, rode the
boom, though without resources in the event of a collapse.

PART II

THE MASTER OF NEW LANARK

CHAPTER 4

'A SPECULATIVE, SCHEMING, MISCHIEVOUS MAN'

In the summer of 1824, when Richard Flower appeared at New Lanark with the prospectus for *Harmonie*, Robert Owen had already been engaged for several months on the detailed planning of the first of his ideal villages. It was to be constructed as a perfect square—thus improving upon New Lanark where the nature of the site dictated that the buildings be arranged in rows—and it was to occupy land which had been dedicated to the purpose by Alexander Hamilton of Dalzell, the son of a Scots landowner, who was an ardent supporter of Owen's plans as expounded in *A New View of Society*. The scheme might have been expected to provide Owen with an excellent way of testing his theories, with New Lanark so conveniently near. Yet Owen insisted that *Harmonie* offered an unprecedented opportunity for the experiment he had in mind. According to his eldest son, 'here was a village ready built, a territory capable of supporting tens of thousands in a country where the expression of thought was free and the people unsophisticated'. The price asked by the Rapps was also attractive—some £30,000 at the current rate of exchange. It was less than a third of what Owen had calculated such a village would cost anywhere in the British Isles.

No doubt he also counted on the same increase in value if he invested there as he understood the Harmonists to have obtained; from only $25 a head on arriving in America, after 21 years 'a fair estimate gave them *two thousand dollars* for each person—man, woman, and child, probably *ten times* the average wealth throughout the United States'. Profit was always a factor, as Hamilton of Dalzell made clear. He told Owen he was convinced the village on his land would pay subscribers 10 per cent on their money in a few years time: he proposed to take up £2,000 in one lot and more under fictitious names. 'The share will be saleable as any other share of a canal, Tontine etc', Hamilton declared. The supposition that Owen's interest in *Harmonie* was not as philanthropic as he represented it to be, is strengthened by the fact that he nowhere made it clear what kind of people were to be the subjects of his 'experiment' at the furthest limit of civilization. He did not count the cost of transporting paupers, or anyone else, to the American West; indeed he was on record as disapproving of emigration as such, fearing that it would deprive the country of its fighting men.

Yet it may be that he envisaged a settlement in Indiana as an outlet for the working people of New Lanark at a future date. He was concerned about the increase in population that had inevitably gained pace since David Dale built the mills. As they grew up the children of the workers threatened order in the village and were an unwelcome charge on the means of subsistence. In 1824 the departure abroad of skilled artisans was prohibited under the Combination Acts, and penalties could be exacted from those who encouraged such a move. But a few weeks before Richard Flower's arrival at New Lanark, and as a result of a campaign brilliantly conducted by Owen's colleague, Francis Place, a Parliamentary Committee had recommended that the Acts should be repealed. The way was about to be opened for Owen to export New Lanark lock, stock, and barrel if he so desired.

The cotton mills at Lanark were built by David Dale in 1785 in a remote ravine twenty miles from Glasgow. His regime was widely admired as an example of enlightened management. The school he established for the pauper children, who proved to be the most readily available labour, was famous. John Marshall, a prominent Leeds flax spinner who visited New Lanark in 1800, shortly after Dale had sold it to Robert Owen and two partners, noted in his journal that the children were not only taught reading and writing after factory hours, but also the 'polite accomplishments', including dancing. 'The present proprietors it is said, wished to give that up, but could not because it was contracted for by Mr Dale in the indentures.' Dale's other preoccupation was as chief preacher of an independent sect which, under his leadership, turned aside from undiluted Calvinism towards a more direct experience of the love of God. As the Rappites did, Dale and his followers leaned towards the practices of the early Christian church, including love feasts and the holding of goods in common. Even after his death in 1806 the Independents were strong at New Lanark, and occupied influential positions at the mills, a fact which argues against the universal vice and drunkenness described in *A New View of Society*. Dale's eldest daughter, Ann Caroline, who married Owen at the same time as he bought New Lanark, was fervent in her father's religious belief, and in its practice, which she imparted to her children.

Up to the time that Owen, in partnership with two well-established firms, Borrodaile and Atkinson of London and Bartons of Manchester, bought the Scottish cotton-spinning village, the progress he had made had depended on his own resourcefulness and effort, or so he would have people believe. In fact he relied on David Dale for many years, especially in matters of finance. As he portrayed himself in his autobiography, *The Life of Robert Owen, Written by Himself*, he resembled the hero of a book which he confessed had caught his imagination when he was very young and remained with him for the rest of his life—*Robinson Crusoe*. Struggling to survive on his desert island with nothing to assist him but his own sharp wits, Crusoe was kin to Robert Owen in what the latter once described to his eldest son as 'the contest of myself against the world'. Like Crusoe Owen saw himself as a castaway, obliged to make the best use he could of whatever came to hand.

New Lanark was Robert Owen's island, subject to his will, as far as he was concerned without a history until he would write it, or create it. A vivid picture of the place which played so crucial a role in Owen's life, and dictated his thinking on the subject of reform, emerges from his earliest literary effort, *A Statement regarding the New Lanark Establishment*. It was written in 1812 as a prospectus for the sale of the mills. It contained suggestions aimed at making the running of the village easier; but the overall impression was that Owen regarded its inhabitants as part of a machine.

It was a dangerous machine owing to the peculiar situation of the village. It was about a mile below the ancient burgh of Lanark, where the river Clyde encountered a series of shallow waterfalls whose power was harnessed to drive the mill machinery. Together with the rows of workers' houses the factory buildings were jammed on to a very narrow piece of ground between the steep escarpment and the fast-flowing river. The poet, Robert Southey, who was one of thousands of visitors after Owen's writings had made the place famous, thought the hill so steep that you could drop stones into the chimneys of the houses. These, with the irregular and grey appearance, reminded him of an enormous convent, of the kind he had encountered when travelling in Portugal.

There was scarcely any open ground belonging to the village; it was surrounded by gentlemen's estates barricaded against trespass. Two thousand people had nowhere to go after working hours except to the single room inhabited by whole families, or into the space between the rows of tenements. The lade—the channel carrying water that drove the huge wheels—ran unprotected through the centre of the village, a constant threat to young children. Whoever was in charge had to consider how to deal with an overlarge population crowded into an unsuitable space, with the added risk of fire.

Owen's prospectus suggested improvements to accommodate a daily influx of workers from Lanark; so as to run the mills on a double shift and keep wages down. The road, which was steep and impassable for young children in winter, must be repaired to make the population of the old town available for the manufacturing processes of the new. The improvements were to include a playground for the youngest children (to free their mothers for work in the mills and to keep them from falling into the lade); a communal kitchen where the workers could be more economically fed; a dining-room; a hall of recreation; and a school. This school would train the children specifically for their employment in the mills, and all their habits, bodily and mental, would be formed to carry them to a high state of perfection. Such perfection was desirable, not for its own sake, but in Owen's words in the prospectus, because these people were to be entrusted with New Lanark's other prime asset, 'nice and valuable machinery'.

This indisputably detached view of the inhabitants of New Lanark was typical of Owen. Paradoxically the man who more than any other manufacturer of the time was represented as having taken the welfare of his workers to his heart, regarded them not as individuals but as forming a substance which, subject to certain rules which he devised, might be moulded into whatever shape he desired. As he explained in *A Statement*, children who were exposed to this system at an early age would 'receive any fixed character which may be deemed the most advantageous for them to possess'.

The people of New Lanark can be discerned only as a group, their faces turned aside; with one or two exceptions their names are unknown. None of the work people left an account of their experiences. It is only in the volumes of evidence before Parliamentary committees that a solitary man or woman provides a glimpse of what life was like for them during the 25 years of Owen's management; their comments contradicting his sanguine account of what he had achieved. It was not so in *Harmonie* where many people observed and recorded Owen's conduct from day to day. Their remarks show that, just as George Rapp proposed to recreate Iptingen on the banks of the Wabash, Owen had in mind an ideal New Lanark there.

The details of Robert Owen's American experience have only fairly recently become available to scholars; they cast a good deal of light upon his personality and on motives which he preferred to keep to himself, until such time as he presented a considered version in his autobiography. But in the United States he was to be exposed to question and comment, far more so than he was in England; Americans were naturally disposed to get to the bottom of whatever interested them, and uninhibited in the process. At the same time Owen met people there in whom, unusually, he was disposed to confide. One of these was George Courtauld's close friend, the Pittsburgh glass manufacturer, Benjamin Bakewell. According to Bakewell, Owen's whole attitude to life stemmed from his aversion to what he described as 'the most revolting system of ultra Calvinism' in which he had been brought up. Owen could not believe that the thing called religion stemmed from God, said Bakewell, that great and good Being whose tender mercies were over all His works: 'without examining further he seems to have rejected revelation altogether'.

Just as George Rapp had done, Owen detested the concept of original sin, of salvation available only to a chosen few which formed the pivot of Calvinism. His attempt to escape from its consequences led him to adopt an alternative belief that excluded sin and denied free will. In the process he abjured Christianity, for though he firmly believed that God created man he could not bring himself to acknowledge that Christ must die to save him. He seized instead upon the idea that man was wholly a creature of circumstance and published it to the world as a discovery. At the same time he proclaimed the power of education—properly directed—to mould men's characters. Others might struggle to reconcile the inconsistency in his thought; Owen never allowed it to disturb him. 'Thus was I forced', he wrote in his autobiography, 'through seeing the error of their foundation, to abandon all belief in every religion which had been taught to man. But my religious feelings were immediately replaced by the spirit of universal charity—not for a sect or party, or for a country or colour, but for the human race, and with a real and ardent desire to do them good.'

There can be no doubt that Owen was sincere in this desire. But his tremendous and lifelong effort to translate it into action by means of establishing what he called 'favourable conditions' within his Villages of Unity and Mutual Co-operation was limited and frustrated by the demands of his singular personality. He was prey to a monstrous egotism that distorted his perception of reality. It prompted him to intervene disastrously in matters that, begun by others, were better left to them. It cut him off from a most effective source of power—a seat in Parliament. Owen's inability to sustain the dialogue with other people required by the democratic process was as marked as George Rapp's, and moved E. P. Thompson to remark that he 'had a vacant place in his mind where other men have political responses'. Many people avoided him as a result; he became what the *Dictionary of National Biography* described as 'one of those intolerable bores who are the salt of the earth'.

In August 1812 Owen had been dismissed as Manager of the New Lanark mills. His co-partners were displeased by his inability to meet calls for extra capital to sustain the spinning business, which was in difficulty as a consequence of adverse trading conditions during the Napoleonic wars. They were also affronted by his financial activities which, to say the least, were questionable. Eventually they voted to wind up the New Lanark Company. Owen, who was on the verge of being declared bankrupt, was desperate to preserve the business as his only source of income, in which he placed all his capital. He set off for London to seek what he called 'new arrangements'—new partners rich enough to refloat the business. He left in such a hurry that his wife, Ann Caroline, had to borrow £100 from the under-manager to feed her large household.

One of the first people to read *A Statement regarding the New Lanark Establishment*, after Owen arrived in London, was William Godwin, who met him at a dinner party given for him by the Scot, Daniel Stuart, a supporter of the Tory government and owner of the evening newspaper, the *Courier*. It was Godwin who took Owen along to the book-lined room behind the tailor's shop at 16 Charing Cross where Francis Place kept open house. Godwin's diary shows that during the next few months, while Owen was composing the essays that have the title *A New View of Society*, he was frequently at Godwin's house for breakfast, tea, and dinner.

It was hardly surprising, therefore, that Owen's work owed a great deal to the ideas in Godwin's celebrated book, *An Enquiry concerning Political Justice*. It was a distillation of all the most liberal ideas that had bubbled to the surface of the Enlightenment. Published in 1793, its theme was the need for a new social order under which the individual would experience justice and equality, but above all, freedom.

When Owen's essays appeared William Hazlitt pounced at once, disliking their pretence of revelation, and in particular Owen's use in the title of his favourite word—a *new* view of society. 'It may be true but it is not new', Hazlitt said. 'It is not coeval whatever the author and proprietor may think, with the New Lanark mills, but it is as old as the royal borough of Lanark; or as the county of Lanark itself. It is as old as the Political Justice of Mr Godwin, as the Oceana of Harrington, as the Utopia of Sir Thomas More, as the Republic of Plato ...'

Though Owen never acknowledged their help it was Francis Place and James Mill who edited *A New View of Society* which bears the stamp of their lucidity. All Owen's other writings were, as one of his disciples was later to admit, very woolly. Their influence, and that of William Godwin, breathed warmth into the calculating attitude which Owen displayed towards the work people of New Lanark, as it was expressed in his prospectus of the mills. This was as foreign to Place and his friends as was Owen's superior manner which became more pronounced as he assumed the role of philosopher–reformer; 'he nodded to me as if crowned with laurels', an irritated friend of Bentham wrote. At one of the meetings called to discuss Owen's plan for villages, a journeyman got up and opposed his theories, speaking with authority and judgement, according to the political economist, Robert Torrens, who heard him and told Place: 'all my respect and kindness for Owen, as a benevolent man, could not restrain some movements of indignation at his daring arrogance in charging with brutal ignorance and stupidity a people from amongst the labouring classes of which such admirable displays of intellect are daily breaking forth'.

Place himself was deeply offended by the second edition of *A New View of Society* which came out in 1816. In this, Owen, having given him an assurance to the contrary, included a passage he had written which Place had already seen and condemned, for it expressed contempt for the electoral process and for the common people, people whom he and his radical friends were passionately anxious to see enfranchised and in whose interest Place was later to draft the famous Charter. 'Now I have to complain of want of candour, of want of honesty and of falsehood in these passages', Place wrote to Owen, 'faults which you of all men should have been the last to commit ... You have done the people an injustice and if the Essays could be widely distributed you would have made man enemy to man.' The people were not responsible for the riots which attended elections, those riots which intimidated Owen and of which he complained; they were the fault of the repressive government, Place insisted, of the Home Secretary, Lord Sidmouth, and his fellow Ministers—'the very persons whom you laud to the skies'.

Though Robert Owen wrote constantly about the need to make people happy, the word that best conveyed his meaning in this connection, and which he often used, was docile. Justice, and the liberty of the individual which Godwin venerated, did not enter into his philosophy, nor play much part of New Lanark. Instead there was the paternalistic device of the silent monitor which hung beside each worker and showed one of four colours to show how well he or she had performed; itself a contradiction of Owen's saying that man was not a fit subject for praise or blame. There were other rules supervised by certain individuals that Henry Grey Macnab, who made a visit of inspection to New Lanark in 1819 on behalf of the Duke of Kent, described as military police. Difficult families, it was said, were relegated to a part of the village which became known as Botany Bay; there was a curfew, and random searches of the person to prevent theft.

Owen treated those of his workers who behaved themselves with condescending kindness, but in the mass he was frightened of them. His attitude may have owed something to his friendship with the gravely harassed man who, as Home Secretary, was for far too long responsible for the maintenance of order in a disturbed country. *A New View of Society*, however, caused its readers to conclude that Owen was not only in favour of equality but went so far as to advocate a community of goods, an impression that was sustained by Owen's frequent references in his propaganda to the example of the Harmony Society. The discrepancy arose from his view of mankind as it was and as it might be, if his new scheme of things were put into effect. The leap was too great for some who, observing how far Owen's actions departed from his declared belief, either condemned him as a hypocrite, or had recourse to the view that he was not quite sane.

A public debate about his scheme for Villages of Unity held in 1817 ended in complete defeat for his proposals, according to Robert Torrens. Yet Owen wrote to *The Times* to say that the meeting was more favourable in its result than he had ever expected it would be. 'The most barefaced and impudent thing which ever appeared in print', Torrens exclaimed. 'I shall not attempt to decide whether it is composed of wilful falsehoods or of the vain imaginings of a disordered intellect. But as I feel a strong repugnance to believe that Robert Owen is a knave, my inclination is still to consider him as an interesting enthusiast in whose brain a copulation between vanity and benevolence has engendered madness.'

The undeniably odd aspects of Owen's character did not come to the notice of his last partners at New Lanark until after they had committed themselves to a share in it. The first consideration that occurred to them when Owen appeared in London with his prospectus at the beginning of

1813 was that here at last was the opportunity they had been waiting for. New Lanark offered the utilitarians what they most desired, a proving ground on which to try their new ideas, above all those concerning the simultaneous instruction of large numbers of children.

When Owen came in contact with them, Bentham, Place, Mill, Allen, and others of their associates were in the grip of a great excitement about a new method of imparting knowledge. Though its invention was disputed between a Doctor Andrew Bell and the Quaker, Joseph Lancaster, its introduction into special schools was principally effected by Lancaster, a dedicated teacher, but a wayward and extravagant man. The chief feature of the method was that a certain number of boys (or girls) chosen to be monitors passed on lessons learned by rote to the other children. It was the factory system as applied to education. The Benthamites who had the greatest respect for their fellow human beings, saw nothing wrong in that, but proclaimed Lancaster's method with evangelical enthusiasm, speaking of the power of education made widely available by this method to regenerate the world.

From about 1802 Lancastrian schools had been opened in many parts of England and from 1808 in Scotland, but its founder encountered financial difficulties, and by 1812 his schools were being run by an organization called the British and Foreign School Society. On its committee were Francis Place, William Allen, and another Quaker who took a share in the New Lanark Company, Joseph Fox.

A joint stock company was formed at the end of 1813 to buy the New Lanark mills at auction. Robert Owen had 5 shares in it, Bentham 1½, William Allen 1, Joseph Fox 1. John Walker, a Quaker who was to beome a close friend of Robert Owen, had 2½, Joseph Foster and Michael Gibbs, 1 each. The first project the company agreed to introduce into the village was a school organized according to Lancaster's method, to which the British and Foreign School Society contributed teaching aids. The articles of partnership of the new company specifically called for the establishment of this school, and also that, as in every other sponsored by the Society, that there should not be religious instruction of a sectarian kind; only that the Bible should be used as an aid to learning to read. This limitation was considered vital by the men of various religious persuasions, and of none, who were members of the committee.

Robert Owen's behaviour after the mills were bought at the beginning of 1814 and he was reinstated as Manager gave the new partners cause for concern. His vehement opposition to organized religion had been concealed from all but a few so far, among whom were Godwin and

Francis Place. When William Allen discovered that Owen was proposing to make his attitude public—which he did most dramatically at the meeting in 1817 called to promote his scheme for Villages of Unity and Co-operation—Allen was not only disturbed by reason of his own piety but also feared for the precarious existence of the British and Foreign School Society. At the same time, Allen and his partners had sent in an accountant to examine the New Lanark books. Allen, alarmed by the state of confusion they were found to be in, was obliged to remonstrate with Owen, and to call attention to his failure to do anything but talk about the proposed school. He had not yet even signed the articles of partnership, a year after they had been drawn up.

On 20 October 1815 Allen wrote to Robert Owen reminding him that the articles included an agreement,

To make the work people as comfortable as possible in their temporal concerns by economic and judicious arrangements. To remove as far as possible from them temptations to vice and immorality. To provide a savings bank for their relief in sickness and comfort in old age. To provide education for the whole of their children and to form in them the habits of morality and virtue. To encourage all in following that system of religion which their conscience shall approve.

Elsewhere Allen noted that the articles also stipulated that the children should not be employed in the mills belonging to the partnership until they were of such an age for it not to be prejudicial to their health—one of the cardinal points of Robert Owen's programme as a factory reformer.

These were the objects that brought him and his colleagues into the concern, Allen told Robert Owen,

but though nearly two years have since elapsed we have not specific and satisfactory information as to the progress made in any of them, and are very much at a loss to reply to the queries put to us by those who have heard of what was intended to be done at Lanark. The eyes of the people are upon us, many for evil and some for good; we wished to have some particulars respecting the population and the progress made in realizing the above objects, but have only received a list of the members. Do write to me, [he urged Owen], not in vague terms but definitely.

When the New Institution was finally completed in January 1816 the public was invited to inspect the amenities available. These included the hall of recreation and the school proposed in *A Statement regarding the New Lanark Establishment*. The school was the greatest attraction. Owen was genuinely fond of children, and they of him; his strongest claim to innovation lay in the infant classes established at New Lanark, whose pupils were allowed a freedom to develop at their own pace rare in those days, and treated with obvious affection. Those who were older but not yet of an age to go into the mills were instructed in the elements of geography, science, and history by the use of maps, drawings, and charts, rather than from books. These lectures, which were open to visitors, became famous; they seemed to show that Robert Owen, who frequently asserted his belief that education was vital to the development of mankind, was doing his charitable best to bring it to the children of his workers. Yet a larger purpose was inferred from the sight of children answering questions on these subjects than was intended; their other lessons went no further than the three Rs, and included instruction in the tasks they would have to perform in the mills.

Nor would the picture alter much when Owen's Villages came into being. Having read his speech at the opening of the New Institution, Fanny, daughter of Gilbert Imlay and Mary Wollstonecraft, whom Godwin adopted when he married her mother, took fright at the statement that the inhabitants would study nothing but 'Mechanics and Chemistry'. 'I hate and am sick at heart at the misery I see my fellow human beings suffering', Fanny told her foster sister, Mary Shelley, 'but I own I should not like to see the extinction of all genius, talent, and elevated generous feeling in Great Britain which I conceive to be the natural consequence of Mr Owen's plan.'

It was Robert Owen's contention in later life that his lack of success with his village scheme in England resulted from the immediate desertion of all his powerful supporters due to his public denunciation of sectarian religion in the summer of 1817. No doubt some did abandon him but many remained: Sidmouth and Vansittart, for example, went on supporting him for several years, as did the Duke of Kent until his early death in 1820. The falling off was gradual and occurred when people divined what an obsessive nature lay beneath his composure, and his famous candour progressed to wild exaggeration. Hazlitt gives a glimpse of him at about this time.

Mr Owen is a man remarkable for one idea. It is that of himself and the Lanark cotton-mills. He carried this idea backwards and forwards with him from Glasgow to London without allowing anything for attrition, and expects to find it in the same state of purity and perfection in the latter place as at the former. He acquires a wonderful velocity and impenetrability in his undaunted transit. Resistance to him is vain, while the whirling motion of the mail coach remains in his head ... He even got possession in the suddenness of his onset, of the steam engine of the *Times* newspaper, and struck off ten thousand wood-cuts of the Projected Villages, which afforded an ocular demonstration of all who saw them of the practicability of Mr Owen's whole scheme. He comes into a room with one of these documents in his hand, with the air of a schoolmaster and a quack doctor mixed, asks very kindly how you do, and on hearing you are still in an indifferent state of health owing to bad digestion, instantly turns round and observes, 'That all will be remedied in his plan; that indeed he thinks too much attention has been paid to the mind, and not enough to the body; that in his system, which he has now perfected, and which will shortly be generally adopted he has provided effectually for both: that he has been long of opinion that the mind depends altogether on the physical organisation and where the latter is neglected or disordered, the former must languish and want its due vigour: that exercise is therefore a part of his system, with full liberty to develop every faculty of mind and body: that two objections had been made to his New View of Society, *viz* its want of relaxation from labour, and its want of variety; but the first of these the too great restraint he trusted he had already answered for where the powers of mind and body were freely exercised and brought out, surely liberty must be allowed to exist in the highest degree; and as to the second, the monotony which would be produced by a regular and general plan of operation, he conceived he had proved in his New View and that the co-operation he had recommended was necessarily conducive to the most extensive improvement of the ideas and faculties, and where this was the case, there must be the greatest possible variety instead of a want of it'. And having said this the expert and sweeping orator takes up his hat and walks down stairs after reading his lecture of truisms like a play-bill or an apothecary's advertisement; and should you stop him at the door by way of putting a word in common ... he looks at you with a smile of pity at the futility of all opposition and the idleness of all encouragement.

Owen's most alarming trait was noted by Francis Place: he 'takes the politeness of great men for a promise to act'. This suggests either an enthusiast or a rogue. Like Torrens most people were anxious to give such a demonstrably benevolent man as Owen the benefit of the doubt; hence the fact that references to him often went hand in hand with an assurance that he was 'sincere'. But the habit made him dangerous, so that people began to distance themselves from him, an attitude which emerges from the account of a visit made to New Lanark in 1821 by Mrs Mary Townsend, a widow, and her father, Lord Stowell. Mrs Townsend was shortly to become the second wife of Lord Sidmouth to whom she sent a description of Owen, whom she had not met before, but whom she described as Sidmouth's 'intimate friend'.

The Stowell part had been warned to ask for the foreman to show them round so as not to be delayed by Owen but he saw their card and waylaid them.

He said it was impossible to see all at once, & that we must dine with him and attend in the Evening again ... we entered the courtyard where all the Babes came round to have their heads *patted* ... We then passed through some of the Schools, Apartments, saw the Shops etc. etc. and went to B[raxfield House] to dinner. I lamented at the onset to hear Mr O talk in so visionary or I may add, insane a style as to his views and expectations. I had feared there must be something very unsound in his plan from that conceited shallow coxcomb my Uncle, Sir William de Crespigny, having advocated his cause, but I was most distressed that a person acting on such benevolent principles as I *really* believe guide Mr O to be such a victim to his own folly and irrationality. I think it is quite of a piece with the Laputan extracting sunbeams from cucumbers or any other of Swift's absurdities for him to suppose all the world in the dark up to the present time, and that *he* alone can hold a Lanthorn to Mankind, and as he asserted, 'this wisdom was derived from causes over which he had had no controul'. I really think my dear Friend you (as an intimate of his) should *try* to stop the torrent of Absurdity that so blinds him

After two visits to see the children at the school, the party escaped to the inn at Lanark for the night. In spite of a polite note declining further tours, Owen and Captain Donald Macdonald, a young Army officer who had been at dinner the previous night, appeared at 8 a.m. the next morning. When Lord Stowell refused to go once more to the mills, Owen put a heap of tracts into their carriage. 'Altogether I regret the visit', Mrs Townsend wrote to Lord Sidmouth. 'I fear it will excite hopes of support and countenance which I am sure ought not to be given to any plan so Chimerical.'

In the autumn of 1822 Owen went to Ireland where he sought out those places where riots had occurred as a result of famine. The potato crop had failed and as they had no work the people lacked the means to buy other food. Owen spent six months touring the country and saw with his own eyes the miserable state to which parts of it were reduced. Public anticipation grew as a consequence of his repeated announcements, as he went about, that he would soon reveal a 'secret' that, when known, would at once relieve the situation. People flocked to hear this at a meeting called by him in Dublin in May 1823. His speech was a shock to those who came in hope that what he had seen would have prompted a special concern for Ireland. Instead they were obliged to listen to a diatribe against the people in their unreformed state. In spite of the misery he had seen Owen showed no pity for the Irish but ranted on about his Village scheme to such an extent that he was denounced as a charlatan. Just as he had in 1817, when Torrens found him out, Owen refused to acknowledge that anything was wrong and, in his written account of the proceedings, presented the result as an unqualified success.

Many, however, were still prepared to give him the benefit of the doubt. Because of their pressure for something to be done to help the

Irish poor, and his unrelenting propaganda, he was called to give evidence before a Select Committee of the House of Commons in June and July 1823. Its members promised to give Owen's scheme for the Villages of Unity and Mutual Co-operation a minute examination since a petition lay before Parliament asking for support. Owen's answers to the Committee's questions are revealing, not only of his plan but of the measures he had devised over the years at New Lanark. He was not a good witness, as always preferring to present his own proposals rather than answer questions. The Committee, which had David Ricardo among its members, often pushed him further than he wanted to go.

It was concerned to establish what effect the villages would have upon the commerce of their neighbours. Owen meant them to be self supporting like *Harmonie*, as well as to produce a surplus of manufactured goods for sale. It may be that members of the Committee had heard something by then of the disruptive effect the power of the Harmony Society had had upon the fragile commercial life of Indiana. Certainly they pressed him on this point. He could not answer. When it was remarked that his village must only flourish at the expense of others, Owen could only suggest that the solution was for everyone to become a member of his scheme.

The Committee was most anxious to discover how Owen justified the requirement for complete equality among the villagers. They saw this as a moral issue. Given the fact that men's natures inevitably differed, how should the industrious and skilful receive their just rewards? It was the crucial question, the issue on which every community however constituted must stand or fall; to which the answer had been found—if it had indeed been found—by people whose example Owen had often cited, the Moravians, the Shakers, and the members of the Harmony Society. Their purpose was spiritual; what could Owen offer in its place? His desire to meet this point was very strong but he could only do it by abandoning logic. Owen asked the Committee to believe that the nature of the people in his villages would be transformed by the very fact of their living in them. As a practical example he pointed to the 'experiment' on which he had been engaged for many years, to New Lanark; proof, he claimed, that the Villages *must* work.

There, Owen said, he had encountered 'the very dregs of the Highlands ...., a more demoralised population I have never seen'. He began, he told the Committee, with 'the withdrawal of unfavourable circumstances'. These included the presence in the village of about a dozen retail shops (which Owen replaced with one general store), and various public houses. But to his mind the most unfavourable circumstance prevailing on his arrival at New Lanark had been the right to which its inhabitants were entitled of appealing to a court to settle disputes.

Owen hated lawyers and the law almost as much as he disliked 'priestcraft'. As Mrs Townsend reported to Lord Sidmouth, Owen described lawyers, with public houses, as one of 'the evils of Society', regardless of the fact that her father was an eminent judge. Now he insisted on telling the Parliamentary Select Committee that he had abolished recourse to the law at New Lanark; for many years, he claimed, there had been no disputes for the magistrates to settle. 'Having the immediate direction of these individuals I can take it upon myself to say that I never had occasion to imprison any one of them for an hour during the course of 24 years, nor to inflict one legal punishment.' Instead he levied fines, as he proposed to do in his villages.

His vehemence betrayed him: according to George Mudie, who started *The Economist* and was an ardent supporter of Owen for a time, he lost his case before the Select Committee purely by harping on the word equality, when he ought to have stressed the virtues of co-operation, which as a system was far more acceptable to them. His appearance cost Owen dearly; it was the last chance to enlist official backing for his scheme. Whatever Mrs Townsend's opinion of her uncle, Sir William de Crespigny MP, he had been one of Owen's best friends and most useful advocates. In 1819 he had sponsored an earlier move to appoint a Select Committee to examine the village scheme. He had been much at New Lanark and had canvassed widely on Owen's behalf. Now his patience was at an end. In May 1824 when Owen's petition for an examination of his scheme was finally laid before Parliament, Sir William told his fellow Members, 'I have asked Mr Owen not to bring it before this House again.'

The rebuff was savage and gravely harmed Owen's standing. It caused him to retreat to New Lanark where, a few weeks later, Richard Flower found him. Of course Flower, who had spent the last several years isolated in the back country of America, was not privy to recent events in England. On his arrival in Scotland he looked to Robert Owen as a famously enlightened, benevolent, and practical man. A closer acquaintance with the cotton master inspired lasting doubt in Flower, a pious and charitable person, but if this assailed him at their first encounter the absolute necessity of finding a buyer for *Harmonie* caused him to set it aside.

CHAPTER 5

THE 'HALFWAY HOUSE'

FLOWER was as amazed as Chester Harding at the eagerness with which Owen pursued the purchase of *Harmonie* and his lack of concern for the difficulties involved. Such impulsiveness was characteristic of him when things were going wrong, as they were at New Lanark. *Harmonie* then must have appeared to him as a mirage conjured up by the mysterious source of all his other inspirations, the wilderness of America offering as attractive a refuge to him as it had to George Rapp.

Owen's supremacy was under threat. Typhoid fever at New Lanark had drawn attention to the poor housing conditions in the village; the other shareholders were disturbed by this evidence of neglect. But their chief concern was Owen's sudden move to ban the Bible altogether from New Lanark—it was anathema to him, representing as it did to Calvinists the Word of God revealed. He later denied that this was his intention, but the argument was fierce and provoked his associates into giving him a month to comply with the articles of partnership, or again to be dismissed as Manager. He gave in, but grudgingly, since he was obliged to accept the presence of a teacher sent from London to supervise the schools. He took his revenge in the *Life*, in a passage written specifically to refute William Allen's account of the incident. Owen described Allen, who was his chief opponent, as 'a man of great pretensions in his sect, a very busy, bustling, meddling character making great professions of friendship to me, yet doing all in his power to undermine my views and authority'.

At the same time reports were circulating calling into question the reality of the improvements in the village, objecting to Owen's criticism of David Dale, and bringing to public notice the enlightened administration at other mills, especially those of J. Finlay & Co. at Catrine. In early 1824 the workers at New Lanark were outraged by Owen's dismissal of seven of their number for objecting to his interference in the running of their benefit scheme, whose assets he took into his own hands. And as the summer advanced, unrest spread throughout the cotton industry in Scotland as the workers fought for better wages. It is not known precisely what happened at New Lanark but many of the factories in the neighbourhood were idle for weeks at a time.

It was hardly wise for the Manager of the largest cotton spinning establishment to desert his post just then, nor was Owen in a position to speculate. He had spent so much money in Ireland and in publicizing his village scheme that he was already hard put to it to go on paying the rent of Braxfield House, where he lived just above the mills, and to support its ample style. Nevertheless he quickly made ready to depart and, in October 1824, took ship at Liverpool for New York.

In the course of the past few years, during his frequent absences from New Lanark, he had been much in the company of Americans. The country itself had taken shape in his mind as a place not altogether real but, as he told Chester Harding, a 'halfway house' to the kind of special new world he wanted to create. As the leaders of English society steadfastly refused to see where their best interests lay, Owen had issued public warnings to them by means of letters to the press, that the United States was fast catching up and with his help would soon outstrip the British Empire in power and influence.

As US Minister to London, John Quincy Adams had been one of the first to receive a copy of Owen's village plan, together with newspaper cuttings and pamphlets, and a visit from the author. Quincy Adams noted that Owen's project resembled that of the Moravians which, he thought, could only succeed with very small societies and to a limited extent. His courtesy towards Owen concealed a certain caution even then. Richard Rush who succeeded him in the post proved far more friendly and was ready to spend hours listening to Owen expound his plans. When Chester Harding arrived in London to try his luck at painting portraits, Rush got him commissions, including that of Owen himself, of the Duke of Sussex, and of Thomas Coke of Norfolk, who was a scientifically-minded agriculturalist and MP, as well as a very wealthy patron of the arts. Coke and Owen were already well acquainted, having been attracted to each other by their refusal to accept Malthus's warning about overpopulation. As an experimental farmer Coke was convinced that, given the right methods, the land could be made to sustain a greater number of people than it already did, a view that Owen enthusiastically endorsed.

Coke of Norfolk's high regard for all things American made his name well known in that country, which is why a young man called John Dunn

Hunter appealed to him for help. Kindly received by Coke at his great house at Holkham, Hunter made the acquaintance there of Robert Owen whose plan for a new social system he seized upon as a means to assist him in what he saw as his life's work; the rehabilitation of the Indian race. Hunter lent his romantic presence to the platform at many of the meetings called to discuss the Villages of Unity and, some two years before the venture to *Harmonie*, appeared as Owen's protégé in London society.

Hunter was a highly controversial figure in America for he represented himself as one of those unfortunates who, having been taken hostage by Indians as children and brought up far from civilization, yet returned to tell the tale. Hunter's book written shortly before his arrival in England in 1822 was the subject of bitter dispute in the United States, being denounced as a fraud by such very influential figures as Lewis Cass, sometime Governor of the North-West Territory, and Peter Duponceau, a member of the Academy of Natural Sciences of Philadelphia. But when Coke of Norfolk received him at Holkham, Hunter found himself lionized by the English whose attitude towards the American Indian was quite different. The Americans, with the recent memory of terrifying acts of brutality committed in the war between the two races, often regarded children who returned from living among the tribes as somehow tainted by the very fact of their survival. The British were confused by the idea of the noble savage, burdened with a feeling of responsibility towards the tribes who had fought on their side, and prejudiced against the American assumption of sovereignty over the whole continent, as expressed in the Monroe Doctrine.

As William Hazlitt rather crossly pointed out, Hunter was living proof of the inconsistency of Robert Owen's thought; if his character had been formed solely by circumstances, as Owen insisted was the case with every living being, Hunter would never have left the wilderness. According to his narrative Hunter had been stolen from his parents when he was a baby and brought up among the tribes. The Osage had taken him across the Mississippi where he had lived a wandering life, going with them as far as the Pacific, long before that coast was seen by white men. When Hunter was about 18 a single incident transformed his life. He and his Indian companions came across a group of white men whom they decided to kill. But something moved Hunter secretly to save them and go with them back to civilization. So far there was nothing really extraordinary in his story. But then Hunter put himself to school and, apparently in a very short time, became proficient not only in the manners and customs of contemporary American society, but in the learning of an older world: in mathematics, Greek, and Latin, so that he could, and did, hold his own in the most polished society—a male Pocohontas at the court of the Prince Regent.

Owen chose to ignore Hunter's inconvenient upsurge of instinct, a quality which he did not value, and fixed instead upon the splendid example he afforded of man's ability to educate himself out of the savage state. To Hunter, Owen's triumphant disregard of all the obstacles standing in the way of his new society must have come as a most welcome endorsement of his own gigantic and self-imposed task: whether his narrative was genuine or not, there seems little doubt that he was totally sincere in his desire to do something about the forlorn state of the Indians. They were being driven further and further West, away from their traditional hunting-grounds, vulnerable to disease and famine. Hunter sailed for the United States before Owen, but planned to accompany him to Indiana.

When he left for New York in October 1824, Owen was accompanied by Richard Flower, returning to English Prairie, and two young men. As the ship, after its six-week voyage, raised the Sandy Hook lighthouse, one of the latter wrote in his diary, 'Mr Owen looked with delight upon the New World considering it the field for great improvements in Society; and Mr Flower viewed it as the nursery of independence. I could not wander far in the delightful regions of fancy; for my recollection of its history always led me to the expectation of seeing Society much as I had seen it at home'.

What the young man had seen there in the past had so disgusted him that he was seized by what he described as a restless anxiety to transform the world according to Robert Owen's Principles. This was Captain Donald Macdonald of the Royal Engineers, who had been dining with Owen on the occasion when Mrs Townsend was there. She thought him a silly youth. 'In talking to my Father', she told Sidmouth, 'he said, Now I command Soldiers, but they would not mind if force and punishment were not used and here Mr O commands by Love, why can't the Army do so?' Macdonald could not bear constraint; rules, regulations, and every form of written agreement were odious to him. What the Army thought of this, and how long he survived as an officer is not known but by 1821 he was on half pay. His first experience of social reform was as a member of a group calling itself, significantly, The Practical Society. Its work was among the poor artisans of Edinburgh. In 1822 he accompanied Robert Owen to Ireland, and latterly he had been engaged in helping with the planning of the first experimental village on Hamilton of Dalzell's land which, in due course, was named Orbiston.

The other young man on the voyage was Owen's second son, William, aged 22, who had spent four years at the famous school conducted by Emmanuel de Fellenberg, at Hofwyl, near Berne in Switzerland. William was thus fluent in German, an attribute that, it was hoped, would prove of value in negotiating with the Rapps. His elder brother, Robert Dale Owen, had also been at the school, by a kind of special dispensation. De Fellenberg took only those boys who would stay with him for six years—and there were to be no holidays nor parental visits. Owen persuaded him to allow the boys to go for only three of these years in view of the unusual role they would be called upon to play in life. Owen asked that they should be instructed in the methods of teaching the poor which had been separately developed at Hofwyl by a single teacher, a natural genius, the famous Wehrli.

When they arrived in New York the young men were left to themselves as Owen went about the business of publicizing his presence and his plan. Among the people who came to him were land speculators, for he seems to have invited offers of property in the East. His plan for communities of equality was already fairly well known in America, not so much through the sale of *A New View of Society*, as from comment on it in the widely read and influential *Edinburgh* and *Quarterly Reviews*. Among the first and most enthusiastic of the people to greet him was a Quaker, Dr Cornelius Blatchly, who kept an apothecary shop in New York. He was the moving spirit behind a pamphlet published in 1822 called *An Essay on Common Wealths.* Besides noting the attempt of the Harmonists and the Shakers at community living, it referred approvingly to Robert Owen's essays.

But Owen's entrée to New York circles really came about through the good offices of the Professor of Chemistry at Columbia College, John Griscom, a very old friend of Owen's partner in the New Lanark Company, William Allen. Like Allen, Griscom was a Quaker; like him, a scientist, and an enthusiast for bringing education to as many people as possible. In 1818 Griscom went to Europe where Allen provided him with introductions to eminent scientists and leading theorists of education. When, after many years of strict confinement to the British Isles, the end of the Napoleonic Wars opened the way for ordinary people to travel on the Continent, William Allen was one of the first to take advantage of the new freedom. Soon, with his plain words and sober dress, including a tall dark hat, which after the Quaker fashion he never removed in company, he was a striking and familiar figure in the presence chambers of Europe.

In Allen's journal and letters concerning these early journeys on the Continent beginning in 1815 are to be found the names of all those people whom Robert Owen mentions in the *Life* telling of his tour of France, Germany, and Switzerland in 1818. Presumably Allen was responsible for the introductions. Griscom followed much the same path as Owen and at roughly the same time. He spent a year inspecting prisons and orphanages and such celebrated educational establishments as the school founded by Heinrich Pestalozzi at Yverdun in Switzerland and the one run by Emmanuel de Fellenberg. His visit to Hofwyl coincided with the arrival there of Robert Owen's two eldest sons.

He noted that de Fellenberg believed in bringing up the two classes of society side by side, 'So that they shall have each other constantly in view without any necessity whatever of mixing or associating. The rich by observing the industry, the skill and the importance of the labouring classes would learn to entertain just sentiments respecting them, and the poor, by feeling and experiencing the kindly influence of the rich would regard them as benefactors.'

When Griscom had reached New Lanark he had declared himself much impressed with the neatness and order of the village, which he put down to strict discipline, and by the cheerfulness of the inhabitants. But he paid no special homage to the teaching in the schools and expressed great reservations about Owen's declared intention of reducing the mind and character of the people under his control to a deliberate uniformity. It was not part of sound philanthropy to pare down the exuberance of the human mind, Griscom thought, and pronounced Owen's method 'destitute of the principles lying at the root of true benevolence'. Nevertheless, like many others, Griscom was impressed by Owen's demeanour which he described as having the openness and candour of a child.

It was Griscom, born and brought up a Philadelphia Quaker who, on Owen's leaving New York for that city, provided him with introductions to a group of people who afforded a fine example of the human mind at its most exuberant. They were members of the Academy of Natural Sciences of Philadelphia who were to form by far the most important group to accompany Robert Owen to Indiana. In about 1823 and probably as a result of reading Dr Blatchly's pamphlet, several members of the Academy took it into their heads to try to live together as a community. John Speakman was the chief advocate of this enterprise. As soon as the necessary funds were raised, he wrote to a friend, Thomas

Say, that they would buy 'some isolated spot and there form a community something like the Harmonists and Shakers who we see have arrived at the height of prosperity although governed by phantoms'. Would it be stretching common sense, he asked, to suppose that a group of rational beings could not do equally well in a community organized so that the interest of each individual depended upon the prospects of the whole? They did not expect to be rich; they just wanted to found a school for themselves and their children; to lead a life in which the knowledge of nature would be their guiding star. They hoped a combination of talents would be as productive as the combination of labour and, Speakman concluded, 'our happyness will be necessarily in proportion as we acquire knowledge, for man cannot lose but from ignorance and disease'. The Academy had been founded in 1812 in the back room of Speakman's apothecary's shop, and was one of those amiably eccentric institutions that flourished like the green bay tree in Philadelphia, a city of enquiring minds, and may be described as 'amateur' in the original sense of the word. The members were united in admiration of their common purpose which they magniloquently expressed: 'Nor is it the least of our hopes that by the communication of our several observations on the operations of mind and of nature, we may have the happiness to promote important sciences and rescue from heedlessness many valuable facts which are not to be found in books or in the ... discourses of persons who garble the thoughts of other men without using the observing or reasoning power themselves.'

Among the leading members at the time of Robert Owen's arrival were the ornithologist, Charles Buonaparte, Prince of Canino (Napoleon's nephew); his colleague, George Ord; the ichthyologist, Charles Alexandre Lesueur, who was also a brilliant artist; the chemist and mineralogist, Gerard Troost; and perhaps the most dedicated entomologist the United States had ever seen, Thomas Say. Speakman was librarian and treasurer.

Their President, a close friend of John Griscom, was William Maclure, a wealthy man who had been appointed to that distinguished post by reason of the generous contribution he was in the habit of making to the Academy and to the dissemination of scientific knowledge of all kinds. Maclure's own reputation as a scientist stood high for his work in describing the geological formation of the known United States, a pioneering feat for which the field work was conducted from 1807 to 1809.

It had involved tremendous and lonely journeys back and forth across the Alleghenies. Geologists were rare in those days so people who observed Maclure inexplicably tapping rocks were apt to close their doors to him. When Robert Owen arrived in Philadelphia Maclure was away in Europe, having been involved for the past few years in attempting to found a School of Industry at Alicante in Spain. Even so he served his office well, sending back case after case of specimens collected in the field, financing the publication of the journal, and helping to support the more indigent members of the Academy.

John Speakman was the first to come forward to greet Robert Owen and his party when they arrived in Philadelphia towards the end of November 1824. Speakman breakfasted with Owen and organized a meeting at the Academy where Owen expounded his plan to its members, including the most enthusiastic supporters of a community: Say, Lesueur, and Troost. William Owen's diary, which recorded their names, did not mention how much, if anything, his father said about the financial implications of the scheme. Indeed Owen remarked elsewhere that he would rather not make these public until the purchase of *Harmonie* was settled. But it is clear from the subsequent correspondence of Speakman and Say that they understood him to have proposed the setting up of a community of property in which each individual would contribute according to his special ability and in which scientific knowledge would be valued in proportion to assets like manual labour or invested capital.

This understanding was crucial since it offered those members of the Academy who were far from well off an opportunity, or so they thought, of exchanging their learning for a decent and honourable way of life. It was essential that Owen should be aware of the expectations of the group, and that his own intention in buying *Harmonie* at least roughly corresponded to the aspirations of the learned men prepared to venture with him. It seems, however, that he allowed at least one fundamental difference to go unremarked—their divergent attitudes to knowledge. Speakman and his friends were dedicated to the dissemination of pure knowledge. As the Harmony Society was bound together by its particular religion, so the members of the Academy saw service to knowledge as the unifying factor in any community they would form.

But Robert Owen thought of education as a means to an end, the forming of character.

Children are, without exception, passive and wonderfully contrived compounds; which, by an accurate previous and subsequent attention, founded on a correct knowledge of the subject, may be formed collectively to have any human character. And although these compounds, like all the other works of nature, possess endless varieties, yet they partake of that plastic quality, which, by perseverance under judicious management, may be ultimately moulded into the very image of rational wishes and desires.

In his ideal village the children would be trained to acquire 'useful' knowledge, 'valuable' knowledge. 'It is obvious', Owen remarked, 'that training and education must be viewed as ultimately connected with the employments of the association.'

This was the true foundation of Owen's proposed community and as such was open to the criticism that Robert Southey levelled at the prototype which he visited in 1819. Southey liked and admired what he knew of Robert Owen and, as he confided to his journal, though there would be drawbacks to the kind of ideal community Owen envisaged, he thought it probably a better system than any other. Southey in his youth had contemplated founding a Pantisocracy on the banks of the Susquehanna River with Wordsworth and Coleridge. Then they had thought that common ownership of land would have to come. But having considered all aspects of New Lanark—and found it as difficult as Lord Stowell to escape from its master—Southey said that Robert Owen 'keeps out of sight from others and perhaps from himself that his system, instead of aiming at perfect freedom can only be kept in play by absolute power'. New Lanark, Southey went on, differed more in accident than in essence from a Southern plantation.

The persons under him happen to be white, and are at liberty by law to quit his service, but while they remain in it they are as much under his absolute management as so many negro slaves. His humour, his vanity, his kindness . . . lead him to make these human machines as he calls them (and too literally believes them to be) as happy as he can, and to make a display of their happiness.

Nothing of this was revealed to the hopeful communitarians of the Academy in Philadelphia. Instead it seems that Robert Owen took his cue from them and presented his plan in the most liberal terms; speaking of equality, of a community of goods rather than of co-operation, as he did before the Select Committee of 1823. As his eldest son remarked, whenever he encountered the slightest encouragement, the slightest interest in his plan, Robert Owen put himself entirely at the disposal of the people concerned. Though no firm commitment was entered into in Philadelphia he and the members of the Academy of Natural Sciences parted as fellow enthusiasts. It remained to be seen whether Owen would extend his original concept of the villages to accommodate the larger vision of the scientists. John Speakman, roused to a new pitch of interest, determined to accompany Owen on his journey to the West.

Before he set out Owen availed himself of another of Professor Griscom's introductions. This was to Madame Marie Fretageot, a French woman who, in only three years, had succeeded in winning the approval of the Quakers of Philadelphia for that most desirable but most delicate of enterprises, a school for girls, which she conducted with faith, energy,. and love according to the principles of her master, Heinrich Pestalozzi. It said much for her character, and the Quaker sense of priority, that though she was well known to be a deist, the Quakers trusted her not to suborn their daughters' faith. Her reputation as a teacher in Paris sufficed, but she also had the advantage of William Maclure's patronage, and Professor Griscom sent his own daughter to her school to be taught the Pestalozzi method.

This emphasized the importance of common sense and kindness as the guiding principle for all teachers. Children were to learn from obser- vation and experience, proceeding step by step from the known to the unknown. In this way people of all levels of ability and from every class might find fulfilment through education. Pestalozzi's system emphasized subjects like the natural sciences and geography, and brought occu- pations like farming and gardening, and crafts like printing, book-binding and, a very new one, lithography, into the learning process. Owen had little time for this disorganized genius whom he had met on his con- tinental tour at the same time as he had encountered de Fellenberg. Owen deferred to the superior administrative talent of the latter while dismissing Pestalozzi in the *Life* as well-meaning but ineffectual.

Madame Fretageot was very anxious to meet Owen and discuss with him ideas about the education of infants which she supposed to coincide with hers. She described the meeting in a letter to William Maclure, written in the fractured English she was passionately determined to improve. She said she was delighted to be in the presence of a man whose principles were so much in harmony with hers.

When he said that children must be taken just when born in order to write in the blanck [*sic*] paper but what is correct, I felt an encrease [*sic*] of desire to arrive at that part of my life where as much as by my economy and the help of some friends I shall be able to put into practise that projects of taking little babies that will be absolutely mine.

Evidently Owen had the same effect upon her as he did upon most open- minded people, of provoking the desire to exercise 'benevolence', as William Godwin called the impulse to act with charity towards one's fel- low men. And, like most women, Madame felt the impact of Owen's charm.

She was intrigued by the plans he unfolded about *Harmonie*, though she had not at that stage decided to join. She had discussed the so-called 'community of wealth' with members of the Academy who favoured it, and whom she knew well. Lesueur taught drawing at her school, Say and the others lectured to her girls. They would never put such a project into execution, she teased them, 'if they can't have some ladies among them'. As it happened her shrewd judgement and common sense and peculiarly Gallic toughness outdid that of any of the men who went to *Harmonie*, and put her in command at times of stress. To these qualities were added an embracing warmth, irrepressible spirits when she was in health, and a dashing sense of style.

From Philadelphia, Owen and his party, which now included John Dunn Hunter, went on to Washington. There they came in contact with a group of Choctaw and Chickasaw chiefs who had come to transact business with the President, James Monroe, over land. According to William Owen, his father cautioned the chiefs against adopting what had been found to be injurious in civilized life. 'He said he had come more than 3,000 miles to promote plans by which he hoped to make the red brethren superior to the whites. He said the Indians taken when young amongst whites would become like whites and vice versa and he concluded that it would be possible to unite the good in the Indian and in the civilized lives so as to make a being superior to both.' And William, anxious to get it all down, went on, 'He further said it would be possible to bring all knowledge of the world together in one place so that each might enjoy the benefit of it.' John Dunn Hunter told Donald Macdonald that the encounter with these Indians gave him an anxious feeling in the breast, a great longing to set out for the West.

The journey by coach to Pittsburgh took nearly a week. William Owen, Macdonald, and Hunter rode together talking about 'Indians, and past recollections and future anticipations, more particularly regarding a new state of society'. Hunter named the trees, identified the plants that Indians used for cures, and picked a sassafras root from which he had tea made at a wayside inn. Macdonald thought these inns along the busy National Road very snug; so much wood lay about on the ground that great fires were kept burning at all times. The food was good too; wheat and rye bread, broiled chickens, preserved pears and apricots, wild honey, venison steaks, and sausages.

Pittsburgh, when they reached it, lay under a dense cloud of smoke from the many chimneys belching evidence of its already considerable industrial prosperity. There, or preferably just outside it, in order to get a better price, settlers making for the far frontier had to sell their wagons in order to get the best possible floating transport which would take them on the next stage of their journey down the only highway, the Ohio River.

It was at Pittsburgh that Owen was introduced to Benjamin Bakewell, one of its leading citizens. He may have known of him already, as a friend of George Courtauld who had died in his house, of fever, the previous year. Bakewell was an enthusiast for 'commonwealths' and was delighted to have the opportunity of discussing Owen's plans with him. Like Courtauld, Bakewell was a devout Unitarian but so free from bigotry and so apparently easy in manner that Robert Owen was drawn deep into conversation with him on the subject of religion.

Owen's progress to the West had been monitored with great anxiety by George and Frederick Rapp, who feared there would be efforts to keep him in the neighbourhood of Pittsburgh to buy land there. People did come to Owen with the daunting information that many had died of fever at *Harmonie*. Father Rapp, who was nearby at the site for the new town which he had already begun to build, wrote to Frederick, who had remained in charge on the Wabash, telling him to urge Richard Flower to keep watch on Owen, who seems to have been their only prospective purchaser. The Rapps were so eager to sell *Harmonie* that they had already decided to reduce the price to $125,000, and they hoped that Owen would also buy movable objects in the town. Their anxiety stemmed from the fact that they had bought new land before being assured of the sale of the old. For the moment it looked as if the second *Harmonie* might suffer the fate of the first town on the Connoquenessing which had not prospered under its new owner, Abraham Ziegler. George Flower had stumbled across the old town on his way West three years later. Brick buildings seen against a wall of trees had startled him; many of the houses were abandoned and the place looked desolate.

Economy, as the Harmonists' new site was called, was only 18 miles from Pittsburgh on a flat bank of the Ohio itself. George Rapp moved up there in the spring of 1824; he and an advance party of 100 men had already cleared the ground of trees, laid out streets, and begun to build. It was probably not a coincidence, as Owen's party thought, when George Rapp met them in a street in Pittsburgh. They were all invited to go with him to Economy where they stayed for several days. Cordiality was extended on both sides.

According to William Owen, Rapp was very pleased to meet his father. 'He said he had often exclaimed to himself, "My God is there no man on

God's earth who has the same opinion as myself and can help me in my plans? I am now lucky to have come in contact with such a one." ' Rapp pronounced himself well pleased with Owen and his village scheme which was explained to him. He asked Frederick, who would have more time to 'test' him, to keep an eye on him and write frequently. When they were together at *Harmonie* Owen apparently told George Rapp that he envisaged between 4,000 and 5,000 people settling there. Between them and the people of Economy there must always be a close and friendly relationship.

A strange coincidence now became apparent. Owen showed Rapp the model he had brought with him of an ideal village which, with its massive buildings crowned with towers and arranged around a central square, closely resembled, as Professor Arndt has pointed out, the drawing of Christianopolis, the utopian city described by the seventeenth-century writer, Johann Christian Andreae. He had been born not far from Iptingen and he had taught at Tübingen University. Rapp recognized Owen's plan at once, remarking that he had had it in mind to build in such a fashion himself. But he had yielded to Frederick who was an experienced architect and had planned *Harmonie* the way it was.

They had more in common. They were both prophets jealous of the power wielded by others in the name of religion and society. They both required that the disciples who followed them must submit to direction that ordinary people would find irksome but which was essential if the system they envisaged was to be put into effect. But whereas Rapp's offer of salvation was extended to a small group of people shut away from the world, Owen desired to transform the world itself and welcomed all who seemed ready to believe in him.

The two men shared a language which proclaimed that the millennium was at hand. In George Rapp's case there was no doubt that this was the natural expression of a religious belief which he shared with his followers. With Robert Owen the question has provoked debate, some scholars contending that he used such language taken out of its religious context merely because he knew it would be readily understood by his audience. Owen may well have come across the practice during his years in the textile trade, many of whose workers believed in the Second Coming. At New Lanark, talk of revelation, of salvation, of extraordinary events to come, was familiar to members of Dale's Independent sect. They looked for Christ's Return to earth at a given time as did the Harmony Society. Owen himself remarked upon this special use of language in his address at the opening of the New Institution to house the school and the hall of recreation in 1816; the millennium was something he knew would arouse his audience. Very likely it was real to him too.

He and Rapp were sustained by a sense that they were always right. As Francis Place remarked, this belief in his own infallibility was Owen's genius, the quality that enabled him to look above and far beyond obstacles that hampered other men. Rapp in the beginning acknowledged God as the separate source of his power, but, as many prophets do, he came in later life to believe that the spirit was present in his own body; he was not entirely convinced that he would ever die. Owen also believed that he was inspired by a superhuman power; his faith in this did not abate as he grew older.

Rapp belatedly realized that aloofness was dangerous, for it needlessly antagonized his neighbours. In an attempt to retrieve the situation he wrote a book, translated into English as *Thoughts on the Destiny of Man*. It contains much that is attractive in his philosophy and is of great interest to students of the Harmony Society, but it found scarcely any readers, and did not alter the public's perception of him.

The move to Economy hardly disturbed the Harmonist dream. Rapp employed the same means there to preserve the illusion of a Swabian town; dress, language, music, habit, and, above all, a collective memory. They were happier there, nearer to the city and among their own kind. 'We here have had more guests at our table than on the Wabash in six years', Father wrote to Frederick in the summer of 1824. His constant and active presence in the midst of his followers was the focus of it all, but the impulse that created the Harmony Society was still so strong that when he eventually died at the age of 90, other members soon filled his place and kept it going into the twentieth century.

Before they left Economy on their way to Indiana, Owen asked Rapp point blank why he had decided to move. Rapp prevaricated, muttering about the will of God, and his work on the Wabash having come to an end. It was an exercise in mystification that Rapp much enjoyed, as he recounted in a letter to his second in command. Macdonald, who did not miss the implication, made a point of questioning other members of the Society, and noted in his journal that 'the Society found New Harmony unhealthy as well as subject to heat and confined air arising from flat land, rich vegetation and stagnant water'.

On 6 December Owen, accompanied by Captain Macdonald, Richard Flower, John Dunn Hunter, and his son, William, boarded a steamer at Pittsburgh for the voyage down the Ohio. The boat was small, an advantage in that she drew little water at a time when the low level of the river deterred other craft, but it also meant that her single cabin was cramped and unbearably hot. Outside the weather was freezing and sometimes foggy. Regular stops were made to take on wood, on which occasions John Dunn Hunter, Donald Macdonald, and William Owen went on shore to amuse themselves, as Macdonald described in his journal. They built large bonfires in the woods and sat up round them until the middle of the night. 'We set fire to 3 large trees, and burnt one down. We then roasted some beef steaks at the fires and drank porter. The cottager on whose ground we were, staid with us, and amused himself much seeing us clearing his land from him.'

With calls at Cincinnati and Louisville the journey took nine days. It was with considerable relief that they found themselves at the Ohio landing some two hours' horseback ride from *Harmonie*.

On reaching there at last Macdonald noted that to a traveller just emerging from a forest, remembering the many days spent wandering through a thinly-peopled and badly-cultivated country, the rich plain, flourishing village, and picturesque river at *Harmonie* was a highly gratifying sight. Then were his eyes opened to the benefit of numbers, Macdonald wrote, and he hurried forward to meet these beings who had achieved such wonders, expecting them to be of a superior kind. Riding in to the village they were greeted by Frederick Rapp, 'a tall, rawboned, sallow complexioned, serious and plain german'.

CHAPTER 6

AN INVITATION TO NEW HARMONY

THE solemn appearance of Frederick Rapp seems to have depressed the spirits of Owen's party. When they wrote up their journals of the first day at *Harmonie* both William Owen and Donald Macdonald were hard put to it to find anything positively encouraging to say. William's account reads like the catalogue of an auctioneer merely concerned to list everything in its place. No doubt they were jaded, the journey had been tremendous, but there is more than a hint of anti-climax in their reactions.

In the first place, as they looked down on it from the top of Father Rapp's house, the village appeared very small. On the ground it measured some 600 yards by 400 or 500, the streets arranged at right angles, the houses 'motly' as William put it; log, frame, and brick dwellings jumbled together though always respecting the line of the streets. These were roughly made and when it rained, as it frequently did at that time of year, became deep in mud. *Harmonie* had a dark appearance, Macdonald noted, occasioned by the fact that wood exposed to the air turned a dusky slate colour to which the red brick houses formed an agreeable contrast. There was less building in brick than they might have wished. The 'manufactures' were small and had few of the more recent improvements, and the work people did not appear to be very expert at their task. As soon as he caught sight of the Rappites spinning cotton Robert Owen was impelled to show them how to do it better. In fact, after all that had been said about the efficiency of the Harmony Society and its superiority over its neighbours, it is interesting to see, through the eyes of the newcomers, that the town was really a modest place, bearing obvious signs of improvisation, and not a little ramshackle.

At first the people struck the travellers as withdrawn, unhealthy looking, and listless, the result in part of the close warm air of the rooms they lived in. Each group were obviously shy of the other. One cannot tell what Robert Owen thought, but as the three young men saw more of them, respect and liking grew. They were mild-mannered people,

Macdonald decided, after he had seen them at service in their still unfurnished church, patient and content. Much hospitality was provided by the members of George Rapp's family who had remained at *Harmonie*, and, to his pleasure, William discovered that the 16-year-old Gertrud, daughter of the ill-fated Johannes, was a natural and pretty girl. He was able to converse with everyone; his German was fluent for he had been allowed to speak nothing else at school. Nevertheless there was a distinct lightening of mood as most of the party rode off to spend Christmas at the English Prairie.

After the small, low, shut-in space of *Harmonie*, they rejoiced to see the rolling prairie with its far horizon, huge free-standing trees, and immense sky. But the fate of the English who had settled there on the Illinois side of the Wabash in 1817 had been unexpected and peculiar; their life in consequence was harder than it ought to have been and their experience the subject of gossip in two continents. Building was hardly begun, and the need for co-operation at its most pressing when a quarrel broke out between the leaders, Morris Birkbeck and George Flower, which split the group into opposing factions. Two struggling settlements were the result: Birkbeck at Wanborough, the Flowers at Albion. There was no communication between them; though their land marched together, the line dividing it was never crossed.

The author of the dispute was Morris Birkbeck. Having been ten years a widower in England, at 52 he had apparently intended to crown his new life in the United States by marrying Eliza Andrews, a girl half his age who, as a friend of the family, had accompanied him, his two daughters and two sons, when they left England in 1817. But on the way West she and George Flower, who was not much older, had fallen in love, and, in spite of Birkbeck's obvious but unspoken distress, were married when they reached Vincennes. But George was already married—as Birkbeck knew. It was because he had found life with his English wife too awful to endure that he had decided to leave the country. According to Henry Crabb Robinson, a relation of the Flower family who knew her, she was indeed a woman of quite intolerable disposition. In 1816, after making provision for her (though without divorcing her), George had departed to find a new life in the United States. Birkbeck's chagrin at the loss of Eliza was made worse by the fact that, having acted as the father of the bride at the Vincennes ceremony (which was bigamous), he was then obliged to share a house with the newly united pair while the land at the English Prairie was surveyed.

The first victim of this unwise arrangement was Eliza herself, for relations were so strained as to oblige George to take her with him when he set out for England in the autumn of 1817, to muster recruits for the new settlement. Eliza was already pregnant, but she rode several hundred miles with George to a tavern on the eastward slope of the Alleghenies. There he had to leave her since his story was known in the East and she could go no further as his wife. She waited alone at the tavern and in the spring of 1818 gave birth to a child. Shortly after George returned, and the three of them went back to English Prairie. When they arrived they discovered that Birkbeck, a man of hasty temper usually kept in check by a Quaker rigour, had succumbed to his long-standing resentment. The scandal was in the open, and made worse when he had Flower prosecuted for adultery and bigamy. The action failed since the first Mrs Flower could not be called to give evidence, and the Vincennes marriage was upheld.

The bitterness that divided the two former friends and partners gravely weakened the settlement, for many who would otherwise have come out from England to join them shrank from the necessity of taking sides. But the chief drawback arose when it became known that Birkbeck had seriously underestimated the difficulties of cultivating the prairie. As he had described them in his *Notes*, nothing but fencing, and the provision of water for stock, was needed to turn the great open spaces into useful grassland, and from that state to arable would be a simple process. Birkbeck's opinion was respected, for it was based on long farming experience in England. But it was mistaken. The cultivation of prairie land was to prove at least as hard in the beginning as clearing land under timber, with the added problem of a serious shortage of water. The natural prairie grass was not much good for grazing as it died if eaten down too far. As for turning it into arable, the earth was desperately hard to break up, being skeined with tough and very long roots.

It was hard, slow work; Birkbeck and Flower were unaccustomed to manual labour and had little help. In the first three years hardly any crops were grown at Wanborough or Albion; both settlements survived by purchasing goods from *Harmonie*. Flour, corn meal, beer, whisky, implements, and clothing figure in the accounts. Even simple tasks such as mending saws or making window frames which ought to have been within the competence of anyone settling in the back country were sent to the Rappites to be done. It was fortunate that the English were not short of money; Flower's first bill from the Harmony Society was for the enormous sum of $11,000, and from 1818 to 1824 he calculated that the Society drew a total of $150,000 in cash from English Prairie as a whole.

By the time Robert Owen came to visit them the towns of Wanborough and Albion were just about managing to survive. Though
Birkbeck and the Flowers had built substantial houses many of the others
had little comfort and no luxuries. They lived under threat from roving
gangs who considered them fair game. As English they were the targets of
a general animosity more bitter even than that directed at the Rappites,
for it arose as a result of the war in which the English were held to have
incited the Indians against Americans. More particularly Birkbeck and
his grown up daughters had made themselves disliked for putting on airs.
But in the last few years a more serious and immediate cause of tension
had appeared. It lay in the fact that at a time when Indiana and Illinois
had to decide whether to vote to admit slavery Birkbeck and George
Flower separately spoke out vehemently against it.

As he talked to the inhabitants of Wanborough and Albion, Donald
Macdonald found them very much alive to the benefit of mutual
assistance, regretting their lack of it. Several hundred people turned up at
the meetings called by Robert Owen to explain his plan. For his part he
was very pleased to see them. It may be that his peculiar, leap-frogging
mind already saw them installed at *Harmonie*. In so far as he was at all
concerned with practicalities, their presumed availability may have
prompted the decision to buy *Harmonie*. Apart from the interest of the
scientists at Philadelphia and some few of Bakewell's friends almost as far
away at Pittsburgh, he had no idea even at this late stage who would
inhabit it, let alone work its land and factories.

It was at Albion and in the presence of Frederick Rapp, who had ridden
over to continue negotiations, that Owen was drawn into a lengthy
discussion of the connection between his system and orthodox religion.
Richard Flower and some of his neighbours contended that man *was* a
subject for praise and blame, of reward and punishment. According to
Macdonald, a fascinated observer,

they supported their opinion by connecting it with the Christian dispensation of
a belief in a God, in a resurrection, a heaven and hell and future rewards and
punishments, and by endeavouring to show that Mr Owen's statement of the
Formation of Human character and his Exposition of the influence of circumstances over human nature, were in contradiction to such creed.

Owen's response showed an extreme reluctance to be branded as an
unbeliever.

He was not aware how his statement that the child was created by a power
over which he had no controul [*sic*] could be considered as a denial of a Supreme

Being; his endeavour to draw public attention to the consideration of the influence of circumstances over the child after birth, was no denial of a Resurrection; and his wish to do away with all human artificial rewards and punishments, was no interference with the future state of man after this life, or with those natural punishments which necessarily follow ignorance and bad habits, and those natural rewards which ensue from knowledge and good habits.

The argument was continued until late in the evening when Frederick Rapp remarked that he agreed with Richard Flower; two other gentlemen were favourable to Mr Owen's views; and a third declared that he would not have missed being present at the discussion for $500.

By the end of December, according to his son, Owen had almost decided to buy *Harmonie*. William described him as being in high spirits, enjoying life in the woods, riding about, picknicking on cold meat and Harmony wine. Then, with the arrival of the newspapers from Vincennes Owen's vivid imagination was seized with an enormous, controversial, and beguiling scheme. The papers carried reports of President Monroe's State of the Union message in which he lamented the condition of the Indian tribes and proposed that they should be brought together in a territory of their own. Who better than Robert Owen, with John Dunn Hunter at his side, to act as Agent between the US government and the tribes, and where else but at *Harmonie*, the very place, as he had told the chiefs at Washington, where all useful knowledge in the world might be assembled? It was with such stimulating ideas at the forefront of his mind, the anticipation of enhanced prestige, that Owen sat down with Frederick Rapp to negotiate the purchase of the town.

On 3 January 1825 they signed a memorandum of agreement whereby Owen was to pay $125,000 (about £25,000) over a period of time in return for more than 20,000 acres of land, the improvements made to it, all the buildings, and sundry items, including the town clock, the famous bell, and implements of manufacture and trade. Considering that the uncleared wilderness cost Rapp $2.50 an acre in 1814 the price was painfully low. In part it reflected the disastrous fall in the value of western land, which was also felt by Birkbeck and the Flowers. It showed how anxious Rapp was to be gone from Indiana and, remembering that the first *Harmonie* in Pennsylvania had been disposed of equally carelessly, confirmed what little value he placed on worldly goods as such. It also demonstrated the wisdom of engaging in industry as well as agriculture for, however difficult it had been for his followers to master the techniques, it was from their manufacturing enterprises that the Society's labour had brought its best return.

In the afternoon of the day on which the memorandum was signed Robert Owen departed in haste for Washington, having spent altogether fourteen days at *Harmonie*. The purchase was not complete; though William Owen and Donald Macdonald had instructions—couched in the vaguest terms—to acquaint themselves with the management of the place, Frederick Rapp remained very firmly in charge. John Dunn Hunter had gone down river to settle some business at New Orleans.

When Owen reached it the Federal capital was seething with the excitement of the approaching inauguration of John Quincy Adams to succeed James Monroe as President. The atmosphere was more highly charged than usual, emotions more readily aroused owing to the presence in the city during the past winter of one of the greatest American heroes of all time, the Marquis de Lafayette. From the moment he landed in the country in the summer of 1824 Lafayette had been caught up in a tremendous surge of love, respect, and pride in the memory of the War of Independence and in a celebration of the achievements of the Republic since that time. The Marquis—or General Lafayette as he insisted on being called—was a towering and a romantic figure, a symbol of the ultimate triumph of idealism and humanity in two revolutions, the American and the French, and of the friendship that existed between the two countries in those dark times. Moreover, as a close associate of George Washington, Lafayette was one of the few remaining links with the founding fathers of the United States. In his astonishing career the General seemed to personify the high qualities of patriotism, valour, charity, and unselfishness with which they had hoped to endow the citizens of the new Republic, qualities which, as they approached the fiftieth anniversary of their independence, the American people were very concerned to uphold.

In these circumstances it would not have been surprising if the Welshman Robert Owen, perceived as English by most Americans, had been politely ignored. He did not suffer such a fate, to him the unkindest of all. Instead he was borne up on the celebratory tide; the Americans took him as an example of one of the most admired qualities of their Revolutionary forebears, one which they feared had since deserted them—disinterested benevolence. On his arrival in Washington the previous autumn, one of its leading newspapers, the *National Intelligencer*, had praised his generosity, his resolution, his mental and moral faculties as demonstrated by the experiment at New Lanark, carried out, it believed, at his own expense, and which, the paper declared, placed his endeavours above those of any lawgiver in ancient or modern times. The United States was fortunate indeed that he had come among them with the intention of establishing a similar institution. Since Owen could announce that Indiana was now the chosen site, his plan became a matter for further congratulation. The American people were keenly alive to the fact that a new society really was in the process of forming in the Mississippi Valley and that very soon its nature would be irrevocably determined. They were concerned that every effort should be made to give the West the most admired, the most enlightened institutions at their command. Since Robert Owen appeared to have precisely such a purpose he was welcomed back with pleasure and anticipation, and much fêted.

One of those who gave him hospitality was Margaret Bayard Smith, a notable Washington hostess, and wife of a former editor of the *Intelligencer*. At first sight Owen struck her as ugly, awkward, unprepossessing in manners, appearance, and voice. It was difficult for her to see in this cool and dispassionate man, as others described him, a visionary and an enthusiast. But after a few hours with him she decided, to her regret, that he was a visionary after all. From her report of their conversation it appears that Owen gave a longer rein to his imagination in the United States than ever he did at home. The people of New Lanark, he told her, were in the beginning the very dregs of society. Now they wanted for nothing and, being wholly without temptation, were entirely happy. 'I require my people to work only eight hours out of the twenty four', he explained; the rest of the day was for instruction and amusement. Among the many hundreds of children at New Lanark there had never been an instance of jealousy, anger, or hatred. *Never?* marvelled Mrs Smith. And did he see the little angels when they grew up? No, was his reply. A truly benevolent and good man, she decided, but 'an amiable madman'.

On 28 February 1825 Robert Owen was privileged to give the first of two discourses on his plan in the Hall of Representatives, in the splendid but not quite finished Capitol. It was a measure of the confidence and expectation placed in him further emphasized by the distinguished audience, which included the President, James Monroe; the President-elect, John Quincy Adams; and members of the Supreme Court, the Cabinet, and of Congress. Speaking from what he called 'this chair from which you have been accustomed to hear so many important truths', Owen began with a survey of his career. At New Lanark, he insisted, the population had been indolent, dirty, imbecile, and demoralized to a lamentable degree until his system had altered them. In the United States, he went on, proof of the gigantic superiority of union over division in the creation of wealth had come from the very important example of the Moravians, the Shakers, and the Harmonites. Now he was prepared to begin his own system. In spite of the memorandum between him and Frederick Rapp it seemed that he had not yet settled the form of ownership at *Harmonie*, for he expressed himself ready to proceed either on his own responsibility, or with partners having the same principles and feelings as himself, or by joint-stock companies incorporated by the states of Indiana and Illinois, or by general incorporated companies formed by the leading persons of each state.

Whatever the means of raising capital the system to be introduced was no different in Robert Owen's mind from all the other Villages of Cooperation; that is, it was to be a profit-making scheme made workable through the well-directed and unremitting labour of its members. Security for capital invested would lie in the land, the buildings on it, and the goods there produced. Owen was convinced that these would increase in value every year; when others were similarly persuaded, the money would flow in. There was never any question at that stage that he was to be the sole proprietor. That situation only came about as a result of subsequent events. The existing Rappite town was only temporary, he told his audience, a place of first resort for the population he would collect for training. Once they satisfied his requirements the people would move into the great rectangular edifice to be built on high ground with a view of the Wabash River, the place he now proclaimed as New Harmony, where his new system of society would first be realized and where the community of property and equality would eventually be introduced.

He now issued an invitation to 'respectable families and individuals' to propose themselves for Indiana. According to their respective resources and inclinations separate arrangements would govern their position in the community. Those who had capital and did not wish to work would pay a sum towards their upkeep. Those who had nothing would pay for their keep with their labour; at building, gardening, spinning cotton, teaching, or other occupations of benefit to the whole community. In return they were assured of the best lodgings, food, and clothing that 'the circumstances of the establishment'—a crucial phrase—would permit. The old and sick would receive the best attention, and the children would be brought up as members of one family, receiving a good and superior education. Those who wanted to leave could do so at any time. In return for their contribution to the community they could take with them 'in the produce of the establishment as much in value as shall be placed to their credit at the annual balance immediately preceding the time when they cease to become members of the society'.

In other words quitters would not be paid in cash but in kind, and would be obliged to sell goods obtained in this way in competition with their former associates. The practical result would be that as in the case of those members of the Harmony Society denied a parting contribution by its leaders, there would be those among the followers of Robert Owen who could not afford to leave.

Owen's discourses on Capitol Hill attracted much attention; the *Intelligencer*, for example, giving them as much prominence as it had devoted to John Quincy Adams's Inaugural Address. In the months that followed, the paper printed a lively debate on the pros and cons of the plan, as did many others. At the same time there appeared an American edition of *A New View of Society*. So it was as a prophet honoured in the country he had long considered ready to receive him that, armed with introductions from no less a person than James Monroe, Robert Owen went into Virginia to stay at the great plantation houses of two other former Presidents: Thomas Jefferson at Monticello, James Madison at Montpellier. Once again it seemed that the most influential people were eager to listen to what he had to say; after the humiliation inflicted by Parliament, the coolness of Ministers, the flight from disaster at New Lanark, he must have felt like Napoleon re-entering the Tuileries.

CHAPTER 7

'I SHALL HAVE WONDERS TO RELATE'

Owen's absence from Indiana, as it happened, lasted precisely 100 days. It was long enough for Donald Macdonald and William Owen, left on their own at Harmony (as the name of the town will now be spelt), to discover what strains the place imposed and what resources they had to withstand them. Of the two, Macdonald was the more adaptable, sustained as he was by a passionate belief in Robert Owen's Principles, and longing for the moment when they would be put into practice. Once Harmony seemed likely to change hands he looked about him with an approving eye, marking down opportunities for building, for increasing trade, for opening up vistas in the countryside. And he watched the Rappites as they went about their business, curious to define the spirit which he understood possessed them and gave its special nature to the town. Yet he had to admit that a certain monotony prevailed. 'Our time was passed from February to April, getting information at *Harmonie*, conversing with the neighbours and sometimes pruning trees', he wrote in his Diary.

As soon as reports of Owen's progress began to appear in the newspapers, 'conversing with the neighbours' became a matter of explaining the finer details of the system and trying to correct false impressions. Either people had not understood the terms whereby a profit must be made before a community of equality and property could be set on foot, or they had been misled by Owen's reference to the Moravians, the Shakers, and the Harmonites to suppose that his system was exactly the same as theirs. William Owen gave the clearest explanation of the position in answer to a query from William Pelham, who was shortly to become one of the earliest members of the new community. The proposed Society, William Owen wrote, was to be formed on the Principles of united Production and Consumption. It would be composed of persons practising all the most useful occupations necessary to the well-being of a complete establishment, to whom lodgings, food, clothing, attendance during sickness, and a good education for their children would be secured. The profits would accumulate in order to form a new community on the Principle of complete equality—'as soon as a sufficient sum shall be realized'.

It might look simple on paper but where were the people to be found? William was alone in fretting about this; he had been given no guidance by his father. He went prospecting to Vincennes but found no comfort there. He saw the leading citizens and reported them favourable to Robert Owen's plan. Few of them impressed him as anything more than possible working hands. As for the poorer families, they lived on 'hog and hominy', which they obtained by working a few months only in the year. The rest of the time they spent drinking and talking politics. Those with a bit more money did little but speculate in land. Wherever William looked, he told his father, he saw listlessness and inactivity (no doubt due in part to malaria). Better by far, he thought, to rely on people brought out from the Old World.

Nor could he accomplish anything more at Harmony. In the prolonged absence of Robert Owen, Frederick Rapp would not allow any intending settlers into the town, though he was forced to make an exception in the case of some who, having sold their farms, arrived on the borders of Harmony with nowhere to live. When Frederick was absent, as he often was, William could not discover which of the Rappites, if any, took charge. One very pressing subject concerned the preparation of the ground for the new season's crops; this could not be done, for there was no authority from Robert Owen and no idea as to who would harvest them. The two young men had to content themselves with measuring the dimensions of the village with a very long piece of string, delving into abandoned and collapsing log houses, helping to correct the English translation of George Rapp's *Thoughts on the Destiny of Man*, and gazing at Miss Gertrud, an occupation that William found congenial. The longer he knew her, the prettier she appeared.

Apart from that he found life tedious and, departing from his normal practice of recording a frugal amount of comment and no emotion in his journal, burst out: 'I find the rainy weather particularly dull. I am tempted to think that it is very difficult to get over one's old habits, even at the age of 22, and that those are the happiest who, having had one mode of life chalked out for them continue to preserve it through life'. With a perception sad in one so young, but obviously arising from his own experience, he continued,

the enjoyment of a reformer, I should say, is much more in contemplation than in reality. For surely one who thinks all around him equal or superior to himself in intellect must receive more pleasure from associating with them than one who thinks all with whom he converses less intelligent and less correct in their views of human nature than himself.

William now expressed grave doubts as a result of his sojourn in Harmony about whether the present generation would find living in a community agreeable. 'I doubt whether those who have been comfortable and contented in their old mode of life will find an increase of enjoyment when they come here', he wrote, and confessed himself unable to determine how long it would take them to accustom themselves to life at Harmony.

William's newly-acquired pessimism was the more striking since he indulged it at a time when his journal was otherwise full of the signs of spring. The winter had been mild and by early March the trees were covered with blossom. Soon the town was smothered by thick clusters of peach flowers. Windows were thrown open during the day and the Harmonites arranged a demonstration of planting Indian corn. Frederick Rapp took off his coat and with Donald Macdonald went along the furrows, sometimes talking to the workers, sometimes dropping corn; at 4 o'clock they all sat down under a tree for bread, beer, cheese, apples, and a song. Macdonald was enchanted by the sight of men and women sowing corn together. It was a pity American females had an aversion to working out of doors, he remarked, for there was nothing so conducive to a good spirit among neighbours as regular exercise taken together in the open air. As the season advanced the woods came alive with birds; great flocks of doves, wild geese flying lower than the housetops, partridge, blackbirds whose note William described as that of a rusty wheelbarrow, and the noisy groups of yellow parakeets which had wintered there.

On 19 March their rustic isolation was relieved by the arrival of two young women bringing William news of his father's doings in Washington. They were the Misses Frances and Camilla Wright who, travelling unaccompanied on horseback, were on their way to join Lafayette at New Orleans. Tactfully, the Nation's Guest had left Washington before the Inauguration, leaving the Wright sisters, whose presence in his entourage was not clearly explained, to follow by a different route. This circumspection was due to the curious relationship between the General and the elder Miss Wright.

For the last three years Frances, and Camilla who was her uncomplaining shadow, had lived as members of the General's huge family—*La colonie* he called it—at the Château de la Grange outside Paris. As the author of a youthfully enthusiastic book, *Views of Society and Manners in America*, Frances enjoyed a certain fame. The book was the means whereby she had come to know Lafayette for it had been sent to La Grange by the General's old friend and Frances's mentor, the man she called her 'good old Socrates', Jeremy Bentham. His interest had been aroused in her by the ability displayed in her book and in particular by its warm regard for all things American, especially the institutions of the new Republic. This was an attitude Bentham shared but it was uncommon among Europeans when her book was published in 1820. Having met her, Bentham doted on her, as did the General in his turn. Frances's official reason for remaining so long at La Grange was that she was collecting material for a biography of Lafayette.

She and Camilla were orphans, their position in English society some-what ambiguous. Their father, James Wright, was a Dundee merchant who, like their mother, had died shortly after Camilla's birth in 1797— Frances was the elder by two years. They had few close relations and no desire to remain in Glasgow where they had been partly brought up. Their isolation was made conspicuous by Frances's restlessness and imperious disposition, and her highly developed taste for celebrity and adventure.

Layfayette became more than a hero to her. As she was admitted into his confidence so she pressed for recognition of their intimacy and formed the idea, odious to his son and married daughters, of being formally adopted as his daughter. She was in her late twenties while the General was in his seventies, and had been for many years a widower.

His family suspected that Frances's aim was marriage. They were mistaken: the last thing *she* would do was 'dwindle into a wife.' But she was also accused of unduly influencing him in political affairs, of pushing him into foolhardy enterprises. This was another misconception. Lafayette was perfectly capable of embarking on adventures on his own account; he had been doing so throughout an eventful life. Frances had been informed of his dealings with the Carbonari, the secret society that in 1822 aimed to overthrow the Bourbon King of France. She plunged at once into the heart of the affair, carrying clandestine messages between Paris and London and badgering those in office in England for help in advancing the cause of liberalism, not only in France, but in Italy, in Spain, in Greece, in Poland. 'I dare say you marvel sometimes at my independent way of walking through the world', she wrote to Lafayette, 'just as if nature had made me of your sex instead of poor Eve's. Trust me my beloved friend, the mind has no sex but what habit and education give it and I who was thrown upon the world like a wreck upon the waters have learned as well to struggle with the elements as any male child of Adam.'

When the Carbonari conspiracy collapsed and Lafayette was saved from disaster only by the loyalty of his co-conspirators, Frances and Camilla retired with him to La Grange where Frances occupied a room in a turret directly below his sanctum, remote from the domestic business of the Château. Her presence aroused the hostility, which she did nothing to conciliate, of Madame George and Madame Louis, the ladies of La Grange, who did everything they could to make her leave. In 1824 the Misses Wright were openly asked to depart. The General's display of distress forced a last minute compromise in which the invitation to him from the United States government played a significant part. It was agreed that Frances and Camilla should travel to America at the same time but keep their distance whenever Lafayette was in the public eye. All those concerned hoped that this break in the pattern would somehow unravel the complex tangle of their lives.

Instead it emphasized the awkward position the Wright sisters were in. George Washington Lafayette was his father's official companion on his triumphal progress; Frances and Camilla languished in the rear, their presence ignored except for occasional sniping in the newspapers. Six months of such camp-following was more than enough for Frances and was the reason why she chose the more arduous route to New Orleans while the General went round by sea.

The journey, unaccompanied except by her sister, held no fears for Frances. Her courage which was quite out of the ordinary and surpassed that of any normal man stemmed from an illusion which was so strong upon her for a time that it affected her appearance. Frances believed herself entirely free from the conventions of the time—which were particularly rigid in the United States—but through her own physical nature: she behaved as though she were a man, and looked like a slender pretty boy. In the American wilderness she courted risks no sensible man would have contemplated. It says much for Camilla's courage that she followed her elder sister unswervingly on a course that, as will be seen, had its origin at Harmony.

William Owen noted in his journal that Frances Wright was a very learned and fine woman; though her manners were free and unusual in a female yet they were pleasing and graceful. She improved upon acquaintance, he rather gingerly concluded. Though he was to come to know her well, their first meeting was short. Having inspected the town and the Rappites with a thoughtful eye, she and Camilla rode off to the English Prairie. She was to report upon Birkbeck's progress for the General who was himself a scientific farmer and had taken an interest in the Englishman since exchanging farming notes at La Grange in 1814, where Birkbeck and George Flower had been received.

Frances's special interest in Birkbeck and Flower arose from their long standing and active opposition to slavery which, she had been forced to admit in *Views*, was a dreadful stain upon the record of the United States. She had already been introduced to George Flower in Virginia where he had gone to greet Lafayette. After spending a few days at Albion, his home on the English Prairie, she and Camilla proceeded down river towards New Orleans where they were to see slavery at its most brutal.

It is likely that before they left Washington Frances and Camilla had attended Robert Owen's discourses on Capitol Hill. The effect of the proclamation he made then and the resulting publicity in the newspapers now weighed heavily on Harmony. People began to arrive in the town asking for work and shelter, in the belief that the communal experiment had already begun. Yet, as the season advanced beyond the possibility of planting sufficient crops, there was still no news of Robert Owen. At last he arrived, on 13 April, on board the Rappites' own steamer, *William Penn*, which had been sent to carry the remaining members of the Harmony Society to their new home at Economy. Their departure was a very moving one, in the presence of the Owens, Donald Macdonald, and the Wrights, who had become friendly with Frederick Rapp, and who had returned in time to witness it.

All the Swabians assembled at George Rapp's house where the band played and the women sang hymns. Then they marched in procession behind the band, towards the river landing. At the edge of the town they stopped, turned, and sang a final hymn, blessing the settlement. Robert Owen took the opportunity to address the assembled crowd, which included the new settlers who had come to join him. He praised the Rappites for their integrity, strict justice, and kindness, and found himself so moved he could hardly speak. All the men and women then shook hands before going on board the steamer. A gun was fired, and the waving of hats and handkerchiefs continued while the band played a march. Donald Macdonald, who recorded all this in his journal, concluded: 'I never in my life returned home after parting with friends, with so sad a feeling as that (to me) melancholy afternoon.'

As soon as Robert Owen returned to Harmony, notices were sent to the neighbouring towns and settlements convening a meeting. On

20 April he spoke for nearly three hours to upwards of 600 people. The following week saw the formation of what Owen called the Preliminary Society. As its Constitution defined it, it was a Society 'particularly formed to improve the character and condition of its own members and to prepare them to become associates in independent communities, having common property'. Since Owen as Proprietor of the settlement, and founder of the system by which it would be run, had purchased the property and in the process subjected himself to risk, the Constitution recognized the necessity for him to appoint the committee that would direct and manage the Preliminary Society's affairs. William Owen was named as a member, as was The Revd Robert Jennings who had thrown up an advantageous position as a Universalist Minister to preach, with an unimpaired evangelical fervour, the duties and benefits of life in a community.

During the next three weeks hundreds of people flocked to the town, most but not all from neighbouring parts. They were nearly all very young and poor, clutching by the hand dozens of small children, their scanty belongings carried on their backs. The back country of America yielded babies in abundance; as one of the inhabitants of Albion put it, 'every log cabin is swarming with half naked children. Boys of 18 build huts, marry, and raise hogs and children at about the same expense.' Unlike in England, where the doctrine of The Revd. Malthus had induced feelings amounting to despair, a fast increasing population was a matter of congratulation in the West. Though the frontier people might be poor, there was enough to eat, and room to expand and grow more food. Children were welcomed for the work they could do, the warmth they brought, the strength they gave to the family. It was the essential, because the most secure and productive, unit in the development of new lands.

But at Harmony, under the system of credit advanced in return for labour, the high proportion of children was soon perceived to be a disadvantage, for they consumed a great deal while contributing nothing to the credits, at least at first. As one of its first acts the Committee fixed a limit to the sum on which members of the Preliminary Society might draw for food and clothing. And so it became apparent that belts would have to be tightened. This was no more than the practical effect of Robert Owen's phrase about the best provision 'circumstances would permit', but it caused considerable anger. As one new member wrote, he had expected Owen to furnish them with every necessity. On discovering the limit his feelings had not been of the most agreeable kind—'and Pittsburgh and its smoke and its friends were never more valuable to my eyes'. But Owen spoke to all of them and their dissatisfaction vanished. 'I do not know how it is—he is not an orator', this correspondent wrote, 'but here he appears to have the power of managing the feelings of all at his will'.

It was a power that had been re-kindled by his exhilarating reception in Washington, and which sprang from a renewed conviction of the importance of his vision. It was the single most effective asset of the new community. For in the absence of any kind of planning or preparation, success or otherwise would depend on Owen's capacity to inspire effort and co-operation in the motley crowd gathered at New Harmony. The transition from the closely supervised and well understood operation of the Rappites to whatever Robert Owen had in mind might not go smoothly.

Yet exactly a week after his return from the East, in a letter to his New Lanark partner William Allen, he revealed that he proposed to leave for Europe not later than the beginning of June. The letter was marked by an unreasoning enthusiasm, a millennial fervour, that must have disturbed anyone who read it. The United States had been prepared for his coming in a most remarkable manner, Owen wrote; his new System of Society would soon be in operation in all the States north of the Ohio River, and not later than the end of 1827. The empire of public property was about to commence, and private property to be discarded; the transformation would soon extend to the blacks and the Indians who had been prepared in a special manner for the change. 'I shall have wonders to relate to you', he told William Allen.

It was typical of his 'crafty crazy' mind that in another part of the same letter Owen gave William Allen details of the purchase of Harmony. He had now decided to pay in cash, since it would be cheaper; the total sum was $95,000, or just over £21,000. Owen gave Allen details of the bills drawn on Barclays Bank in London and promised further information later. It was the letter of one partner in a business enterprise to another, and it presumed that Allen was about to take a share in the joint stock company to run New Harmony.

Owen went on to tell Allen that he had also bought from Frederick Rapp the flocks and herds and implements of husbandry, a large stock of store goods, and provisions for one thousand people for a year—'as in England would have cost a princely fortune'. As he could either pay for this with two or three years' credit, or at the end of 1825, he said he would wait to decide until he had seen Allen.

On the face of it Allen seems an eminently suitable partner in such a venture. Not only was he familiar with, and sympathetic to, community ideals, having visited many of different religious persuasions all over Europe, but his links with America, and more particularly the Wabash country, were close and personal. He gave an early prominence to the Rappites when his journal, the *Philanthropist*, published Melish's account of the first *Harmonie* in 1815. He was foremost among the English Quakers who, in 1816, helped the Württemberg Separatists to migrate to America (for much the same reasons as the Rappites). They settled at Zoar and established contact with the Harmony Society. Allen knew the history of the English Prairie at first hand; his third wife, Grizel, was Morris Birkbeck's cousin; his dearest friend, William Forster, was another Birkbeck cousin.

Robert Owen left Harmony for Europe on 5 June 1825. The reason given was a piece of special pleading. He said it would be folly for him to 'fall a sacrifice' to the climate, and represented himself as in great need of relaxation. The people believed him and, as one member dutifully recorded, 'the obliging us to rely on ourselves may be productive of much good'. They also trusted him when he promised that he would shortly return accompanied by his wife and family, and 'almost the whole town of Lanark'.

As the great experiment got under way, circumstances seem propitious in spite of the limit imposed on the drawing of supplies. Hundreds travelled long distances over painfully rough roads to pursue the vision Owen had displayed to them. It was so vivid to them that his absence from the town caused little concern at first. Soon it was so full that log cabins the Rappites had abandoned were being hastily repaired. The mood of optimism that prevailed found its way into the first report of Thomas Pears to his wife's uncle at Pittsburgh, Benjamin Bakewell.

Pears expressed himself astounded at the progress already made at the time of Owen's departure: it is clear that enthusiasm lent colour to his report. Schools had been organized, boarding-houses established, smiths, turners, and carpenters employed and, it seemed to him, agriculture was going on as well as if they had been a year in residence already. He was no farmer but he was no stranger to the backwoods either. In 1815 in partnership with J. J. Audubon, the naturalist, and Bakewell's son, he had tried to establish a steam grist mill in the wilds of Kentucky. When that failed he went into partnership with Bakewell, making glass at Pittsburgh. By 1825 he and his wife Sarah had seven children with them at Harmony, ranging from Maria, aged 18, to William de Witt Clinton Pears, the baby.

They were typical of those families most hard pressed by the regulations introduced by the Preliminary Society. But anxiety as to how they
were all to survive was at first outweighed for Thomas Pears by his pleasure in the important task allotted to him, that of a bookkeeper at the
store where he issued goods according to the value of labour performed,
as certified by the superintendents of the various departments. With a
head full of Debits and Credits, he told Bakewell, he rejoiced that he had
dedicated himself to Owen's Social System. That was just as well since he
might have despaired at the difficulty of balancing books whose entries
read: 'Credit. To Mr Smith for weeding a garden—three hours. Debit. A
pot of molasses and four pounds of corn meal'.

Before he left Owen recommended the inhabitants of Harmony to
meet together three times a week for discussions on matters pertaining to
business, for concerts, and for public balls. With regular social intercourse, as rare in those parts as it was eagerly anticipated, a mood of light
heartedness prevailed for a time, at least among the younger members of
the community. According to Sarah Pears, the girls' heads were just as
full of dresses and beaux as in any other place. But in this place, to the sur-
prise and disquiet of a neighbour riding by, the sound of a fiddle playing
reels was heard even on the Sabbath Day. Outside school hours the children ran free, too free for some, who complained of their loud laughter
and their depredations in the orchards. Someone, who had doubtless not
yet heard that man was not a fit subject for praise or blame, flogged
the boys for stealing plums.

But as the season advanced, bringing with it heat and high humidity,
the mood became more sombre. To all of them, even to those accustomed
to it, the Indiana summer was a severe ordeal; frequently the thermometer
rose above 100 °F. Mercifully there was no epidemic among the adults;
but nine small children died. Thomas Pears recorded a host of minor
complaints; slight bilious fever, boils, sore eyes, and the lassitude that
comes from hot and sleepless nights: 'I would not willingly pass another
such a summer', he told Bakewell.

With time to look about him, Pears perceived that the enterprise was
running into trouble. There was no effective organization among the
farmers and the neglect of fencing particularly worried him. 'The hogs
have been our Lords and Masters this year in field and garden', he wrote,
and feared they must go without vegetables in the winter except for what
they might buy. He was equally gloomy about the prospect of earning a
surplus in the immediate future from their manufacturing operations; as
left by the Rappites the cotton factory had proved to be not in good

order and the steam engine that drove the spindles was old and under-powered. The entire output of blacksmiths, shoemakers, carpenters, and tailors was absorbed by members of the society, leaving nothing to sell. As for the brick-makers, by the end of the summer they had turned out 250,000 bricks which were stacked to await the construction of the quad-rilangular village in which the Community of Equality was finally to be housed.

That Pears was not alone in progressing from euphoria to serious dis-quiet is demonstrated by the letters of William Pelham to his son. He was a journalist, a former Editor of an Ohio newspaper, and had been a doc-tor in the War of Independence; he was, therefore, well into middle age. In spite of this he had been attracted to New Harmony by his belief in the community ideal, everything seemed good to him at first. 'I have become a Harmonite and mean to spend the remainder of my days in this abode of peace and quiet', he wrote, shortly after he arrived. He had not found everything in order, nor had he expected as much, but he particularly approved the freedom he was given to mix with his fellow citizens with-out fear or imposition, ill humour, censure, or suspicion. 'Each one says what he thinks and mutual respect for the sentiment of each other seems to pervade all citizens.' Such was his peace of mind, he told his son, that though there were many mosquitoes at Harmony, he felt their bites far less than he had at home.

Yet as the summer of 1825 wore on and more and more people came in to the town, the lack of planning began to make itself acutely felt. Pelham became apprehensive, particularly as to how they would all survive the winter. He was dismayed at the sight of whole families with young chil-dren crowded into the flimsy shelter of log cabins the Rappites had long since turned over to animals and stores. He was himself most uncomfor-tably perched in an unfinished attic where he sweltered in the summer heat but feared even more exposure to the winter cold. In fact some people who lacked warm clothing began to leave as autumn drew on and no extra garments were provided for them. Funds for these were not available, and William Owen thought fit to warn his father in October that the expense of setting up the establishment had already exceeded what Owen had anticipated.

The problem could only be solved if and when the members of the Preliminary Society began to produce a surplus. It was essential that all should work their hardest. Work as a duty and a pleasure was the text taken by The Revd Mr Jennings who, as part of his contribution, occup-ied the pulpit of the Rappite church on Sundays where he delivered a strongly secular address. He was one of the more prominent communitarians and appeared in several roles. On week day evenings, 'Major The Revd Mr Jennings', as William Pelham dubbed him, led the boys and young men in marching and counter-marching, as was done at New Lanark. It was Robert Owen's wish that the town should now play its full part in the Indiana militia. When it was his turn to occupy the pulpit William Owen gave readings from the first book by his elder brother, Robert Dale Owen, *An Outline of the System of Education at New Lanark*, which had been published the year before. William was so busy as to be almost unapproachable, Pelham noted.

As for the women, their lives were more arduous and less interesting than those led by the men. Thomas Pears's wife, Sarah, wrote home to Pittsburgh at the same time as he did; her letters are not so buoyant. It was not that she was unsuited to the life; her connections gave her the strongest claim to a part in an egalitarian and non-sectarian experiment. Sarah Pears's father was The Revd John Palmer, who taught for many years at the centre of liberal dissent in England, Warrington Academy, and who stood by Joseph Priestley in his effort to introduce the principles that inspired the French Revolution into England. But although Sarah had confidence in Owen's sincere desire to promote the happiness of all, when she considered her family's lot she owned herself very depressed. And it was the same for all the women who came to Harmony; all suffered from cramped living quarters and heavy domestic work. Though it was undeniably useful to the community, washing, cooking, mending, and cleaning was labour which did not qualify for credits, unless these tasks were done for bachelor members, and such extra work was necessarily limited. While the Constitution stated that all members of the Preliminary Society were to be of equal rank, it turned out that wives were not members, not entitled to maintenance in their own right. The effect was to create a separate and inferior class; and, like women, blacks were separate and inferior too.

'Persons of colour may be received as helpers to the society, if necessary', the Constitution stated, 'or it may be found useful to prepare and enable them to become associates in communities in Africa, or in some other country, or in some other part of this country.' In other words blacks were not to rank as equals at New Harmony; better by far for them to develop separately. Though the actions of some of Owen's associates on the Wabash, including his eldest son, were to earn them a place in the history of Negro emancipation, he himself regarded the institution of slavery with equanimity; in certain circumstances with approval. He

chose to believe, or at least to state, that all slave proprietors were benevolent since it was so clearly in their interest to be so. He wished slaves
could be left alone by abolitionists—prominent among whom was his
partner, William Allen—for in their present state he felt they would be
the 'happiest' members of society for years to come. Once they acquired
knowledge they would become dangerous, as the manufacturing classes
in Great Britain and Ireland were at that moment. This was because the
power of science was hourly diminishing the amount of manual labour
available to occupy them; the resulting idleness appeared to Robert
Owen too frightful to contemplate. 'Let not therefore the existing slave
population be urged forward beyond the present happy ignorant state in
which they are', he begged, 'until some wise arrangements between the
existing white producers and non-producers shall be adjusted to their
future benefits.'

Such a process of adjustment was now to be set on foot at New Harmony, and it was the Committee's role to supervise it. In the absence of
the Proprietor, as Owen was styled in the Constitution, the ultimate
power of decision lay with his representative, William Owen, who was
virtually unsupported in this daunting task. Except for the ubiquitous Mr
Jennings, his fellow Committee members, though enthusiastic, were
inexperienced and lacked force. Donald Macdonald had gone back to
Europe with Robert Owen, and all summer long Frances Wright, whose
organizing ability matched her energy, was caught up in a visionary
scheme for Negro emancipation.

Under stress, the government of Harmony became a desperate affair
whose frequent changes of course and fright at the consequences, were
disguised under a strict and authoritarian manner. The Committee did
not hesitate to threaten, and sometimes to use, the sanction of expulsion,
a fate at all costs to be avoided in that remote place. Though by this
means it managed to avoid disaster, it suffered the erosion of its members' good will. Who they were was the subject of a report printed in the
Co-operative Magazine in August 1825. There were then some 1,200 persons in the town, with a large proportion of children. They were chiefly
from the surrounding countryside, but also from Cincinnati and some
Eastern cities. About half were 'mechanics'—skilled workers—and the
rest backwoodsmen, 'men capable of learning anything they please—
many will be good but many others find the life incompatible with their
high notions of independence'.

At Economy the Rapps received a regular flow of information from
private sources about the state of their former home. As the summer

advanced their correspondents painted a scene of Biblical desolation, fields unsown, grapes rotting on the vine. A spirit of carelessness prevailed, it was said, and the new system appeared sadly out of balance. Storekeepers, clerks, and committee men outnumbered artisans and farmers, to the detriment of production.

Some of this gloom was undoubtedly exaggerated, the kind of thing his Rappite correspondents thought Father would like to hear, for shortly after their meeting the previous winter he had denounced Robert Owen as a tool of the Devil. Blame for the decline of Harmony, such as it was, may not have lain all on Owen's side; there is some evidence that the Society allowed things to run down before the final decision was taken to depart. Macdonald's diary contains information that sounds plausible.

When the Harmony Society purchased the Estate [in Indiana] and removed from the neighbourhood of Pittsburg [*sic*], they hoped to be joined by a great number of their countrymen, and therefore took a much greater extent of land than they immediately required. Two years back, finding that few joined their association, they sent some to the old country to try to obtain an accession to their members. Their missionaries however proved unsuccessful and returned about this time twelve months. Soon after they resolved to sell this property, and purchase a smaller one in Pennsylvania nearer to that part of the country which is peopled by germans [*sic*].

A recurring question, put to George and Frederick Rapp, was how could Mr Owen, rich as he was, pay for it all? As early as 7 June the Harmony Society's agent at Vincennes reported that the provisions in the town were nearly exhausted. This was obviously not true but as they contemplated the large numbers flocking there, people who had allowed themselves to become involved financially began to look for reassurance. As one of the principals in the sale Frederick Rapp's opinion was much canvassed. 'Respecting the responsibility of Mr Robert Owen', he wrote to one anxious enquirer, 'I would venture that he is considered a man of great property and very respectable in Scotland, he has almost paid for the purchases from our Society ... However whether he will be able to succeed with his plans in this country is yet very doubtful to me, nevertheless, I think small credits in short terms would be safe enough, at least for some time to come.'

PART III

PROBLEMS OF THE OLD,
IMMORAL WORLD

CHAPTER 8

A FAMILY FORSAKEN

HAPPILY for Robert Owen's credit in the Wabash country, the bills he drew on Barclays Bank in London, amounting to over £20,000 to pay for Harmony, were honoured when they fell due at the end of June. After some discussion his partners in the New Lanark Company, William Allen, Jeremy Bentham, Michael Gibbs, and Joseph Foster (Walker and Fox had died), agreed to back them: 'acting a kindly and liberal part in this matter', Owen's eldest son, Robert Dale, noted in evident relief. It is unlikely that any of them, especially William Allen, to whom in April Owen had written as to a partner in the enterprise, had anything more to do with Harmony than that. In the summer of 1825 their first concern had to be the survival of the New Lanark Company.

From the beginning of 1824 the economic situation in England and Scotland had become so threatening that prudent men were securing their affairs against a violent storm. A rage of speculation enveloped the country, prompting the formation of dozens of joint stock companies to deal in everything from mines in Mexico, sheep in New South Wales, to canals, turnpikes, and Tontines at home. In all these speculations only a small investment, seldom exceeding 5 per cent, was paid at first, so that a very moderate rise in the price of shares produced a large profit on the sum invested. The consequence was that people of every sort—even, as the *Annual Register* put it, women—rushed to buy. The price of raw material therefore soared, and this was why the New Lanark business was at risk: raw cotton became impossibly expensive. It was a situation that Robert Owen had always feared, to the point of discouraging buyers from placing orders when the price was high. In 1825 the reaction set in; shares collapsed; companies failed; and a considerable number of banks closed their doors.

William Allen's papers have mostly disappeared, but enough remain to suggest that he was deeply worried. 'The times', he told Jeremy Bentham, 'have been tremendous.' Although in the *Life* Robert Owen spoke of the large profits made while he was Manager at New Lanark, Allen's experience indicates that, from 1824 to about 1828, the partners received little or no return on their capital, while the nominal value of their holdings in the company—including those of Robert Owen—fell.

So, was Allen willing to enter into partnership in a company to run New Harmony, with the man he had made strenuous efforts to have dismissed from his post as Manager at New Lanark in 1823? The answer must be that he was not: that in the letter written to him from the Wabash in April 1825, Owen presumed an acquiescence that Allen was not prepared to give. To proceed to action upon the basis of an unfounded assumption was a habit of Owen's: William Maclure, who eventually did allow himself to be drawn into association with Owen at New Harmony, noticed the practice even before they got to Indiana. On that occasion he decided that Owen had taken silence for consent, when it was only 'indifference bordering on contempt'.

Precisely what source of capital was found to support New Harmony for a time must remain a puzzle. The Rapps were paid the original sum, amounting to some £20,000, but, as will be seen, the account for the goods they left behind was not settled without great difficulty. No money appeared to come from appeals to the public. Although the Select Committee of 1823 was very firmly told by Owen that £50,00 had already been subscribed to found a Village of Unity and Mutual Co-operation, he apparently had no access to any sum approaching that amount; perhaps promises made at the time never materialized. His own shares in the New Lanark Company were not converted into cash until 1828.

It may be that conditions in England in June 1825 forced an entire change of plan. For in spite of the impression he left on the minds of those in Indiana, he made no attempt to recruit in England. Yet there would have been no shortage of offers had he sought them. During his absence in the United States, the idea of co-operation had begun to take hold among the working classes in various parts of the country, fostered by two publications, *The Economist* and the *Co-operative Magazine*. They made of Owen a figurehead for what was to become a genuine popular movement, and gave much space to accounts of developments at Orbiston and New Harmony.

It was to a large audience of enthusiastic members of the new movement at the London Co-operative Society that Robert Owen gave an important address on 25 August. He told them that the climate of Indiana exposed persons going from England to risk: on the whole, he said, he would sooner direct his friends to form societies in England where they had greater opportunities of happiness, and of doing good.

Turning to the question of property, he gave a specific assurance. The property of each community was to be invested in the members of it. For himself, he said, he never would again invest in property with a view to profit. Whatever he had done, or would do, in America, he would be content with the simple interest of his capital invested there.

If Owen did not recruit any of the enthusiasts in England then, of course, he would do so in Scotland: at New Lanark as, in order to reassure the members of the infant society on the Wabash, he had promised he would. New Lanark, after all, was the prototype, the 'colony' which, as he had written to George Rapp in 1820, he had built up so carefully over the years—'the half new world' which he had already called into being. People with experience of communal living were essential to the success of new communities. He even charged the Rapps with breaking an agreement to leave some members of the Harmony Society behind on the Wabash in order to ease the introduction of his new settlers. So when he reached home at the end of August 1825, surely that was the time to gather the workers and their families who were prepared to emigrate? Moreover his own family, his wife and the six other grown up children, were also expected at New Harmony where their presence would have been a great encouragement. But although the repeal of the Combination Acts in 1825 had freed skilled artisans to go wherever they chose, that did not happen. As far as can be known, none of the workers from the mills, who numbered nearly 2,000, chose to depart, and Owen's visit to his home was only to take leave for a second time.

Robert Owen planned to return to Indiana at the beginning of October and only his eldest son, Robert Dale, aged 24, was to be permitted to go with him. For his wife, Ann Caroline, their imminent departure was almost too much to bear. She was ailing that summer, frequently obliged to rest during the farewell visits she paid with her son. Desolate at the parting she wrote to Harmony, 'Notwithstanding you think the New System brings happiness, it certainly, my dear William, in the first instance has created a good deal of uneasiness to *some individuals.*'

She was the victim of her husband's obsession. From the moment of his impulse to become a reformer he left her for months at a time to pursue his mission. Later, when the crowds flocked to New Lanark— 'benevolent individuals, committees of philanthropic societies, speculative regenerators of mankind, gossiping judges and jail gadding ladies'—she was obliged to play hostess to those who, if they did not condescend to her face, spoke of her afterwards as a nonentity. In manner perhaps she was, but not in effect; she played a leading part in her children's upbringing and that, in turn, was to give a special feeling to their life and that of their descendants, at New Harmony.

By the autumn of 1825 a change had taken place in the fortunes of the Owen family, whose price for Ann Caroline and her three daughters—Anne, Mary, and Jane Dale—was to be inordinately high. Their life at Braxfield, the handsome and commodious house above the Clyde, standing on a grassy plateau and sheltered from the sight and sound of the cotton-spinning establishment—'so as not to be annoyed by it', as Robert Owen said—was in its most pleasant aspects, all but over. So much of the money left by David Dale to Ann Caroline and her sisters had already gone to finance Owen's passion that the women of the family were to be reduced in time to what in Dale terms was genteel poverty. In September 1825 the other partners combined to dismiss Owen as Manager of the mills, and then his salary ceased. Although her letters are unfortunately not available to scholars, from other evidence one can say that Ann Caroline did not blame her husband for these misfortunes. The Owens were a close-knit family, very affectionate towards each other, and to the father who, if they did not share his views or comprehend his genius, to the end of his life received their loyal and forgiving support.

One member was elated at the prospect of emigrating to Indiana, namely Robert Dale, the eldest son. William was told, 'he thinks that he himself is spoilt for any life but that of a community'. Robert Dale's state of mind was of continual interest to his family and monitored with some anxiety. Ever since a severe illness struck him at the age of eleven, in the year of his father's gravest financial crisis, he had suffered from weak nerves while at the mercy of a conscience which, tempered by a rigorous moral training and supervised by his deeply pious mother, gripped him like steel.

Of all the Owen children he was the one most proud of their heritage, most attached to the way of life at Braxfield House. Its sense of privilege, of rank, of duty to others less fortunate at the gates; as well as its fine furniture and silver, were eventually transferred to Indiana where, with his singular personality, they made of Robert Dale a separate, almost a pathetic figure. (In his biography he was respectfully referred to as 'the well born Scot'.) Although he spoke with pride of their grandfather, David Dale, and cherished the reputation he had for philanthropy, Robert Dale derived the greatest satisfaction from his grandmother's side of the family. She was a Campbell whose proud boast it was, handed down to her daughters and by them to their children, that among their ancestors was a kinsman of the Earl of Breadalbane.

Robert Dale was educated until the age of 16 entirely at home. 'I thus acquired timid, retired habits', he wrote. He had scarcely recovered from the grave illness he suffered at the age of 11 when, in 1815, his father took him on a tour of manufacturing establishments in Scotland and the North of England. The elder Owen's intention was to discover evidence of the misuse of child labour in the textile trade in order to support a Bill restricting hours of work. Robert Dale was greatly disturbed by the sight of small children shut up in the foetid and dusty atmosphere of the mills, pale and deformed by the unnatural conditions. He accompanied his father wherever he went. He was present at his discussions with Sir Robert Peel, who undertook to steer the Bill through Parliament, and attended sessions of the committee appointed by the House to hear the evidence. Owen's mauling at the hands of more than one MP who judged his reports on the ill treatment of children to be exaggerated, and his evidence too frequently based on hearsay, inspired in the 14-year-old Robert Dale an aversion to declamation, to eloquence even, which led him ever afterwards to rely on fact, 'carefully prepared and consolidated'. In particular he never forgot the onslaught of a committee member who happened also to be a wealthy cotton manufacturer. 'This oppressor of childhood questioned my father as to his religious opinions and other personal matters equally irrelevant, in a tone so insolent that, to my utter shame, I could not repress my tears.'

Robert Dale deplored what he called his lack of 'pluck', yet after much heart searching he was brave enough openly to endorse his father's anti-religious views, whilst knowing what distress it would cause his mother. She did not spare him from the sight of her bitter disappointment and reproach.

It was his father's intention that Robert Dale should succeed him as a benefactor to mankind. All the Owen children were destined to play a particular role in the new system of society; that was why they had been kept so carefully apart. In 1818 Owen judged the time had come to broaden the experience of the two eldest. As he declared in the *Life*,

with the aid of well selected governesses and tutors . . . their characters, physical and mental, had been so far formed on rational principles, that I had no fears to send them from home . . . to become more practically acquainted with the ways of men in the old world,—so different in many respects to the half new world in which alone to this time they had been trained.

Three years at Emmanuel de Fellenberg's Hofwyl left Robert Dale with an even stronger sense of responsibility than his mother had been able to impart, and the deepest respect for the democratic principles on which the day to day running of the school appeared to depend. As he described it in his memoirs there was no coercion by masters of their pupils; an elected council of the boys themselves decided matters and upheld discipline. Less committed witnesses, on the other hand, accused de Fellenberg of absolute control which rested on the system of informing that he encouraged among the boys. Robert Dale placed entire faith in him, addressed him as 'foster father', and wrote to him for years after he had settled at Harmony.

While at the school he conceived a passion for gymnastics, believing, as de Fellenberg did, in the power of exercise to regenerate mind and body. He practised on horseback—riding was a skill for which he awarded himself high marks. When in London he kept himself in trim at Astley's famous circus, where he tried acrobatic stunts. At New Lanark, in the summer of 1825, he prepared for the egalitarian society he expected to find on the Wabash by taking lessons from his groom on how to care for his own mount.

Since 1822, when he returned from Switzerland, Robert Dale had occupied himself teaching in the village school and writing a book, *An Outline of the System of Education at New Lanark*, which was published in 1824. It was to be the first of many, for writing came easily, and was a solace to him. Under the impulse to advise, improve, reform, which had been nourished at Hofwyl—and further cramped his disposition—polemical discussion leaked incessantly from his pen.

According to the preamble of the *Outline*, the system of education at New Lanark differed essentially from that of any other institution in the United Kingdom, or possibly in any other part of the world. It was no less than an experiment to ascertain the capabilities of the human mind. No praise or blame was permitted to be used by the teachers; kindness was all and a general happiness the overriding aim. But the curriculum remained largely unchanged: reading, writing, arithmetic, and, for the girls, sewing. Though the New Institution which housed the school had been opened eight years previously, the author remarked that it was only in the last two that some innovations, such as mental arithmetic as practised at Yverdun, had been made. From Robert Dale's account it also emerged that books were few and classes large, and that most lessons consisted of one person reading aloud to the other pupils. The famous classes in natural history, geography, and ancient and modern history which attracted so many visitors to New Lanark, were *extempore* lectures by the teachers who had a set of maps and drawings to assist them. In fact, the New Lanark school was similar to other Lancastrian institutions which, according to William Allen, were having grafted on them at that time the Pestalozzian ethos.

With the publication of the *Outline* Robert Dale's reputation, which had been founded on his father's interest in the same field, took on a momentum of its own. For the Philadelphia scientists and teachers the prospect of his joining them was an added incentive to their moving to the West. In 1824 a colleague of theirs, the young Quaker doctor, Philip Price, who was already an ardent supporter of community living, made a pilgrimage to New Lanark where he spent the winter teaching in the school. He sent glowing reports of Robert Dale to Marie Fretageot and told her that, when they all set out for the Wabash, Robert Dale would bring a class of his pupils with him.

That was not to be. Nor was Robert Dale to be accompanied to Indiana by the girl he hoped one day to make his wife. She was secretly the reason why his reaction to the prospect of buying *Harmonie* had been as enthusiastic as his father's. His feeling for her, which began shortly after his return from Hofwyl, both obsessed and frightened Robert Dale. Self-conscious in the extreme, inordinately proud of his Campbell heritage and the Breadalbane connection, he was appalled to find himself desperately in love with the 11-year-old daughter of a worker in the New Lanark mill. Margaret's humble birth and what he saw as her grotesque youth were a serious impediment to his future happiness. While he struggled to conceal his infatuation from the rest of his family, he wildly hoped that a removal to the wilderness, to a backwoods community where all must surely be equal, would solve the problem.

Margaret (no other name is known) was one of a number of village girls taught music by Anne, the eldest Owen daughter. Disliking the idea that such a pretty creature must shortly go to sweeping floors and minding throstle frames, Anne Owen requested her parents' permission to take her into Braxfield House, apparently to train her as a teacher or a governess. But in his memoirs written in old age, Robert Dale insisted that Margaret was received as a member of the family and being as clever as she was pretty, soon outshone the Owen girls in grace, talent, and ultimately ease of manner. According to his journal kept at the time, in 1825 there was some question of Margaret going to America with his party but as things turned out she stayed at home. However plain it may have been to others, Robert Dale did not declare his love to her before he left.

When the Owens, father and son, sailed from Liverpool on 1 October 1825, with the faithful Donald Macdonald who was returning with them, there were only two other members of their group. One was Joseph Applegarth, who had left his bookselling business in London to devote himself to Owen's views. He taught for a time at New Lanark and was often a guest at Braxfield House. His dedication to the Owen system led to his appointment as a Trustee at Orbiston where he also served for a time as Manager of the store. The other, Stedman Whitwell, was involved at Orbiston too; as an architect he began the planning of the village. Whitwell's sister had been brought from London by Robert Owen to teach in the New Lanark school; the drawings of animals and plans for the Stream of History as used in the lectures were done by her. She held views on the desirability of free love which resulted in her dismissal by the other partners in the New Lanark Company. She thereupon took over the school at Orbiston. Whether her brother shared her views is not known. But his head was full of bad poetry and curious schemes.

In his charge for the journey to America, Whitwell had a six foot square model of the ideal village destined to be built on the high ground at Harmony. In Washington, President John Quincy Adams allowed it to be displayed in the White House. Diagrams, models, architectural drawings were favourite devices of Robert Owen, by which he hoped to gain the attention of the ordinary man.

When the party landed at New York at the beginning of November, some of the reports circulating about New Harmony were good, some hinted at disaster, even an exodus. In spite of this uncertainty, and the fact that he had been absent since the previous June, Robert Owen lingered in the eastern states throughout November. To and fro between New York and Philadelphia he went, preaching the gospel of the new social system, sounding his favourite note, the utter depravity of 'buying cheap and selling dear'. Robert Dale who attended his meetings was moved to record his unease at his father's attitude—perhaps for the first time. He confided to his journal, writing in German for better security, 'My father criticized the existing system in a too violent and absolutely irritating manner. However all the people have accepted it all very well and have even applauded the points that hit them hardest.'

At Philadelphia Owen issued what he called a Proclamation calling once again for workers and their families to go to New Harmony. He did this without considering what might actually be going on there, and in response to nothing more substantial than a rumour that numbers of the people who had answered his first invitation to New Harmony, the previous summer, had either left, or were preparing to do so. When news of his father's action reached William Owen at the beginning of December he let fly in a manner that was as unprecedented as it was apparently justified. Besides coping with an immensely difficult situation during his father's prolonged absence, William was still smarting under a jibe that his letters home, giving an account of his stewardship, were unbusinesslike.

They already had sufficient workmen of the kind that Owen had requested, William began. For instance, they had an excellent foreman cotton-spinner, with a hasty temper admittedly but valuable as he at least understood the steam engine. They had good weavers, plenty of distillers, a brewer and maltster. There were plenty of tanners, two superior brickmakers and some inferior ones, plasterers, an excellent stonemason, and a journeyman watchmaker. What they did need was a good superintendent of farming, together with saddlers, potters, smiths, ropemakers, and above all good cooks.

'But although I have said we want these men to make our workshops full and perfect, I would at the same time repeat and impress upon your mind *we have no room for them.*' Building houses was impossible, William explained.

We have *no lime, no rocks* (ready blasted), *no brick, no timber*, no *boards*, no *shingles*, nothing requisite for building, and as to getting them from others, *they are not to be had in the whole country.* We must dry and burn the lime, dig and blast the rocks, mould and turn the bricks, fell and hew the timber, fell and saw the boards and split the shingles and to do all these things we have no hands to spare, or the branches of business in the society must stop, and they cannot stop or the whole Society would stop too. *These are the facts as they really are,*

William wrote.

Alarm at the thought that Owen would bring too many people with him when he came set William off again. 'We have no bedding for anybody . . . we have *no* feathers, no *ticking*, no *sheets*, no *blankets*. You must buy some or *everyone* must bring along with them enough for themselves. The *sugar* is gone, *quite* gone and the river being low we can get *none* till it rises. We use about two barrels a week. The store will be quite empty in six weeks.'

William's apprehension was well founded, for even as he wrote, Owen was collecting a considerable number of people from Philadelphia to go with him to New Harmony. As soon as he had signed the agreement to buy the town with Frederick Rapp in April 1825 he had issued a pressing invitation to the various members of the Academy of

Natural Sciences who had welcomed him at his first appearance in the city to join him on the Wabash. Consequently Thomas Say, Gerard Troost, Charles-Alexandre Lesueur, and John Speakman were now making ready to accompany him, as was Marie Fretageot.

She had not been proof against Owen's charm and his argument—one that Jean-Jacques Rousseau must have approved—that the secluded spot on the Wabash was the only place where, the distractions of the world banished, their collaboration would demonstrate what the effect of a good education could be. There is nothing to suggest how Owen explained away the fact that, contrary to what Madame Fretageot had been given to understand, he had none of the workers from New Lanark with him, and no children. She had used the promise in her strenuous campaign to persuade her friend, and the patron of all of them, William Maclure, to join the expedition. Now, in November, she was overjoyed that he had seen fit to commit himself, his vast library, and extensive collection of mineral and botanical specimens—but only a canny amount of his money—to Owen and to the Wabash.

Maclure's surrender was only partial; he did not believe in a community of property and equality and said as much. His passion was for education, for the widest possible dissemination of what he referred to as 'positive knowledge'. He was perhaps the more disposed to join his friends since the school of industry at Alicante in Spain, on which he had lavished much time and money since 1819, had recently been obliged to close following the collapse of the liberal government at Madrid. His presence lent a solid air which the enterprise had wanted, for though hasty, dictatorial, and prone to take people at face value, Maclure was an experienced businessman.

He was already familiar with the philosophy of Robert Owen, and with him personally, though they had met only briefly at New Lanark in 1824. His visit had been in the course of a tour of educational establishments in the British Isles, including several Lancastrian schools, the famous one at Edgeworthtown, and Glasgow College. The three days he spent at New Lanark were the most pleasant of his life, he wrote to Marie Fretageot. The views expressed by Owen exactly matched his own and pre-disposed him to admire everything he was shown. Owen's courage and perseverance had made a vast improvement in society, Maclure decided, and that in spite of malignant opposition—his dislike of priests was almost as intense as Owen's. In his journal which, like his letters, was badly spelt, unpunctuated, odd, and earnest, he noted; 'Mr O's opinions go far before any I have ever expected to hear touches upon the favourite fancys I have indulged opportunity in looking through a telescope at the probable progress of civilisation.'

It was an apt description of the effect of Owen's special genius. But, however much they appeared to have in common, however auspicious their association promised to be, it was not to last. That it occurred at all was a kind of retribution imposed by circumstances, exacted by events. Maclure eventually had the experience of seeing through Robert Owen, of watching the shifts he used to escape from a situation that trapped them both. In the course of it the nature of their beliefs became extremely clear. Maclure's were in his heart as well as his head and governed his behaviour totally. Owen's were expedient, external, whatever it suited him to say; the makeshift garments Crusoe wore, pieced out from fragments discovered on the desert island.

CHAPTER 9

THE *PHILANTHROPIST*

HARMONY was in just the right place for William Maclure. It was a maxim of his, or rather one of his famous 'opinions' the circulation of which among his numerous and learned acquaintances he fostered with care, that the geography of the United States made it likely that sooner or later war would destroy the Eastern seaboard. Settlements would flourish in the Mississippi Valley long after foxes looked out of the windows of Philadelphia, he said. It was curiously precise as well as picturesque of fate to deposit Maclure on the banks of the Wabash just south of Vincennes. As its name implies Vincennes was founded by the French as a post on the route between Quebec and New Orleans. Maclure had an early connection with the Wabash region through a friend, while the philosophy which shaped his life was quintessentially French.

After the outbreak of the Revolution there had arrived in Philadelphia men whose ideas and actions had directed the course of its first few years, but who had been obliged to flee from the anarchic passion of Robespierre. They made a little Paris, a Gallic focus in the squarely sober city. For these men, one of whom was Talleyrand, the old French presence in the West was less a matter for nostalgia than a challenge to re-establsh empire. Various reconnaissances were made before the US government called a halt, but many of the first accounts of the Wabash country are in French.

One of the most vivid appears in the *Tableau du sol et du climat des États-unis*, written by a fellow *émigré* of Talleyrand, Constantin-François Volney. When he set out on his journey to the West in 1796 he did so from the house in Philadelphia of the friend who had offered him shelter in the United States, the geologist William Maclure. Volney had become known to Maclure when the latter was in Paris in the last days of the *ancien regime*. They had a mutual acquaintance in the American Minister to France, Thomas Jefferson. To Jefferson, Volney wrote from the Wabash describing the flatness and the propensity to fever, which he had not escaped. The experience obviously depressed him for he was moved to remark of the Wabash country that though one might eventually possess broad acres and great flocks and herds, one would in the end be left with 'la tête vide, le cœur fade, les jours bien longs.'

Maclure's connection with France came about as a result of his business activities. It is not known precisely what these were but they may have been to do with the textile trade; in any case they brought him a large fortune before he was 40. By that time he had become a cosmopolitan and a wanderer, at home in Europe, as well as in America. While still a youth he had turned his back on Scotland, where he had been born in 1763, and emigrated to Virginia where he had prospered from the start. It was there that Jefferson took a liking to the young Scot and kept a fatherly eye on him.

Like Benjamin Franklin, his predecessor, when in Paris Jefferson frequented the salon of Madame Helvétius at Auteuil. Among the habitués at the outbreak of the Revolution were Talleyrand, Mirabeau, and Condillac. The inner circle was formed by the so-called *idéologues*— who included Destutt de Tracy, Cabanis, Maine de Biran, de Gérando, and Volney. They resembled their English contemporaries, Godwin, Mill, and Bentham, in that they were preoccupied with the desire to translate ideas into practice. Furthermore the *idéologues* assumed that all known sciences, together with aspects not yet expressed in scientific terms, such as morality and politics, formed an organic whole. When the relationship could be clearly perceived the way would be open for man to achieve a higher state.

This philosophy found an eager response in William Maclure. It was the first time in his life that he had been sufficiently impressed to surrender to instruction for, as his correspondence shows, he possessed all the dogmatism of those who make an early success in life. Though a Scottish education of the kind that Maclure had received was the envy and admiration of the rest of Europe—the reason why, it was said, the workers there were far less disturbed than in other countries—Maclure condemned his teacher for leaving him 'as ignorant as a pig of anything useful not having occasion to practice anything I had learned'.

For Maclure geology was both a serious study and a relaxation. 'I adopted rock hunting as an amusement in place of deer or partridge hunting', he explained, 'considering mineralogy and geology as the sciences most applicable to useful practical purposes but, like most things of the greatest utility, neglected.' The journeys across Europe which he began after he had retired from business were undertaken in pursuit of geological knowledge, above all in search of coal. He and a companion, sometimes Joseph Carrington Cabell, son of a Virginia planter, or Joel Poinsett, who was to have a distinguished career in the diplomatic service, covered thousands of miles by coach in Scandinavia, Russia, Italy, France, and Germany.

Les idéologues considered education vital in the effort to increase man's capacity to help himself. In this Maclure wholeheartedly concurred. Property, knowledge, and power were the three essentials of freedom, according to him. And, unlike Rapp or Robert Owen, he considered freedom all-important. The fact that these three essentials were unfairly distributed was, he maintained, the cause of all crime and distress. Again, unlike his predecessors at New Harmony, he forbore to tackle problems of property or power, acknowledging, as they had not, his own limitations. He concentrated upon the task he felt best equipped to do and in pursuit of which he spent large sums of money: his object was the widest possible dissemination of what he called 'positive knowledge'. He was acquainted with Joseph Lancaster's system which, vigorously promoted by William Allen, was exported to France after 1815 under the name of *instruction mutuelle*. In Maclure's opinion the advantage of the system in giving access to education to large numbers who would otherwise be deprived of it, outweighed the criticism now being heard of learning 'parrot fashion'.

The most effective method in his eyes was that of Pestalozzi whose school at Yverdun he had come upon by chance in the course of a journey to the Alps in 1806. What Maclure found there was, as he confided to his journal, 'the most rational system of education I have seen'. From the beginning of their acquaintance Maclure provided the school at Yverdun with books and instruments of learning on which Pestalozzi placed so much emphasis. He was responsible for sending young Americans there to be taught the method. But his most welcome gift was the loan of capital to ease the financial burden which weighed heavily on the founder of the school. '*Edler, lieber Mann*', Pestalozzi addressed Maclure, in gratitude not only for his sustained material assistance but also for the idea of transplanting his method to the United States, the place in which it could be expected best to flourish. Pestalozzi had encountered much wearisome opposition in his own country. Faithful to the principles of his mentors, the *idéologues*, Maclure did all he could to get Pestalozzi's system adopted. That meant bringing over specially trained teachers, who had to be helped to emigrate to the United States and set up schools. Even there, in Philadelphia, conservative prejudice was a serious problem. It was with a view to the uninhibited development of an ideal that he had long had in mind, therefore, that Maclure accepted Robert Owen's invitation to accompany him to Indiana. As far as he knew Owen combined experience of the Lancastrian method as practised in the New Lanark schools with a firm belief in the Pestalozzian ethos.

The first teacher sponsored by Maclure was Joseph Neef, whose giant stature and forcibly expressed, revolutionary ideas brought a vital charge to life in the New Harmony community. He came from Alsace and fought as a soldier in the *Grande Armée*. Neef's passionate and unwavering allegiance was to democracy, and the greatest betrayal of his life came when Napoleon made himself Emperor over the French. By that time Neef was teaching in Paris, where he met his future wife, and she became a partner in the school in Paris.

Holding the views he did, Neef grew fretful at the contrived ceremonial of the Imperial régime, in spite of much flattering attention from the authorities, including a visit from Napoleon himself, accompanied by Talleyrand, at which Maclure was present. In 1807, therefore, Neef jumped at the opportunity Maclure offered of financial support for three years while he learned English, if he would emigrate to Philadelphia, there to begin a Pestalozzian school. Maclure's trust in him was fulfilled; the school was founded at the Falls of Schuykill, and Neef, having learned English remarkably quickly, set down his pedagogical experience in a book, *Sketch of a Plan and Method of Education*. It was the first of its kind to appear in the United States, and Maclure was as proud as a parent of it.

Neef's success did not last. His refusal to allow sectarian teaching so antagonized powerful religious interests that he was obliged to abandon his school after some years. He took his wife and family to farm in the backwoods of Kentucky, where lack of experience ensured a hard and precarious existence. Need therefore jumped at the offer Maclure made to him in the summer of 1825 offering him a place at New Harmony. He promised to join the main party there as soon as he could.

The majority of those bound for the Wabash—about forty—assembled at the real beginning of the journey, Pittsburgh on the Ohio River, on 1 December 1825. Robert Owen was now in a tearing hurry to reach New Harmony. The river was low and falling, too low for steamboats to operate. He therefore ordered a keelboat which was constructed in the space of three days. It measured 85 feet long by 14 wide and had 16 oars to move it. Below deck there was a cabin for the ladies, which they called 'Paradise' and which served as the galley, as well as a general living area, a small store cabin, and a fo'c'sle for the eleven crew. Owen called the boat *Philanthropist*.

In such cramped conditions it obviously helped that so many of the passengers already knew each other. Some were colleagues, like the three members of the Academy of Natural Sciences, Thomas Say, Charles Alexandre Lesueur, and Gerard Troost. They and Marie Fretageot, who had brought three of the girls from her school with her, looked to Maclure, their patron, as leader. The real author of the enterprise, Robert Owen, had only the slightest acquaintance with his fellow passengers. His original travelling companions had been reduced to his son, Robert Dale, and their manservant. Whitwell and Macdonald had remained in the East charged with sending on the heavy baggage.

All those on board professed enthusiasm for the community idea, but especially Thomas Say. He was, of course, a brilliant entomologist completely absorbed in his subject, but his claim to the special consideration which was afforded him apparently lay in a peculiarly gentle, almost timid disposition. He had been unfortunate. His Quaker family which had come to Philadelphia with William Penn had, in his own lifetime, lost their fortune. Say, who was born in 1787, entered gallantly into the druggist business with John Speakman who soon found himself doing all the work as his young colleague took refuge in the Academy of Natural Sciences. Thomas lived there, and frugally, on bread and milk, eggs and the occasional chop, for besides his lack of money he suffered from a very delicate stomach. That did not prevent him from accompanying Maclure on an arduous expedition to Florida in 1817, which damp and jungly place he had described as not flowing with milk and honey, but something vastly more pleasing to him, insects, 'and if they remain unknown I am determined it shall not be my fault'.

In 1819 official recognition had come with his appointment as zoologist to the famous expedition under Colonel Long which the US government directed to explore the upper Missouri River as far as the foothills of the Rocky mountains. Its purpose was to establish military posts in order to protect the fur trade, control the Indians, and lessen the influence among them of British trading companies. The going in unknown territory was very rough and, according to Long, Say was often ill. The conclusion reached as a result of the expedition, that the country could not support agriculture and was best considered as a defensive frontier, the limit of westward expansion by American settlers, acted as a deterrent to an entire generation.

The wilderness, therefore, held no fears for Thomas Say, and no surprises, or so he must have believed. His purpose in going to Indiana was to enable himself to continue his scientific work while living more easily and decently than he had been able to of late. He placed his trust in the community of equality and property which Robert Owen was about to set up at New Harmony. As to the initial difficulty of accommodating people of all kinds and from different levels of society in an equal manner, Say and his colleagues, Troost and Lesueur, relied on the arrangement which Marie Fretageot described to William Maclure.

Those who will be received the first shall be chosen [*sic*] amongst the best principles [*sic*] being, in order to form by their example those who afterwards will be received indiscriminately. The town already built will be allowed to them for their residence, and [they] will remain there until the community will allow them to take place in the new town ... The first settlers by their wealth, their industry will establish all that is proper to accumulate prosperity, union, peace and consequently happiness.

By wealth and industry Say and his fellow scientists understood the application of their expert knowledge to the achievement of a higher form of human existence. Say confided his hopes to his colleague Charles Buonaparte whose book on American birds he had been helping to compile.

Gerard Troost was a Dutchman, a distinguished scholar who had studied chemistry and, a rare subject in those days, crystallography, at The Hague and in Paris. His expertise had brought him to the notice of an older Buonaparte, Louis, King of Holland. Troost was chosen to take part in another of the great expeditions of the age, to Java, but fell victim to one of the hazards of the Napoleonic era—capture at sea. Escaping, he made his way to Philadelphia, a place he regarded as being on the way to Java, but he liked it so much that he remained. His practical enterprise extended to the founding of the first alum factory in the United States, but his business sense was not so well developed and the factory failed. His urbane wit and splendid manners served him better, and he became the first President of the Academy of Natural Sciences. Troost brought his wife with him to Indiana, and another treasure, a collection of geological specimens so fine that Maclure hated, as much as he envied, and coveted them.

Charles Alexandre Lesueur was a marine scientist, a compatriot of Madame Fretageot's, like her and Neef one of Maclure's pensioners. Lesueur was brought by him to the United States in 1815. The Academy of Natural Sciences was in the nature of a home to him. To him fell the time-consuming task of seeing to the safe landing of the huge boxes marked WM which contained the dead weight of hundreds of mineral specimens his patron dispatched to the Academy from wherever he went.

Lesueur's was another career influenced by the light that shone from Auteuil. He had his early training at the *Muséum d'histoire naturelle*, one of the institutions founded as a result of the influence of the *idéologues*. In 1800 he joined the crew of Baudin's celebrated expedition to the Southern Seas, an exploit which looked back to the adventures of Captain Cook, and forward to the voyage of Darwin's *Beagle*. Lesueur was appointed assistant to the naturalist, Péron. Together they collected and recorded some 100,000 specimens of hitherto unknown plants, animals and birds, and Lesueur discovered a gift for drawing and an eye for detail that made him an artist of very considerable stature. According to his friend and colleague, Baron Cuvier, Lesueur and Péron together discovered more species than any other man alive.

The fine detail with which he recorded the exotic flora and fauna of the Pacific was reproduced by Lesueur when he joined Owen and Maclure 25 years later. His drawings of New Harmony, the Wabash, and the Mississippi, though small, precise, and delicate, sharply convey a sense of puny resources pitted against the wilderness. Lesueur depicted the mess and bleak discomfort that accompanied the settlers wherever they went first; objects dumped ashore from boats in no kind of order, ramshackle jetties propped against bare banks, flimsily constructed cabins with smoke spouting from rusty tin stove pipes, and everywhere the isolation of half-cleared forest, trees girdled and left, leafless and stark, to die, stumps impeding progress in all directions, logs tumbled anyhow, and brush rotting. Lesueur was not attracted to the communitarian ideal as such. He agreed to go to the Wabash partly to please Maclure. He was irked, and his scientific work disturbed, by the business of getting a living at Philadelphia. Either he was confined to his room drawing, designing, engraving, he grumbled, or he was out chasing after pupils whose fees provided him with a mere competence. The prospect of having all his needs supplied at Harmony in return for purely scientific observation much attracted him. The Wabash, moreover, was well on the way to the Gulf of Mexico whose marine life he had long been anxious to explore.

Though pleased to be in company with Robert Owen, Marie Fretageot's whole attention on board *Philanthropist* was reserved for William Maclure. Though she had been associated with him for some five years she had been parted from him for most of that time while he was in Europe. Now she was eager to discuss plans, people, and ideas with him. There is a correspondence preserved at New Harmony, beginning in 1820 and lasting more than a decade, between Maclure and Madame Fretageot. From the moment he encountered her it seems that Maclure decided to entrust her with his business affairs. That confidence would have been a mark of the highest regard for any person so honoured, for Maclure was excessively cautious in such matters; that it was given to a member of the female sex was both an acknowledgement of Marie Fretageot's outstanding ability, and the affirmation of a principle, another of Maclure's cherished 'opinions'. He believed that the female half of the world was disastrously cramped in its ability and forbidden to use its talents. 'I should wish to see the women take their half share of all the occupations in life their strength will permit them', he declared, ' 'tis one of the modes by which the men exercise their physical superiority under the refined pretence of humanity and tenderness to exclude the women from almost all the trades and professions which lead to independence and wealth 'tis the remains of barbarity with the exterior polish of civilisation which ought to vanish before the light of reason.'

Their association prompts questions. The tone of Marie's letters to William Maclure has impressed some people as that of a lover unashamedly clinging on, or of a mistress held at rather more than arm's length. That was the interpretation put on their relationship by Mrs Frances Trollope in *Domestic Manners of the Americans*. She even went so far as to imply that the boy, Achille Fretageot, who passed as Marie's son, had been fathered by Maclure. Though many facts about Marie Fretageot are, and will remain obscure, that is not one of them for her letters make it clear that Achille was not Maclure's son and not even hers. He had been entrusted to her when a baby by his parents, of whom nothing is revealed in her correspondence other than that they were Quakers.

Apparently she separated from her husband, Joseph Fretageot, some years before she met Maclure, though she remained in touch with him after she emigrated to the United States. His letters are those of a simple, uneducated man, greedily intent upon his share of Marie's inheritance.

Her letters to Maclure are affectionate; she was always enquiring about his well being, concerned for his safety when he was in Spain in 1819 and for his health which, in the latter part of his life when she knew him well, was precarious—or so he thought. She lamented his absences for the interruption they caused to the exchange of ideas between them, which she greatly enjoyed. In effect, she displayed a strong desire to cosset and pamper Maclure. That is not evidence that they were lovers; it rather betrays her own loneliness and frustrated warmth. Maclure's attitude, as revealed in the letters, bears this out; he never unbent, never responded in kind to her expressions of affection. He was, one suspects, a very shy man; many bear witness to the diffidence with which he approached his own acts of philanthropy. What distinguishes their relationship is Marie's candour, the absence of false modesty in her gratitude towards him, that sometimes comes to those who have known help in times of great adversity.

That is to speculate, as one must also do in considering her career. Maclure's association with her seems not to antedate by much the year in which the New Harmony correspondence begins. He financed the girls' school she conducted in Paris, as he did her move to Philadelphia in 1822, money which she was determined to pay back. There is no doubt that she was an effective teacher; Maclure considered her one of the few capable of promoting the Pestalozzian system in all its purity. She is described as a mathematician; mental arithmetic was part of the discipline she imposed upon her pupils, and a fearsome instrument of learning called an arithmometer accompanied her to New Harmony.

Maclure's correspondence with Madame is enlivened by references to another of the passengers on *Philanthropist*, a Frenchman who in America went by the decently republican name of William S. Phiquepal. He was born some time after 1775, not far from Bergerac, in the country of Cyrano, whom he much resembled. His full name was Guillaume Casimir Sylvan Phiquepal d'Arusmont.

'Phi' as he appears in Maclure's correspondence was an absurd figure; a bustling, bristling, noisy, pompous little man, a sort of humourless clown; Maclure's remarks about him are often exasperated. As a young man Phiquepal sought his fortune in Martinique but was forced to flee the Negro rising that occurred in 1791. He took refuge in Philadelphia where he survived by doing all kinds of odd jobs. During these years Phiquepal seems to have developed strong ideas concerning the education of the young. When Neef established his school at the Falls of Schuykill, Phiquepal was a frequent visitor with the expressed intention of trying out his ideas on Neef's pupils. Maclure who was introduced to him by Neef, possibly in self-defence, seized upon Phiquepal as the ideal person to translate Neef's book into French. His anticipation soured when Phiquepal failed consistently to produce anything.

In 1814 Phiquepal had gone to Paris where, with Maclure's help, he set up a school whose method owed much to Pestalozzi but something to his own peculiar energy and character. The boys he accepted received a rigorous training, rising early and working late, besides coping with the moods of their instructor. He littered the place with reminders to himself, of which 'Be Calm' was the most frequent. But his teaching attracted such fashionable attention that the Prince of Poland tried to lure him into his service, an offer which Phiquepal declined. In 1824 Maclure made him move the school to Philadelphia. Phiquepal had ten of his pupils with him on board the keelboat, all chattering French. Among them were Achille Fretageot and two of his cousins so-called, Victor and Peter Duclos.

Philanthropist, with Thomas Say as captain, cast off from Pittsburgh on 8 December 1825. They had made only nine miles when, the following day, the boat went aground on one of the Ohio's notorious rapids. Robert Owen, Maclure, Lesueur, and Phiquepal boldly disembarked to summon help from Economy, seven miles away. The Rapps sent six men with long poles who took an hour to dislodge the boat, giving Robert Dale his first opportunity to scrutinize them. 'They appear to understand admirably how to act in concert, to be steady, retired, cautious and industrious, but not to possess, superior intelligence or liberality of sentiment.' When they anchored off Economy the day after, Frederick Rapp in his turn observed the prospective communitarians; '40 heads and only several pairs of hands', was his verdict. Here, rather early in the proceedings, they lost their leader. Robert Owen went back to Pittsburgh to fetch some legal documents.

The cold intensified, and floating ice began to hinder the boat's progress down river. According to Robert Dale's journal, the ladies objected to their cramped quarters and flinched at the thought of greater hardships to come. He discovered he had seldom had a better time, and explained it privately to himself, again in German. 'I find that this way of life becomes me well. I am exposed to heat, cold, and also the hardships much more than otherwise, but I am truly already stronger and more vigorous. I believe I could not have better preparation for Harmony and it will probably also be that way with the others.' On 11 December an eddy caught *Philanthropist* and swung her inshore where she was promptly frozen to the spot at a place which, because it happened so often, a wit had christened Safe Harbour. Here they were stranded for three weeks under conditions that tested the resolve of all of them.

Disaster very nearly visited them for, characteristically, Phiquepal fell over a fence and knocked himself unconscious. Delirium and fever held him in its grip for many days, and his life was in danger. When he recovered he found himself deaf in one ear. Marie Fretageot nursed him with skill and authority. She found another subject for her care in Robert Dale who confided in her about difficulties with his family which the journal does not specify but which may have concerned Margaret. While, to his disgust, certain other females were given to bursting into tears at breakfast, lamenting their plight, Madame's intelligence, good sense, and will to make the best of everything greatly impressed Robert Dale. He played the Leatherstocking role, which pleased him almost more than that of the famous equestrian; spending days in the snowbound woods after elk and partridge and other game. The practice was useful for he had acquired a rifle only at Pittsburgh and learned as he went along how to load and clean it. His journal is full of tips as to the efficacy of turkey fat for lubrication, and how to correct a gun that shoots to the side.

They passed the days of bad weather playing whist, baking bread on the cabin stove and hearing the works of the French communitarian philosopher, Charles Fourier, read aloud. They also discussed at length what was going to happen at New Harmony, and particularly what kind of uniform they would adopt. Though he disguised it from all but close associates for many years, Robert Owen believed that it was essential for everyone in the new moral world to dress alike; it was one of the reasons why he sought out Quakers: their sober habit was evidence to him of sound social discipline.

A certain amount of tension is detectable in reading between the lines of Robert Dale's journal and that of Donald Macdonald who, with Stedman Whitwell, caught up with *Philanthropist* while she was trapped in the ice. On being reunited with his associates at Safe Harbour, Macdonald did not disguise his irritation at the theoretical discussions with which they occupied their time; practical activity was all he was interested in. 'Macdonald seems to possess many false ideas and to imagine things quite differently from us', Robert Dale remarked. He also noted a certain fretfulness in William Maclure, with whom he shared the little store cabin. In fact, when Phiquepal was out of danger, Maclure and Marie Fretageot left the boat for Wheeling, lower down the river. On 9 January a thaw at least released the prisoners. With fine weather they proceeded more rapidly and even attempted singing and dancing on deck. Maclure and Madame rejoined and at Cincinnati they had news that Robert Owen was ahead of them, proceeding by carriage.

On 23 January *Philanthropist* tied up at Mount Vernon, the Ohio landing for New Harmony. Robert Dale could not wait for the wagons to arrive. He grabbed a horse and rode over at once, missing William who had come to meet him. His journal of the 4,000-mile journey from Scotland ends, 'Arrived just in time to hear my father address the inhabitants.'

CHAPTER 10

LORD PROPRIETOR

ROBERT Owen returned to Harmony in the early evening of 12 January 1826. By 7 p.m. he was in the pulpit of the Rappites' first church which, in Quaker fashion, some of the new inhabitants referred to as the steeple house. He told those who had assembled there that a company of people was following him by water, in a vessel which carried more learning than was ever before contained in a boat; by learning, he went on, he did not mean Latin or Greek or any other language but real, substantial knowledge. And so New Harmony was provided with its ark; the name *Philanthropist* receded from the people's memory to be replaced by the slogan Robert Owen had invented, the 'Boatload of Knowledge'.

His influence continued at its most compelling for the next few weeks. His impact upon the former Editor, William Pelham, for example, was shattering. Pelham had not previously encountered him though he had waited upon his coming for many months. On 8 February he wrote to his son: '[Owen] is an extraordinary man—a wonderful man—such a one indeed as the world has never before seen. His wisdom, his comprehensive mind, his practical knowledge, but above all his openness, his candor and sincerity have no parallel in ancient or modern history. Do not think I am dreaming, for in fact, I have closely attended to his language and movements since his return.'

In the days following that return Robert Owen set about the re-education of the inhabitants of New Harmony. With the addition of the forty or so new arrivals on board *Philanthropist*, these now numbered some 1,000 people. Some of the first arrivals had been dismissed for idleness or drunkenness. The latter was a common condition in the West where whisky was cheap and a specific against all manner of complaints. To Robert Owen it was a crime, one of the few for which he always prescribed punishment. So, though Donald Macdonald thought the population about as numerous as when he had left for England the previous June, he saw almost as many strange as familiar faces.

Owen addressed them as if they had all been present since the beginning. Whatever moments of despair they may have suffered in contemplating their situation, he said, he must assure them that it was very satisfactory. In fact it was so far advanced that he had decided to dispense with the remaining two years during which the Preliminary Society, formed in May 1825 (see Chapter Seven), was supposed to exist. Instead he proposed to proceed at once to the creation of a 'community of perfect equality based on the principle of common property'.

Whether this abrupt change of plan was due to Owen's need to find an alternative source of finance for the enterprise is not certain, but it seems likely. The Constitution of the Preliminary Society had contained a clause stipulating that the community of equality to be formed at the end of three years would be independent and would be established on land 'purchased by the associated members.' In other words, if Owen wished to divest himself of the responsibility for New Harmony he had only to advance a step in a procedure which was already laid down. The need for some such action may have arisen even before he left England and may have been connected with his extraordinary failure to bring out new recruits. Or it may have been prompted by the devastating financial collapse which had begun in England in December 1825.

Whatever the reason for the radical change of plan, as soon as the party from *Philanthropist* set foot in the town they found themselves caught up in a fury of reform. Two days after their arrival, at the usual Wednesday business meeting, William Owen moved 'that this Society do form itself into a Constitutional Convention for the purpose of framing a Constitution for the Community about to be established'. It was decided that Robert Owen and William Maclure would hold themselves apart from standing for the committee to be elected to draft the document. Its members included Macdonald, Revd Mr Jennings, Judge Wattles, a young—almost everyone was young—local lawyer, and William and Robert Dale Owen, the last a fervid constitution maker.

The document began with a statement of its purpose, which was 'that of all sentient beings, happiness'. The principles included:

Equality of rights, uninfluenced by sex or condition, in all adults.
Equality of duties, modified by physical and mental conformation.
Co-operative union, in the business and amusements of life.
Community of property.
Freedom of speech and action.
Sincerity in all our proceedings.
Kindness in all our actions.
Courtesy in all our intercourse.
Order in all our arrangements.

Preservation of health.
Acquisition of knowledge.
The practise of economy, or of producing and using the best of everything in the most beneficial manner.
Obedience to the laws of the country in which we live.

With such alterations as experience might suggest, and the special circumstances of Indiana require, the rules and regulations to govern the new community were those already set out in a printed paper available in the town and called, 'Mr Owen's Plan for the Permanent Relief of the Working Classes'.

All members of the Community of Equality were to be considered as one family, eating the same food, wearing the same clothes, and as soon as was practicable, living in the same kind of house. Every member was to enjoy the most perfect freedom in all aspects of knowledge and opinion, especially on the subject of religion. Laws would be made by an assembly of all those over 21. Executive power would lie with a council which would be charged with the supervision of the day to day running of the place, the making of contracts with the outside world, and with determining compensation to be paid—in goods produced by the community—in respect of their services to those who wished to leave. The Constitution also decreed the division of the establishment into branches: agriculture, manufacture, education, domestic economy, general economy, and commerce—each with a superintendent.

The organization of these working departments resembled that introduced by Robert Owen at New Lanark. Each section would elect a certain number of 'intendants' who were to act as the channel of communication between the workers and their superintendent. These embryo shop stewards represented those people Henry Gray Macnab had referred to at New Lanark as the military police. Nor was the silent monitor forgotten, except that at New Harmony it had a human face and voice. The intendants were to be required to make a daily assessment of the character of each worker, based on his or her application and amount of production. Every week these reports would be presented by the executive council to the assembly, together with an assessment of how the intendants themselves had performed.

The Constitution, having been fully and freely discussed by the people, was adopted on 6 February and copied into a book which all members of the Preliminary Society who wished to join the new Community were invited to sign. Most did, but a few declined. After only two weeks of the new regime, the members of the executive council asked Robert Owen to take the direction of New Harmony back into his own hands for the time being. This he did, and though matters were arranged according to the regulations framed by the Constitution his power was absolute. To its members, as to historians, this new body was known as Community Number One.

Though when they signed the Constitution the members of the new Community of Equality accepted the duty laid on them to live as one family, the shock of reality drove the new found siblings into separate rooms. Like cleaved to like and the door was shut against outsiders. It was hard to look upon some of the rough people there as brothers and sisters, Sarah Pears lamented. 'Mr Owen says we have been speaking falsehoods all our lives; and that here only we shall be enabled to speak the truth. I am sure I cannot in sincerity look upon these as my equals, and that if I must appear to do it I cannot either act or speak the truth.'

The first schism took place before February was out, when a number of people went off into the forest, where they built a dozen or so cabins arranged in the form of a parallelogram, on land leased to them by Robert Owen at just over $80 an acre. According to Stedman Whitwell they were fervent Methodists who wanted to be free to observe their religion and to live and cultivate the earth in the way they had always done. They called the place Macluria, in honour of the man Owen represented to them as his business partner.

The second offshoot appeared in March when settlers who had come across the Wabash from English Prairie joined together on land just outside Harmony. The government of both these satellites was similar to that of Community Number One. Whitwell had a lot to do with the second settlement, having spent much time 'electioneering'—the word is Maclure's—at Wanborough. It had lost its leader the previous summer when Morris Birkbeck had been drowned on the way home from Harmony, where he had been to solicit the good offices of Robert Owen in the long-standing dispute with the Flowers at Albion. Now the new community identified itself in accordance with Whitwell's system of naming places, which was designed to avoid the repetition of such favourites as Washington and Springfield. Expressed in letters the longitude and latitude of the spot they chose near Harmony produced the name, easier on the tongue and more pleasing to the ear than it had any right to be, of Feiba Peveli. According to this system New York at 40° 43' N 73° 59' W would be Otke Notive and London, 51° 30' N 0° 5' W, Lafa Vovutu. Writing in the *Co-operative Magazine* after he was safely out of the way in England, Whitwell described Macluria as slovenly, a consequence of its American origin, whereas as Feiba, being English, was neat. Both, as he put it, had the worm i' the bud; 'super- stition in the one, whisky in the other'.

While these settlements, known to history as Community Number Two and Three, proceeded on their way outside the boundary of the town, a much more dangerous threat was aimed at its heart. The agent of this was Robert Dale Owen whose enthusiasm for community building had been raised to fever pitch by his entrance into the town, and the days of constitution making that followed it. By March he could hardly contain his impatience at the failure of certain people to commit them- selves wholeheartedly to the new and equal way of life, and proposed a secession of those who could be guaranteed not to shirk. In this he was supported by his brother, William, and The Revd Mr Jennings, rapt with his own preaching. Community Number Four was to consist of them- selves and the members of the Boatload of Knowledge who would take over certain buildings in the town, and devote themselves with faith and the utmost rigour to the letter of the Constitution. The proposal was understandably greeted with suspicion as a move to promote an élite. The principal challenge was to Robert Owen, though his eldest son may not have seen it in that light. The Proprietor dealt with it by offering the group as much woodland as they wanted, where they could cut down trees to their hearts' content. 'But this did not quite suit them', Sarah Pears wrote, 'as they were not in general very well calculated for hewing down timber.'

The Literati was the name given to the group in question, which included Marie Fretageot, William S. Phiquepal, and the Philadelphia Academicians. It was not altogether kindly meant, for those who had endured the rigours of the first year at Harmony objected to the privileges enjoyed by the newcomers. Owen explained away the slightly higher remuneration and better housing which the passengers from *Philanthropist* enjoyed as a purely temporary measure, dictated by the need to attract their special skills and knowledge to the town. The attempt by the Literati to distance themselves from their neighbours, however, was resented, especially by the parents of children whose education these much vaunted teachers had been engaged to oversee.

In fact the schools made surprising progress in the first two months after *Philanthropist* arrived. In March Maclure concluded that, all things considered, they had succeeded better than they had had any right to expect. To his friend, Benjamin Silliman at Yale, he explained why he had come to Harmony and the arrangements now well under way.

The obstinate prejudices of men against making any useful or radical change ... has, for a long time, prevented me from putting into practice, what I would have called experimental farming schools, for the education of the children of the productive classes, and this sociable system of Mr Owen, offering all the means and materials for effecting the same reform amongst the same useful class, I have joined him in all his undertakings on this side of the Atlantic, and we intend to carry them into execution, as far as a considerable capital will permit. Already part of the boys' school is so far organized that they make shoes for themselves, and will soon do it for the whole community. They will likewise have work-shops for tailors, carpenters, weavers, etc., in the school, all of which trades will be alternately practiced, by way of recreation from their mental labour of Arithmetic, Mathematics, Natural History etc. as a useful substitute for gymnastics; to which will be added agriculture and gardening. We have nearly 400 children belonging to the Society, besides strangers from the different parts of the Union. The girls are taught the same things as the boys, by Madam [sic] Fretageot, and are classed, alternately to work in the cotton and woollen mills, and in washing, cooking etc., (for no servants are permitted in the society and every one must do something for himself) not working above half a day on any one kind of labour, thereby alleviating the fatigue by variety ...

My experience does not permit me to doubt, that children, under proper management, can feed and clothe themselves by the practice of the best and most useful part of their instruction; and in place of being a burthen, they would be a help to all connected with them.

The schools here will be on such a scale, as to location, men of talent, and perfection of machinery, as to constitute them the first in the Union, for every species of useful knowledge.

Shortly before he wrote this letter Maclure had come to an agreement with Robert Owen by which he agreed to advance a sum to carry 'the sociable system' into operation, but which limited his losses, should they occur, to $10,000. The memorandum of these arrangements makes no reference to any other obligation or partnership between the two.

Owen's concern to divert all would-be separatists to uncleared land outside Harmony arose from his desire to keep the land and buildings within its boundary intact, the better to sell them. The bargain he attempted to strike in April 1826, if concluded, which it was not, would have given him a very large profit indeed. He began by choosing from among the members of the Community of Equality a group of twenty-four whom he called the 'nucleus', on whom he proposed to place the burden of future responsibility. They were requested to buy from him the town of Harmony and 2,500 acres of land at a valuation of $140,000. Owen added to that sum $20,000 in respect of the 'credit' he would be extending to them by deferring the repayment of the principal over a period of years. In spite of that, interest on the whole $160,000 would begin at once, and run at the rate of $8,000 a year.

This was no more than a detailed application of the procedure foreseen by the constitution of the Preliminary Society, but it had been generally overlooked by those who had signed that document. To them, and to the various newcomers, the suggestion appeared absolutely contrary to the way Owen had represented the Community of Equality to them, and not least his own part in it. Yet it was quite in accordance with the original system of running the Villages of Unity and Mutual Co-operation as described in detail by one of their chief advocates, George Mudie, Editor of the *Economist*. He wrote,

though strict equality prevails with respect to all the associated members of the community, it by no means extends to the public at large, *nor even to all the persons connected with each concern*. It is, in fact, nothing more than the equality of partners all of whom have an equal interest in their joint concern but whose relation to the community at large remains unchanged. Thus though the basis of affairs remains agriculture, unless a society be rich enough to purchase their own land the community of goods does not include the land, any more than equality in rank includes the Land Owner. The Land Owner and the Society stand in the ordinary relation of Landlord and Tenant; and his rights, his property, his rank in general society remain as unchanged by the fact of his letting a farm to a Partnership as by the fact of his letting it to a single Farmer—with this only difference, that a Society, if required, will *be enabled to pay a much higher rent than any single Farmer can do.*

In giving his account of these proceedings to Benjamin Bakewell, Thomas Pears (see Chapter Seven) did not trouble to conceal his disappointment and dismay. Feiba Peveli had taken all the real farmers and the good land; he doubted if Community Number One, the object of the sale, could produce enough to support its people without further arduous clearing of forest. As for the 'nucleus', there was not a man of business among them, and few whose security he cared to take. 'Whatever may be the terms I have no intention of making myself responsible', he wrote, 'for I can see no prospect of producing enough to maintain us.' How he would rejoice to see Pittsburgh again: 'The System I like but I detest its practice here.'

The unrest communicated itself to Joseph Neef and his family when they arrived in Harmony. Neef was astonished and dismayed at what he found: 'nothing but valuation of houses, barns, stables, land: of making bargains and contracts, of "buying cheap and selling dear", of capital and its interest!' From out of the frying-pan he felt himself plunged into a red hot furnace. Eleven years' experience in Kentucky had convinced him that, short of discovering a gold mine at New Harmony, it would be impossible to discharge such a debt of $160,000, or to pay the annual interest. In the belief that Robert Owen was serious in what he said concerning his desire to found a Community of Equality, Neef proposed that he should either make the Community a present of the 2,500 acres, or be content with what he called the 'very equitable sum' of four dollars an acre—roughly twice what Owen had paid Rapp for the whole estate including the buildings and the improvements on it. Addressing Robert Owen directly, Neef declared,

To talk of common property, co-operation, of industry, economy, etc. etc., as you did, to a set of people that did not own one inch of the ground on which they lived, that were liable to be expelled at any moment, that had no interest in being extra frugal, industrious, economical or careful was just as wise as if one of our southern planters should preach such doctrines to his community of black citizens.

These words were strong enough, but they were feeble beside the bitter indignation of Paul Brown, a Quaker who had come to New Harmony at about the same time as Joseph Neef. Brown was an ardent believer in pure communism who had come upon Robert Owen's *Essays* as upon a revelation which drew him at once to the place where it was to be made fact. His account of what passed during the twelve months he spent there was largely discounted by the first writers who described the New Harmony experiment, who could not reconcile his abuse of Owen with the traditional image. But, in so far as Brown's account can be verified from other sources, it is accurate. His language was strong, for his contempt was scathing. His principal objection was to Owen's insistence upon giving leases rather than deeds over land assigned to other parties, a device which locked them in for if they defaulted on the interest payments, as in bad years they risked doing, the lease reverted to him and they would be left with nothing. But the very fact of Owen asking payment at all was odious to Brown. By that, he said, 'Robert Owen proved himself to be a trading man and not a philanthropist ... proved himself to be lacking in integrity, magnanimity, and all those solid sublime principles essentially requisite to form a character competent to introduce into life an example of a state of society in the true order of human perfection, and of a sort which he had recommended.'

Brown's denunciation came with hindsight. The general disposition at the time was to give Robert Owen the benefit of the doubt; few could afford much more. Some of those who had, or could procure the means to depart, now did so. The others stayed, however uneasy. They could see that Owen might need money; the support of the community was put at $20,000 to $30,000 for the first year. The figure was available to those outside the town, where its creditors marked the absence of production at the same time as the store was thronged. The Harmony Society's agent urged Frederick Rapp to dispose of the bonds he held from Owen for they could not be sold at Philadelphia. This lack of confidence stemmed partly from Owen's conduct in the East before his return to Indiana. His ranting lectures, his admonition against 'buying cheap and selling dear', called in question his common sense.

While Owen was endeavouring to sell leases, Maclure found himself constantly opposed to his methods. 'Owen told me he could do nothing but in his own way', he said, and 'that I did not understand his plans.' By April he was sufficiently alarmed to tell Owen he could not longer be responsible for actions done without his advice and contrary to his opinions. Owen said he was sorry for this, remarking that he would not have spent so much had he been aware of Maclure's intention to pull out.

Eventually, in May, when Maclure discovered that Owen was, as he put it, 'pushed for money', he agreed to pay $50,000 for a lease on 900 acres of land in the centre of Harmony on which stood some of the principal buildings, including Father Rapp's house, the huge stone granary, and the first church. These he proposed to employ for a School, or Education Society. It was the beginning of the lasting division of New Harmony, with Owen on one side and Maclure on the other, though the differences noted by Maclure, and described above, remained confidential at the time, known to only one other person, Marie Fretageot.

The Education Society continued with the schools already under way; they were directed by Phiquepal, Joseph Neef, and Marie Fretageot. Say, Lesueur, and Troost also gave their services. Maclure kept a fatherly eye on them to see that they upheld the Pestalozzian system. 'Let all your practice arise out of experience, and all your conduct be in strict union', he admonished Madame, 'the principles of the System being adhered to, never to attemp [sic] to teach what the children don't comprehend and in the exact ratio of their understanding it.'

It was Maclure's idea to separate the rest of the inhabitants according to their occupations; the unequal contribution made by some workers having been a source of unrest for some time. On 17 May 1826, the town newspaper, the *New Harmony Gazette*, printed a letter from him which said,

the thing most wanted is, to protect the industrious, honest members against the unpleasant, mortifying sensation of laboring for others that are either unable or unwilling to work their proportion necessary to keep up the expenditure of the society, and pay their debts. To accomplish this object it has been tried, by individual reports of production and making public the number of hours each was occupied in a day; the practice of which was rather invidious, and difficult impartially to be executed; and even if it were possible to get correct returns, it was liable to injustice; as one willing workman might do more in an hour than another without the same good will or industry, would do in four.

It was decided, therefore, as Maclure most pungently expressed it, 'to let every herring hang by its own head'. Beside the Education Society two other occupational groups were formed: the Agricultural and Pastoral Society, and the Mechanic and Manufacturing Society. Robert Owen presided over these last which continued to be governed according to the regulations laid down in the Constitution of the Community of Equality; except that he remained Proprietor, for no prospective leaseholders other than Maclure and Communities Two and Three had yet appeared. It was the third reorganization in four months.

The members' subsistence was regulated by their credit at the store on which they drew for food and clothing. For those who had been at New Harmony during the past year this was a figure calculated at the winding up of the Preliminary Society according to the value of the work they were considered to have done. For them and for the newcomers it was set so low as to provide little more than the bare necessities of life. For now began the period which Robert Owen had envisaged in the building of a Village of Unity and Mutual Co-operation when, by leading a frugal existence and working very hard, the inhabitants would create that surplus out of which to pay off the interest and, eventually, the capital cost of the land. One person at least felt it was too soon to introduce this system. Donald Macdonald argued that it was folly to expect newcomers to submit to it at once, especially those with no previous experience of the ordinary hardships of living in a wilderness.

Owen ignored him and in consequence Macdonald left New Harmony. His journal is silent as to precisely what the reason was but he was known to be opposed to continual constitution making and the shifting of ideas and people of the kind that Owen had practised there, as well as at Orbiston. He had spent five years of his life as a devoted follower of Robert Owen, now perhaps his disillusionment was too painful to record.

He would not have been at ease with the personality which emerged under the stress of circumstances in the spring and summer of 1826. Sarah Pears voiced the general dismay, telling Mrs Bakewell; 'Mr Owen is growing very unpopular even with the greatest sticklers for the system. I assure you that Mr Owen of New Harmony is a very different personage from Mr Owen in Pittsburgh, Washington etc.' The orders he now issued virtually broke up families like the Pears.' Small children were sent to the boarding schools while those over 14, girls and boys alike, were to live together in special houses, a move whose impropriety upset and scandalized Mrs Pears. As in the time of the Harmony Society, bells now marked the passing of the day. 'Instead of 4 or 5 hours of labor being sufficient for one's maintenance, as people were led to imagine by Mr Owen's representations', Sarah wrote, 'the bell is now rung at 5.30 to get up, at 6 to go to work, at 7 for breakfast, at 8 for work again, at 12 for dinner, at one to go to work, at 6 in the evening to return home.' Unpunctuality at work was reported to the intendants, and sickness certificates had to be produced. There was an impression that manual labour counted for more than intellectual effort. Excessive consumption was discouraged and a watch kept on articles drawn from the store. Those who indulged in 'luxuries' (things like tea or coffee) were viewed with disapproval, and penalized by an unfavourable balance struck on their account if they decided to leave. The result of this was that only the rich or single could *afford* to leave.

In effect work became the moral basis of the system; it was the means of judging character, of gaining prestige, and of getting favour and reward. Every Sunday night Robert Owen held a meeting at which he read out the particulars of the expenditure of the two Societies, the amount of work achieved by each trade, and the character of each work man or woman. As much as any medieval lord he was the fount of honour, the giver of law, and the arbiter of justice. Though it was something the backwoods people had never thought to encounter, there was no hesitation in putting a name to what was happening. One visitor who spent two months at New Harmony at this time described tasks laid on its inhabitants as a *corvée*. This was Karl Bernhard of Saxe-Weimar-Eisenach, son of the most enlightened ruler of the century, the Duke who had governed Weimar for the past fifty years, whose court was a haven for the most distinguished European intellectuals, including Goethe and Schiller. Karl Bernhard wrote a book (which Goethe edited) in which he expressed his doubt as to the durability of the New Harmony experiment, and dwelt at length and rather mischievously on the awkwardness of its ill-assorted members at living on equal terms. During the time he spent waiting for a carriage to take him on his way, Karl Bernhard observed the effect of the system on the work-force. He concluded that they regarded the tasks allotted to them as tedious and disagreeable, and performed them under protest. In conversation with Joseph Applegarth who had gone over to the School Society, Karl Bernhard agreed that, in producing his Village plan, Owen must have had recourse to schemes of forced service and statutory labour. Joseph Neef was even more forthright. 'You took it into your head to establish a feudal barony', he told Owen.

It was a truth which had been disguised for so long by Robert Owen's public espousal of a very different social system; it was in fact the way he tried to run New Lanark. It had betrayed itself before in certain attitudes and actions—his belief in his own infallibility, his exclusion of any but his own law from the cotton-spinning village, and his designation of himself as laird of New Lanark.

It was precisely how he saw himself. At the same time as he confessed to the influence *Robinson Crusoe* had over him—in conversation with the French educationalist, Jullien de Paris, at New Lanark in 1822—Owen cited the famous story *Adèle et Théodore* by Madame de Genlis, governess to the children of the Duc d'Orléans. The principal character in this fable was an old man, M. Lagaraye, who presided over a large estate in France where there was a cotton factory and a model village. No laws were observed there but those he gave; all was prosperous, disciplined, and safe.

As the summer of 1826 approached, Robert Owen became an increasingly isolated figure. Those friends who had accompanied him from Scotland withdrew their support. Macdonald had gone home in silence. Stedman Whitwell returned to England, ostensibly to seek recruits for a separate community on the prairie; failing to return he became a source of critical comment in the *Co-operative Magazine*. Joseph Applegarth lent his good business sense and energy to the School Society for a time but, suffering from what he called Harmonyphobia—depression induced by the confined situation of the town—eventually departed to English Prairie. Even Robert Dale crossed the divide, becoming superintendent of the School Society. Its leaders welcomed him, liking him the best of the Owen family. What Robert Dale needed, Maclure remarked to Marie Fretageot, was to be joined to a 'Rib of Talent' (he meant a sensible woman), fearing that 'if fluttering about the feminine triffles of the spoiled children of Harmony his ability will be parilised'.

As always in times of difficulty when Robert Owen's emotions were deeply engaged, his instinct was to attack. This battle was more serious than the others, or so he seemed to think, for he went to it not as English reformer, or Scots cotton-master, both of which roles came easily to him now, but in a much more natural guise, his by right of his real ancestry. On 4 July to the inhabitants of New Harmony, and to the world, he delivered, not a speech but an incantation in rhythm quintessentially Welsh and claiming a Druid's power.

CHAPTER II

THE DECLARATION OF MENTAL
INDEPENDENCE

THE Fourth of July had always been kept as a special celebration by the Harmony Society for it was the day on which their first landing in the United States had been made, a day when Father Rapp exhorted his followers to renew their dedication. Now another prophet spoke of good and evil to those assembled in the great hall of the Rappites' second church.

Up to that hour, Robert Owen declared, Man had been in all parts of the earth a slave to a Trinity of the most monstrous evils that could be combined to inflict mental and physical suffering upon the human race. This Trinity, this Hydra, was composed of property, religion, and marriage, which he denounced as Ignorance, Superstition, and Hypocrisy. Though the American people were more fortunate than any other in the achievement, fifty years before, of political liberty without which they could never proceed to mental liberty, ancient prejudice and fear still impeded their advance. Even so, they must not despair because, as Robert Owen told them,

For nearly forty years have I been employed, heart and soul, day by day, almost without ceasing in preparing the means and arranging the circumstances to enable me to give the death-blow to the tyranny and despotism which for unnumbered years past have held the human mind spell-bound, in chains and fetters, of such mysterious forms and shapes that no mortal hand dared to approach to set the suffering prisoner free. Nor has the fulness of time in the accomplishment of this great event been completed until within this hour . . . and such has been the extraordinary course of events that the Declaration of Political Independence in 1776 has produced its counterpart, the Declaration of Mental Independence in 1826.

Owen's objections to individual property and religion were those he had put to the public many times before: that the unequal division of property led to poverty and crime and that religion was the way to keep those deprived of it enslaved. His denunciation of marriage as another

2. New Harmony.

1. Father Rapp.

3. The Harmonists' second church, begun in 1822. Used by Robert Owen for concerts, lectures, and dancing.

4. Brick and frame house built by the Harmonists; afterwards lived in by Thomas Say.

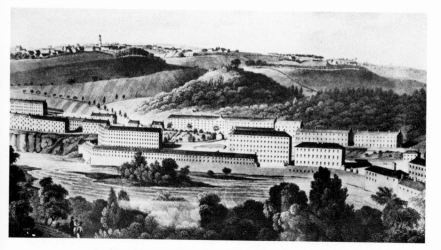

5. The old town of Lanark and the mills of New Lanark.

6. Drawing of the quadrilangular village by Stedman Whitwell.

7. Robert Owen.

9. William Maclure.

8. Frances Wright.

10. (*left*) Charles Alexandre Lesueur.

11. Thomas Say.

12. Marie Fretageot.

13. (*right*) Title page for Thomas Say's *American Entomology*

14. Nashoba.

15. David Dale Owen's Laboratory at New Harmony.

form of private property, and of slavery, was new; and his advice as to what a changed form it would assume under his new social system was startling. 'Among the truly intelligent', he said,

marriage will be respected only when it shall be formed between those who are equal in wealth, education and condition; who are well acquainted with each other's habits, minds and feelings before they enter upon the engagement; and who know also that by their nature the continuance of affection does not depend upon the will of either, but that it will diminish or increase according as they produce pleasurable or disagreeable sensations in each other.

As it was a law of nature that the affections were not controlled by will, it should be as respectable in law to dissolve a marriage when it appeared likely to produce unhappiness as it was to contract it in the first place. 'This Truth has passed from me beyond the possibility of recall: it has been already received into your minds; speedily it will be heard throughout America and from thence it will pass North and South, East and West, as far as language is known,—and almost as fast as it shall be conveyed human nature will recognize and receive it.'

In 1826 time and circumstance combined to make the Fourth of July solemn and memorable above all the others that had so far occurred. As Robert Owen said, it was the fiftieth anniversary of the founding of the Republic and, as the day began, the American people gave thanks for danger surmounted and progress made, an exercise which brought them to identify those qualities that had contributed to success. By evening the deep and general emotion was to be enhanced by the quiet death within hours of each other of two of their greatest men, John Adams and Thomas Jefferson.

Robert Owen's speech, which was reproduced in many newspapers, broke into this moment of national mourning and celebration with the force of an explosion, shattering all hope of success at New Harmony. From that time on it was impossible for any person connected with the town to procure a fair hearing from the public at large, for Owen had called into question those things which the great majority of them cherished, on which they felt the security and good order of the nation to depend, and which had served them well in time of hardship when the country was being hewn out of the wilderness. That was an experience which no foreigner could pretend to understand, or take upon himself the right to criticize.

Especially in the West religion was a living force whose power to inspire and to excite showed itself at the great camp meetings. New Harmony was open to itinerant ministers, for Owen always upheld the right of religious freedom; there were many in the town who preserved their own rituals, among them Baptists, Methodists, Quakers, and so many Swedenborgians that it was worthy of special comment. There were also deists, among them William Maclure and Marie Fretageot. Although ever since he had set foot in the United States there had been a lively public debate about Owen's anti-sectarian views, they were regarded essentially as concerning only himself, as did his attitude to property. But the Declaration of Mental Independence alarmed even the most moderate newspaper reader, and incited his existing opponents to a frenzy of attack.

The fault lay not as much in his views themselves as in his brutal language, expressing a hostility towards the practice of all religion, which one of his own supporters regretfully described as 'phobia', and which harmed his credibility in other respects. Benjamin Bakewell, who more than once referred to Owen's dislike of Calvinism, also remarked upon the lengths to which this went. 'He is bigoted against bigotry as well as religion', he explained, 'and seems to think the two are inseparable.' Owen usually tried to conceal the virulence of his feeling behind that famously composed and candid face; it was one of the aspects of his personality which Francis Place, who watched him closely, observed that he kept hidden from all but a few. For instance in the debate at Albion, described in Donald Macdonald's journal, Owen went to great lengths to try to reconcile his views with the religious belief of his companions. The Declaration of Mental Independence abandoned this restraint.

By attacking religion Robert Owen wounded people's feelings—a private matter: by deprecating marriage he threatened public order under the law. His portrait of an unreformed marriage as a prop to wealth and privilege, a bar to lasting happiness, seemed to many Americans simply a distortion of the truth. As Professor Rohrbough remarked in his recent history of the trans-Appalachian frontier, the family was an institution of central importance, the pioneers moving in family groups both for physical protection and for mutual assistance in economic enterprise. Marriage provided shelter in a strange and hostile world. Nor were its benefits allowed to pass unrecorded; as the journal of the Legislative Council of the Northwest Territory (which included Indiana) declared, 'the foundation of public prosperity and happiness must be laid in private families—every well ordered family is a little amiable community'. The Harmony Society's apparent flouting of this principle was one of the chief objections laid at its door by its neighbours; Robert Owen's speech gravely compounded that offence.

His strictures upon marriage, as upon religion, were not based upon a general truth, but rather proceeded from an intensely personal experience. According to the Declaration of Mental Independence the ideal marriage would avoid precisely those circumstances which attended his to Ann Caroline Dale; disparity in wealth, in rank, in education; above all incompatibility in religion; the fate of two people hastily united after a brief acquaintance. How sinister the threat implied in the Declaration that love would cease with the capacity to please! Did Owen, bearing a grudge against his wife for her attachment to her father's religious belief, and for her indoctrination of their children, isolate her in retribution? Was that the underlying cause of her ill-health, as it was of open tension in the family?

As Francis Place said, Robert Owen saw so far beyond the limit of ordinary human behaviour that only succeeding generations could make sense of what he proposed. The same notion of Owen as a seer occurred to William Maclure, who perceived that the general disappointment with Owen's schemes proceeded from 'his forgetting that there was at least one century between the scenes his fancy was painting and the present'.

Maclure believed that, for a long time to come, the ordinary manual labourer must be the only support of Owen's Community. He ought not to be distracted by ideas like those put forward in the Declaration. Nevertheless, it seemed to him at first that the only part of the establishment at risk from Owen's bold discourse would be the School Society, as parents might draw back from committing their children to his care. As indeed they did. All that needed to be said, Maclure assured Marie Fretageot, was that these were Owen's private opinions; the schools were independent and taught no religion, leaving the children's minds, in that favourite phrase, so much blank paper on which priests and parents might write what they pleased.

It was not enough, as Maclure soon discovered. Disapproval, thick and stinging as the seasonal cloud of mosquitoes, descended on New Harmony and would not be dispelled. Maclure had to try to soothe the irritation. 'I did all I could to bridle the impetuosity of the enthusiastic reformer', he explained in one letter that found its way into the newspapers.

But after all what have the three positions [property, religion, and marriage] to do with the co-operative system? not quite so much as fungus that grows at the root of a tree has with the health or prosperity of the tree. *They are the opinions of one individual, Mr Owen* ... and have no more effect upon the citizens of New Harmony than they have upon the citizens of Philadelphia.

It was precisely to relieve the School Society of any connection, mental or physical, with Robert Owen that, Maclure insisted, he had advanced the money to set them up on their own.

The newspapers also got hold of his efforts to reassure Mrs Sistare, mother of Lucy, Frances, and Sarah, who had accompanied Madame Fretageot on the *Philanthropist.* Maclure described Mrs Sistare as being in a state of misery, fear, and tribulation at the rumours of promiscuous behaviour that clung to the name of Harmony. Small wonder that she was agitated, for one of the stories put about was that Lucy Sistare was pregnant by Thomas Say. This was the work of Stedman Whitwell, a mischievous young man.

Maclure attempted to convince Mrs Sistare that the inhabitants of Harmony were more strict in their behaviour than anyone else he had ever met, but acknowledged that the odds he had to face were too great. 'I did not conjecture that Mr Owen was quite so amorous as the stories make him', he told Madame Fretageot in late August.

The wives of the greatest part of those that have left you lately have declared to their husbands that it was in consequence of the freedom that Mr O took with them that they could not think of remaining under such dreadful risk of their virtue. This, beat up with the discourse on the antient [sic] mode of marriage forms a nostrum that gives currency to all the stories about indiscriminate inter-course and all things being in common.

He foresaw that Harmony was to be made the scapegoat of the whole western country; all the calumny and scandal that side of the Alleghenies was to be fixed on the back of the Harmonians—who were 'without the Jewish advantage of hiding themselves in the desert'.

In spite of his desire generally to promote their cause, Maclure seems to have considered most of the females he encountered at Harmony boring and silly. 'You must manage the women', he told Marie Fretageot, and warned her to take care not to offend their vanity. For instance it was unwise of her to flaunt expensive shoes; she ought rather to adopt the kind of canvas boots Lucy Sistare wore, and on going outside—surely a sacrifice for Madame—she ought to wear sabots.

As he travelled about Maclure began to realize that the purchase of the town on the Wabash had been a hasty and ill-advised act, partly the result of the Rapps playing on William Owen's ignorance of the price of land. Rapp had made a great fuss about selling the place too cheaply, but Maclure now discovered there was an abundance of good land, in Ohio for example, where a mixture of prairie and forest could be got at one dollar an acre so that a mere $2,000 might establish a community. Even old *Harmonie* in Pennsylvania would have been a better place for the schools, Maclure concluded; 'the lands are not so rich but much healthier'.

These were asides. Maclure's overriding concern, as demonstrated by these letters, was to preserve the rest of his fortune in order to be able to support the educational experiment at New Harmony. He knew now that he must separate himself entirely from Robert Owen, not only because of his idiosyncratic opinions, but above all because of business affairs. 'Stay short', he admonished Madame, who was acting as his agent, and warned her to make sure that his name did not appear on any bonds issued by Owen. He depended on her to keep the Education Society out of trouble. 'Mr Owen, when you mention him as my partner', he wrote to Madame on 21 August, 'I have not the smallest connection with anything he has done. Every purchase or sale he has made has been either against my will, or unknown to me, for which I cannot for a moment consider myself responsible'.

Though he never surrendered to the attraction of a community of property, Maclure did come to believe that under the right management, the co-operative system could be made to work. He deplored the way Robert Owen went about it, especially the extravagance with which he considered he had supplied the needs of the Preliminary Society, of whose members he had formed a very low opinion. Most of the trouble at New Harmony could have been avoided, Maclure thought, if the first inhabitants had been obliged to work hard and take care of what they had. To that extent he felt that any community would have a better chance if it was made to settle on virgin land. If Owen would only gather small groups of 20 or 30 families, give them a few hundred dollars and send them off into the forest, even at this late stage he might yet create a sound enterprise.

As far as education was concerned Maclure had not reduced his expectations. He still looked to the day when the experiment at New Harmony might result in scholarly research, tuition at all levels, and publication; each with a view to excellence. He held to the plan of pupils learning at the same time as they produced goods which, when sold, would defray the cost of their establishment.

Phiquepal was already well on the way to achieving this, having thrown himself into the business with frenetic energy. Besides shoes, his pupils produced straw hats, brooms, pottery, and tinware. The little boys had their assembly, workshop, dining-room, and dormitory in the hall of the Rappites' second church. They slept on bunks, filled with corn shucks, arranged on tiers around the walls. Phiquepal, who was so caught up in the concern that he discouraged visitors, lived there too and shared the children's meals: the regimen he imposed began at 4.30 a.m. when they all got up, and ended at 8 p.m. when they retired to their bunks. In August an illness, nervous in origin, drove Phiquepal to seek the open prairie for a time, and Joseph Neef fell sick too. Marie Fretageot was left alone to cope with a crisis.

As superintendent of the Education Society, Robert Dale Owen seems to have been the moving spirit in the decision to charge members of the other two, the Agricultural and the Mechanic, fees for the tuition of their children. The number of pupils from outside had diminished as a result of the Fourth of July speech and there was scarcely any money coming in. The children of all three schools had to live very frugally; they had soup, bread only on Saturdays; milk and corn meal mush cooked in a large kettle was their staple diet. 'I thought if I ever got out, I would kill myself eating sugar and cake', one of the girls remembered. The announcement concerning fees was not well received, and the upshot was that most parents took their children away. On top of that Robert Owen refused to allow members of the Education Society to gather crops from the land they had leased, saying that these had been planted for the benefit of the community at large. It was a move in a contest to determine what kind of education would prevail at New Harmony.

It was becoming clear that Owen's intention, which Maclure's presence threatened, was to establish on the Wabash a better-conducted and better-motivated New Lanark. In the isolation of the wilderness he hoped to put into effect ideas concerning such things as the relations between the sexes, and a uniformity of thought and habit too extreme to be explored on the Clyde. He had begun with labour and proposed to continue with education. In August he caused a series of discourses on education to be published in the *New Harmony Gazette*, which indicated dissatisfaction with the work of the Education Society. When he read them first Maclure was dismissive; 'He rants in big vague undefined words', he told Marie Fretageot, 'out of which he has always many holes to creep.' But at the end of August a detailed plan showed that Robert Owen was determined to replace the Pestalozzian system by the Lancastrian method in use at New Lanark, and more especially to promote the old familiar lectures, complete with maps and globes, that had attracted public respect in Scotland. On 20 August Owen proposed, and the members voted unanimously, that the entire population of New

Harmony should meet three times a week in the Hall for the purpose of being educated together.

From a question and answer session printed in the *Gazette*, it emerged that Owen proposed to make these communal lectures compulsory, arguing that unless and until everyone at New Harmony, above the age of 3, had a mind 'well formed and well informed', they could not proceed to a community of property. He acknowledged there might be some repetition in the lectures—which were generalized accounts of world history and geography—but refused to consider this an excuse for absence. 'It ... requires no more than an honest endeavour on your part to attend regularly, take your seats quietly and listen attentively', he informed his readers. As for the children, besides attending these lectures, they were to have classes in the daytime, a proposal which alarmed Maclure who foresaw that the good work of Neef would all be undone. He denounced the return to the system of New Lanark which operated by'sticking incomprehensibles into the memories of Children as you would do pins into a pincushion'.

Years of dedicated service in the cause of educational reform must give weight to Maclure's considered judgement concerning Robert Owen, who not only claimed but was awarded distinction in the same field. Maclure deplored Owen's attempt to indoctrinate adults in received ideas while giving only a superficial and cursory instruction to the children. It has already been said that Maclure believed the Lancastrian system had its uses, but not at New Harmony, where he hoped the most careful attention would be given to developing their faculties, more especially the power of observation and the capacity to reason. Of Robert Owen Maclure had this to say: 'He has not the smallest idea of a good education and will not permit any to flourish within his reach. His parrot education to exhibit before strangers as at New Lanark is the whole he knows.'

Probably because she was without Maclure's support at the time, and still under the influence of Owen whom she now regarded as a muddled but upright man, Marie Fretageot agreed to conduct one of the classes on the new principle. Maclure gave her short shrift when he heard of it. 'Think you are too full of Owen. Don't allow your enthusiasm to embark your all in his fate ... shall not contradict you in your scheme of having a school on the Owen principle, tho I believe [it] a visionary theory ... for of all the children of New Lanark none got above the merit of twisting a thread of cotton.'

His concern was short lived, for the arrangement lasted only six or seven weeks and was then allowed to lapse as Owen threw himself into another major reorganization, the fourth, and by far the most disturbing to the town. At the beginning of October the Agriculture and Mechanic Societies gave way to a board of trustees consisting of Owen and four of his appointees, who, by virtue of a covenant signed by the members, were to have sole management and control of all property. This government was not to be challenged for five years. According to Paul Brown, 'some called it an oligarchy; others a limited monarchy; others again an absolute despotism'.

The covenant contained provision for dismissing members guilty of a wide range of offences—absence without leave, intemperance, wasteful-ness, negligence, unkindness, and unfriendly and harsh treatment of their fellow members and others. These powers were invoked, and at the beginning of October several were dismissed. Maclure, who had long seen the need for some kind of operation to get rid of idlers and trouble-makers, was obliged to agree with Paul Brown that the way in which it was done had not been altogether just. In the weeks that followed he also perceived that the government of the trustees was openly biased towards a group of Robert Owen's favourites. For instance, while most people had to wait for their scanty provisions to be dealt out on set days, this group was given access to food as well as clothing at the store.

Owen's monopoly at the store gave him a considerable influence over the lives of the inhabitants of New Harmony; it allowed him to value their labour lower than it might otherwise have been, for the necessities were available very cheaply there. This was a repetition of the arrange-ment he had imposed at New Lanark where wages were lower than those of other cotton factories. Under examination by the Select Committee of 1823 he revealed that the introduction of a company store which sold goods at a 25 per cent discount had driven twelve other shopkeepers in the place out of business. Whether this number included itinerant traders who frequented other isolated cotton-spinning villages, such as Catrine, where they were allowed to congregate in 'bazaars', is not clear, but these were also discouraged from entering New Lanark by a tax which Owen levied on their sales.

His justification was that this relieved the workers from the burden of debt built up over the years. But this debt, this dependence, was merely transferred, as henceforth the New Lanark Company was the only source of credit. Wages were paid only once a month by Owen, instead of fortnightly as at other cotton factories, a restrictive process which one critic denounced as coming near to a violation of the Truck Acts.

The system was similar at New Harmony, with the difference that no money at all entered into the transaction. But it never had a chance to function properly. Beside the favouritism shown in the matter of valuing work done, the price of articles on sale was set so low that whenever any of the settlers in the neighbourhood found themselves with cash, they hurried to Harmony which became famous as the cheapest place for miles around.

When on 6 October Maclure returned to Harmony, he was dismayed to find that Owen was once again in need of money, as some $15,000 worth of goods bought for the store earlier in the year, had almost gone. Maclure protested to Madame that he would release no more of his capital to Owen, reserving all his funds for the Education Society. This was maintaining a precarious existence very much reduced in numbers in the wake of the Declaration of Mental Independence. Maclure comforted Marie Fretageot with the thought that the fewer the pupils, the better the education they would receive. Soon the evidence of the excellence of their teachers would become known and then the applications would arrive. He announced the advent of an engraver, Cornelius Tiebout, whose skills would be needed to illustrate the books he proposed to have published at New Harmony. A printing press had been delivered and he directed that the children be taught to set type. Maclure was determined to make a knowledge of science the foundation of the children's education, more especially to counter Owen's maps and globes and diagrams which he detested more than anything in the 'absurd' old system.

During his sojourn at New Harmony that autumn Maclure and Robert Owen came to no open break. Though he grumbled privately about his conduct, Maclure remained in sympathy with Owen's aims, giving him credit for genuine inspiration and honest endeavour, however misdirected. He departed at the end of November, going down-river this time, to winter at New Orleans. His health demanded a warmer climate than that of Indiana; all those arduous journeys had left him with rheumatism and a disordered stomach, a complaint he tried to control with very strict and frugal eating habits. Four days after his departure, Robert Owen mounted yet another attack upon the Education Society.

Through the columns of the *New Harmony Gazette* he accused his members of inconveniencing their neighbours by taking more land in a particular direction than they were entitled to. He signified his attention of taking it back. A furious response, signed by Joseph Neef on behalf of the Education Society, reminded Owen that the dividing line between the property they had and his was embodied in the lease, a perfectly legal document which Owen had signed. According to Paul Brown, this attempt to take back land which was in the very centre of the town was part of an arrangement that Owen had been negotiating for some time. So was the covenant set up in September 1826, whose purpose, Brown charged, was to resolve the various leases granted in order to put the estate back under Owen's direct control. The reason, as Maclure had learned in October, was that Owen intended to quit Indiana in the coming spring. What Maclure had not suspected was that before he went he proposed to dispose of what property he could. In January 1827, Owen announced that he had sold many of the principal buildings in the town, including those which brought in revenue such as the store, the tavern, the flour mill, and the cotton factory—to a William G. Taylor, a businessman from Ohio.

At the same time as Taylor's firm began to trade, Owen gave notice that his support of the inhabitants of the town was to cease. On 1 February, according to Brown's account, some twenty heads of families were invited to hear what he proposed. It was

that they should settle on a half section of Mr Owen's lands, on Mr Owen's terms, on Mr Owen's principles, according to Mr Owen's plans, he advancing them some provisions for the first year: or, being allowed their rations one or two weeks longer, should thenceforth be independent of the society, and make the best of their way through the world by themselves.

Some accepted the first terms, settled on the land and began clearing trees, but when their lease was finally drawn the conditions were so 'intolerable'—Brown's word—that they would not sign. Though it was winter they departed.

In March 1827 Maclure's return to New Harmony coincided with the appearance there of Frederick Rapp, demanding the settlement of two bonds given by Owen of $20,000 each as payment deferred from 1825 for the goods the Harmony Society had left behind. According to Maclure's memorandum of these events, Owen spoke of him to Rapp as his partner and offered the Harmony Society $40,000 in Maclure's name, which Frederick Rapp refused since he was aware it was done without Maclure's knowledge. It was this and another bond issued in the name of Owen and Maclure, a company which did not exist, that prompted Maclure to post public notices at New Harmony and the neighbouring towns disclaiming responsibility for Owen's debts.

Rapp threatened to sue Owen. Maclure, who was by now desperate to be done with the miserable affair, bought the $40,000 worth of bonds from Rapp. With these in hand he went to Owen and offered to pay down the remainder of the money due from the Education Society, plus the $10,000 he had underwritten as his share of any loss, if Owen would give him an unrestricted deed, instead of a lease, to the property. Owen refused, and held out for a further $15,000 as payment for the deed. Maclure noted that, as his confidence in Owen's honesty had put him in the latter's power, he was forced to comply or risk losing what he had already paid.

The affair eventually went to arbitration, when it was decided that some kind of partnership had existed. In the end Maclure found that he had paid Owen $82,500 for not quite one quarter of the land Owen had bought from Rapp; Maclure put Owen's profit at 300 per cent. The memorandum concerning these figures which was found among Madame Fretageot's papers, may have been drawn up by Maclure in response to Robert Owen's version of the affair. If so, it was never published, so Owen's statement remains the more readily accessible of the two.

Owen delivered this after he had left New Harmony on 1 June 1827, at a meeting in Philadelphia called to refute newspaper reports about the collapse of the experiment. According to Owen these reports cast aspirations on his character and conduct. He had been charged with being a first rate speculator, Owen said. Official documents published in the *New Harmony Gazette* would give the lie to this. He was not going to deny it. Nor did he, but he launched into the familiar exposition of his plan. He had time to say, however, that as far as Maclure's involvement was concerned, 'friends' had urged him to join, and that both of them should put $150,000 into the enterprise. Owen implied that he, at least, did this.

According to his speech, Owen's major complaint was about the long delay that attended the realization of the superior system of education which Maclure had promised, a delay for which Owen blamed his supposed partner. Maclure was an old man, Owen, said, a rich man, a man who had done a great deal of good. But he was sometimes impatient and irritable and allowed himself to be worked up into a state 'very much beyond rationality'. The other cause of disappointment was that though *he*, Owen, had wished to make a careful selection of people to form the community of equality, the popular will had forced the inclusion of a large number of unsuitable members.

Getting into his stride he painted a picture of New Harmony as he had left it, composed of a number of small communities outside the town emerging now from a period of hardship and rough work into a time when, under good management, they would exploit first the abundance of products that merely waited to be gathered, namely flesh, fowl, fish, corn, and all kinds of fruit; second, the crops that would bring them money, namely flax, wool, silk, and cotton; and third the reserves that would make them rich one day, namely clay, stone, iron, and copper. His responsibility had been discharged, Owen said, by the fact that before leaving for Europe, he had settled all his debts.

It was an illusion, an account of a mirage which, when Joseph Neef and Paul Brown addressed themselves to it in plain and simple language, vanished. The truth was as follows. Painted signboards had appeared, advertising property for sale and to rent in the town. Feiba Peveli was in existence on its borders. Macluria was empty, abandoned by its members who had defaulted on the payment of interest and capital. Further into the woods were scattered log cabins whose owners scarcely lifted their eyes from the drudging task of clearing ground.

Looking back on his association with Robert Owen, Maclure decided he had been subject to a kind of infatuation; his eyes obscured by a film; 'that mist which the good Mr O had done or got done for him at New Lanark rose before my vision and refracted all objects out of their natural place'. Owen was a dangerous mad man, Maclure concluded, who persuaded many persons to indulge his whims with the sweat of their brows. 'But Vanity is at the bottom. He is I think the vanest [sic] man I ever knew.' And when that vanity is disappointed, Maclure predicted, 'he will go to Bedlam'.

CHAPTER 12

A 'TALL, THIN, TALKING WOMAN'

'SELLING and buying, taking and re-taking, turning and overturning and re-overturning, bargaining, bartering, scheming, manœuvring': by the spring of 1827 the people of New Harmony had been kept in what Paul Brown, whose words these are, described as a state of perpetual agitation ever since Robert Owen's arrival in January 1826. Some spirit remained in them; after the offer of tenancies on Owen's terms, a number of them planned a symbolic funeral: a coffin was made and labelled the Social System, but the procession and interment which might have provoked scenes of disorder—for the people were angry as well as hungry—was frustrated. The night before the funeral was to take place someone smashed the coffin.

At the same time one of the most enthusiastic supporters of that Social System, Robert Dale Owen, was obliged to acknowledge that the experiment was at an end. An editorial in the *New Harmony Gazette* written by him and his brother, William, laid the blame upon difficulties which had arisen because the Community of Equality had been open to all members of the Preliminary Society, many of whom were quite unsuited to that life. According to the editorial, Robert Owen had tried to save the situation by sub-division and some of the groups established then still flourished. 'It is not in the town itself', the editorial said, 'but on the lands outside of Harmony that the Community System is in progressive operation.'

Like his father, Robert Dale saw the fault as lying not in the system, which had no flaws, but in the people whose character and motives he impugned. There was little charity in the view of either member of the Owen family of the individuals they encountered in pursuit of their special doctrine; in passing judgement they seldom took extenuating circumstances into account. For instance, neither then nor later, did Robert Dale Owen ever allude to his father's acquiescence—to put it no higher—in the unregulated admission of members to the Community of Equality, his failure to commit himself to that Community, his efforts to sell the estate at a profit, his quarrel with Maclure, or the hardship caused by cramped quarters, hard work, and scanty provisions.

It was left to Paul Brown to point out the consequence of Robert Owen's belief as it was reiterated in a place like Harmony. If people were constantly told they could not be blamed for their actions, he said, they speedily concluded they need·not be scrupulous about their conduct. The assertion, that man did not form his own character, was odious to Brown; he considered it had a depraving influence on the minds and hearts of many of the people; a view that Maclure came to share. 'A general cupidity pervaded the place', reported Brown,

individual wealth was venerated ... the individual suffering from the privations and embarrassments arising out of the continual shifting of arrangements, as well as undue circumscription of subsistence, deadened the wonted sympathy of many ... souls. The sick could hardly get requisite attendance. Money was in higher repute than in any other town ... The sexes fought like cats about individual marriage.

Robert Dale's disappointment was the more acute since he had begun life at New Harmony with typical enthusiasm, delighting in the freedom from constraint in dress, in the expression of opinion, and in social intercourse. He enjoyed the evening gatherings—the weekly meeting to discuss the Principles, the weekly concert whose music was much superior to anything he had expected in the backwoods, and the weekly ball, attended by crowds of young people whose lack of polish in his eyes was excused by a love of dancing as passionate as his own.

Work was a different matter. Though he was eager to promote the idea of co-operation in all things and volunteered for every disagreeable task, he found his strength was not sufficient for manual labour. One day's trial at sowing wheat left his right arm useless for forty-eight hours, while others accomplished twice as much as he could manage.

At teaching he was naturally much more proficient, and won high praise from Maclure and Madame, but the rift between them and his father made his continuing in the task impossible. In September 1826, at the introduction of the covenant—called by some the social compact—Robert Dale was detached by his father from the School Society and directed to become Editor of the *New Harmony Gazette*. It was a task he found very much to his taste; the paper, then the only one in Posey County, Indiana, bore the imprint of his high moral sense and laborious thought. Under his editorship it was a vehicle for the propagation of those principles that were to govern the new state of society, and it also set out to shape the record of Robert Owen's career as a reformer by printing the text of speeches made on those occasions which he had come to consider most significant. The Proprietor was something of a trial to his eldest son for he exercised close control over the paper, censoring those items he did not like.

With the collapse of the community experiment thus openly acknow-ledged, Robert Dale Owen was faced with a decision on what he should do next. It was a turning-point in his life, the moment when he acknowledged that he could no longer endure doing his father's bidding. So much is clear from the account he gave in his memoirs, in which he mused on what life might have been had he been supported by advice from a cool-headed and dispassionate friend, 'I found no such mentor', he wrote 'but met instead with a friend some ten years my senior possessing various noble qualities, but with ideas on many subjects, social and religious, even more immature and extravagant than my own.' This was Frances Wright (who was six, not ten, years older than Robert Dale). She was at Harmony in the spring of 1827 and had paid many visits to the town since her first arrival there two years before. Her imagination had caught fire then from the example of peace and prosperity presented by the Rappites. It had inspired her to embark upon an enterprise of her own which was, indeed, extravagant, as well as altruistic, desperately hard, and dangerous.

On a small parcel of uncleared land beside the Wolf River, fifteen miles into the forest back from Memphis, Tennessee, and 400 miles down river from Harmony, Frances had established what, disliking the word 'plantation', she called her farm. In those days Memphis, the nearest landing on the Mississippi, was a huddle of 12 cabins, an Indian trading-post. As a gesture to the hunting parties that visited her land Frances gave it the Chickasaw name of Nashoba. Here she and Camilla hoped to put into effect a scheme to educate and eventually emancipate Negro slaves. The slaves would discharge their value to their owners, the Misses Wright, through profit made on agricultural produce. Frances thought that this profit would be easily obtained through a system of united labour copie from that employed by the Harmony Society. She would supply the capital. She and Camilla now controlled a substantial sum, much of which had been left to them by an uncle. Frances had the wildest expectations of the success of the scheme which she intended as a lever to effect nothing less than the abolition of slavery.

It was by far the most difficult and delicate cause she could ever have undertaken. As she told friends in Europe, 'If you knew the horrors connected with slavery, the extent of its demoralizing influence along the western frontier, the ruin with which it threatens the country—its sin, its suffering, its disgrace you will rejoice [at the plan for Nashoba] since I do think it promises fair to pave the way for the destruction of this monster.' As monster many people cast it in the role of Gorgon and shrank from looking directly upon it; the very act of association was degrading. Maclure was of this sort; his distaste at the sight of slaves drove him to exchange New Orleans for Mexico as a place of winter resort. So were Robert Owen and Robert Dale Owen, who were particularly opposed to children being brought up in a slave-holding area.

Frances wrote an account of the circumstances that gave rise to Nashoba.

When I first visited *Harmonie* ... [in March 1825 when William Owen received her] a vague idea crossed me that there was something in the system of united labour as there in operation which might be rendered subservient to the emancipation of the South. After my enquiries in Louisiana and Mississippi had convinced me more than ever of the imperative necessity of some *immediate* remedy being applied to the evil, I revisited *Harmonie* then changed to New Harmony. We arrived to witness the opening of the new community by Mr Owen, we found also still there a large portion of the old occupants awaiting the return of their steam boat to take them to their new settlement in the neighbourhood of Pittsburgh, Pennsylvania. We found also with these the active head of the society, Frederick Rapp. (His father may be considered now in his old age as its religious head.) F. Rapp is a man of the most enlarged and liberal views and possesses more practical knowledge and experience as an American farmer and settler, and also as a practical reformer and teacher of the human species than any other individual probably existing. After considering his system and practice together with those of Mr Owen—ascertaining from the double experience of the Harmonians first in Pennsylvania, afterwards in Indiana ... that the effects of united labor, even in a free state ... so greatly exceeding those of individual labor, as to injure the latter when found in the neighbourhood of the former, it then occurred to me that if individual labor could not stand in competition with united labor in a free state how much less could it do so within the regions of slavery.

Two or three plantations worked on this plan, Frances thought, would be enough to undersell and render profitless *all* the slave labour in whatever state of the Union they were established. The profit motive that inspired the scheme was intended to meet one of the greatest objections raised whenever abolition was discussed—that the plantation owners would be ruined by it and the economy of the South destroyed.

Frances claimed supporters for her plan whose names are already familiar in connection with New Harmony.

'Upon consulting with F. Rapp I found him decidedly of the same opinion and obtained from him the ready promise of his valuable assistance. Our amiable friend George Flower of Illinois who has spent a large sum of money and injured his health by his excertions [sic] in repressing kidnapping [of runaway slaves on the frontier] together with Judge Wattel [Wattles, a member of the Community of Equality] who has worn out his time and patience in the same way, immediately volunteered their cooperation. The former engaged to supply all the stock cattle cows sheep and pigs, to rent out all his lands under cultivation and assist in the direction of the new establishment—A very amiable young man originally a Minister of the Universalist church [The Revd Mr Jennings] and who had conducted schools on an improved system, much similar to Mr Owen at New Lanark engaged to me immediately his services as a schoolmaster . . .'

It will be noted that at this stage 'F. Rapp' bulked far larger in Frances's eyes than Robert Owen. The former helped her a great deal. She went to visit Economy where she was also most impressed by another leading member of the Harmony Society, John Baker. She seems to have believed that one of the two, probably Frederick Rapp, would accompany her to choose and buy the land on which the scheme was begun. That was never likely but Frederick did give her a great deal of advice and information, and sent supplies to her once she was established at Nashoba.

Frances told Lafayette of her plans when they were reunited for the remainder of his American tour. He was gravely worried and confided in the Wright sisters' closest friends, Julia and Harriet Garnett. Their correspondence with him and with Frances and Camilla Wright is a major source of what is known about the Nashoba affair and its connection with New Harmony. Writing to Julia Garnett, Lafayette tried to preserve a detached view of Frances's inspiration. He had the highest regard for Frederick Rapp, and as for George Flower, Lafayette described him as a 'man of an Enthusiastic turn, mingled with a high sense of honour'. Before he left America at the end of his triumphal tour Lafayette exacted a promise from George Flower that he would prevent Frances spending too much of her money on what the General acknowledged was a noble endeavour, but one which he could not approve.

Frances's disappointment at his attitude was heightened by the recognition that Lafayette would never make her his adopted daughter and that she and Camilla could not return to the life they had enjoyed at La Grange. That was the impetus for the Nashoba adventure: it was a means of escape from a situation that had become humiliating.

As one who knew Frances well remarked of her conduct in France on a previous occasion: 'She could pass unnoticed all the wretchedness in the streets [of Paris] at the same time as the struggle for liberty in Poland convulsed her.' However down to earth she seemed in the organization of Nashoba, she was not wholly in command of herself; resentment, a desire to triumph drove her to exceed her strength and to ask too much of others. A hint of angularity, a tendency to domineer was inherent in Washington Irving's description of her as 'a tall, thin, talking woman.' Her letters, with their acute sensibility and loftily expressed ideals foster the illusion of extreme youth. Yet when she went to Nashoba she was already thirty.

Partly as a result of her connection with Lafayette but also because they admired her courage, the most eminent Americans responded to her proposal. Thomas Jefferson who was old and tired and very near to death told her that slavery had been one of his life's anxieties which he must now leave to the next generation. The younger James Madison on the other hand paid her scheme the compliment of careful consideration. He offered wise advice. He was not satisfied that the prospect of emancipation at a future date would sufficiently overcome the natural repugnance to work of the Negro; it would be difficult to introduce the principle of united and voluntary work among them. 'The example of the Moravians, the Harmonites, and the Shakers in which the united labours of many for a common object have been successful have no doubt an imposing character,' he told her. 'But it must be recollected that in all these Establishments there is a religious impulse in the members and a religious authority in the head, for which there will be no substitute of equivalent efficacy in the emancipatory establishment.' Rapp's code of rules by which he managed his conscientious and devoted flock was not relevant to Frances's plan, though his general experience might offer useful aid. She needed managers who were thoroughly conversant with the habits and propensities of slaves, Madison concluded. Generously he gave her leave to use his name if she found it would help, remarking only, 'it will be most agreeable to me on all occasions not to be brought before the public when there is no obvious call for it'.

As the time came for the experiment to get under way there was little competition for the honour of taking part in it. Camilla Wright was undisturbed. 'Rejoice with me', she admonished the Garnetts, 'in the new and glorious career . . . opened to our heroic Fanny by the energy of her own powerful intellect and indefatigable mind.' The Nashoba scheme, Camilla thought, promised not only relief to thousands of oppressed human beings but happiness to the Garnetts, who must shortly join her and her sister and live at Harmony until the Wolf River farm was ready. It was Camilla who declared that she and Frances had no alternative to Nashoba. On their return to Europe what would have been their prospects for the future? 'A Life of constraint and endless solitude', relieved by the occasional *visit* to La Grange. That was a sacrifice to which Fanny, having undergone a great change in America, was no longer equal. Camilla did not reproach Lafayette; 'he is himself too guileless to suspect duplicity in others'. They would soften the blow of parting for him by pretending that it was not final. 'You know how readily he believes what he hopes.'

Camilla was shrewd. She is often presented as the weaker of the two, a victim of her sister's escapades—attractive because she was a gentle girl. Little in fact is known about Camilla, who died young. If her actions are separately considered she was, as will be seen, less susceptible to reason than Frances, willing to risk far more, bolder in defence of the principles in which they both believed. Camilla never flagged in her praise of her sister, and she was always there; they must never part, she said. Camilla, one suspects, was a gentle rod to Fanny's back, a loving spur more often than a support.

In December 1825 George Flower accompanied Frances to Tennessee, helped her to choose and buy the land on the Wolf River, and engaged men to clear it and build the first cabins on it. Then he returned to Albion in order to bring down Camilla who was staying there, his wife Eliza, their children, and a flatboat-load of livestock, hay, and enough pork and beef to last the small community with its blacks for at least a year. Frances was left alone at Memphis.

It had long been in George Flower's mind to promote a scheme for emancipating Negroes but, as Camilla explained, 'He could not undertake it without such pecuniary aid as we can supply while on the other hand *we* could as little have attempted [it] without all the appliances and means to boot which he had it in his power to furnish, not to speak of his personal services which *I esteem as beyond price*.'

George Flower's contribution to the cause of emancipation had already been considerable. Even before they left England and when they were still friends, he and Morris Birkbeck were deeply involved in the movement for abolition of slavery on that side of the Atlantic. On settling at English Prairie they found themselves at the very edge of the split between the States over the Negro question. As a result of the Missouri Compromise of 1820 the citizens of each new State were called upon to vote to decide whether slavery should be introduced or not. The question was an open one on the Wabash for a time: at Vincennes, for example, were a number of prosperous men who hoped to introduce plantation methods into the country.

On either side of the tragic frontier that ran through English Prairie, Birkbeck and George Flower strenuously campaigned for slavery to be held at bay. So did the Governor of Illinois, Edward Coles (an old friend of Maclure), who was ardent in the cause of emancipation. Coles made Birkbeck his Secretary of State, a position the latter held briefly before his death by drowning at Harmony in 1825. Even when Indiana and Illinois voted not to admit slavery the problem was far from being at an end. Their lands, on the border between the two systems, were the scene of innumerable attempts to kidnap and return escaped slaves. Frances Wright was herself involved in one incident, risking her life to rescue a runaway slave from his pursuers. She had him lodged in jail, safely as she thought, only to find him snatched away in the morning. George Flower sought a more satisfactory solution; he was the first person to convey a number of slaves out of the country, to freedom in the black Republic of Haiti on the island of St Domingo.

His stand offended many people and he became the target of abuse. At Albion his son by his first wife was murdered by hooligans; though they were brought to trial and the evidence was conclusive, they were acquitted, an incident which may have contributed to Flower's desire to quit Illinois for Nashoba. Camilla Wright was very much on the defensive in describing her new friends to the Garnetts, the Flowers' bigamous marriage and the quarrel with Birkbeck being the subject of continuing gossip. Camilla exonerated George for leaving his first wife, 'an odious woman', and lauded Eliza for her 'admirable' character, and her 'noble, generous, and candid mind'.

By March 1826 the Wright sisters and the Flower family had settled in at Nashoba. There they received 15 Negro slaves; 5 men and 3 women bought by Frances for between $400 and $500 apiece; a mother and her six daughters donated by a well wisher in South Carolina. The land, the slaves, and expenses to date had cost Frances $10,000 of the $12,000 she had resolved to spend—a large part of her inheritance. 'Without assistance from subscription we must here rest until our farm and store are thriving', she wrote prudently to Julia Garnett. She calculated it would take at least two years. They would raise cotton and sell the surplus to help recoup the cost of the slaves.

Frances's funds in the United States were committed to the care of

Charles Wilkes, an old friend of the Garnett's father, who was President of one of the leading New York banks (and nephew to John Wilkes, the radical Member of Parliament). Wilkes was perhaps the wisest and best friend the sisters had. Lafayette was counting on Wilkes to see that Frances came to no harm at Nashoba; the banker wished her well, though he told her at the same time that he could not have confidence in the success of her enterprise.

At Nashoba Frances performed a wide variety of tasks including working in the fields. The inhabitants of Nashoba were cheerful and happy and growing in industry—an example to the Garnetts, as Frances patronizingly told them. 'Remember dear loves that we are not ladies of leisure with nothing to do but follow up the correspondence of friendship—I wish I knew you engaged in some pursuit that would call forth your energies and prevent your indulging in melancholy and vain regrets'.

From time to time the sisters separately went the two days' journey by steam boat up river to New Harmony to rest, obtain supplies, and observe the Community of Equality. William Maclure, who encountered Frances in the spring of 1826, formed a high opinion of her ability. 'Miss Wright would be a great help to Mr Owen as a Manager', he told Marie Fretageot. A few weeks later when the Education Society was in the course of separating from the main community, Maclure offered Frances teachers trained by his experts for the Negro school she planned to open at Nashoba, in exchange for her assistance while the Society got under way. She was sorely tempted by his offer and as a result performed prodigies of labour at Nashoba hoping to put it in order before she went off to Harmony. Once she arrived there in July she was allowed no rest. According to Camilla, 'her talents and influence had no small share in settling many important matters relative to the interests of the School [and] Society'.

When she returned to Tennessee in August she was obliged to nurse several of the slaves who had fallen ill, as well as catching up on other work: she was constantly out in the mid-day sun and drenched by the nightly dew. The result was a fever which, for ten days, put her life at risk. Camilla described the ordeal.

As you know the danger in all sickness with our Fanny is the tendency to the disease attacking her head, and on this occasion our terror was the fever settling on the brain where her greatest suffering lay and but for the skill and yet more the admirable judgment of our friend Mr Richardson . . . I am persuaded we could not have saved her invaluable life.

James Richardson, to whom Camilla referred, was a Scot who apparently studied medicine without qualifying as a doctor. The Wright sisters had come across him at Memphis where he was lying ill. He went with them to Nashoba and made their cause his own—with what disastrous results will shortly appear.

Camilla did not escape the fever; on nursing her Frances suffered a grave relapse. This time she was unable to move from her bed for three months and, even when able to ride out a little each day, remained too weak to read or write for many weeks. The business of the place might be supposed to have come to a standstill. Yet, when William Maclure called at Nashoba on his way to New Orleans in December 1826, he was moved to admiration by what he found. 'I am here at Miss Wright's', he wrote to Madame Fretageot, 'and as newly astonished at the order and good conduct of the Negroes which contrasts with the disorder and dilapidation of Harmony more than the color of their skins.' Prejudice, he thought, was the reason for reports about the poor state of Nashoba which had been circulating. Marie Fretageot was not surprised. Frances 'has that positive good sense that enables her to calculate every means proper for her undertaking and that knowledge to apply them in every direction', she replied.

What neither of them knew was that Frances had fallen under the spell of Robert Owen whom she encountered in his most prophetic mood. It is not known whether she was actually present when he delivered the Declaration of Mental Independence but she was in Harmony shortly afterwards. It soon became clear her thoughts were concentrated on the radical changes which that extraordinary utterance both stated and implied. The most charitable explanation of her ensuing conduct was to be that the fever had irrevocably upset the balance of her mind.

When it became available in Europe the Declaration of Mental Independence caused the same sensation as it had in the United States. Reading it the Wright sisters' friends were not at first alarmed by their proximity to its author, but curious to know what they made of it. Julia Garnett told Frances that the world thought Robert Owen insane; she was prepared to suspend judgement until she knew what Frances thought. In December 1826, still too weak to hold a pen, Frances dictated her reply to Camilla.

I must reply in person to your observations respecting Mr O—You are in error and I was the same before I *knew* him—*very few do* know him—a few words explained to me at once the *Man* and his object and satisfied me he is to influence the condition of mankind [more] than any individual that has ever existed—Mr

McClure who possesses one of the soundest heads I have met with, knows him as I do and holds the same opinion of him and his principles. This however understand—My feelings here have in view the *principles* not the Man, no change in my sentiments towards the latter could ever affect my view of the truths with which his name will here after stand connected ... The principles advocated by Owen are to change the face of this world as surely as the sun shines in the heavens—this is my calm opinion it does not rest upon the man but upon the principles with which that man stands connected—these principles have been mine ever since I learned to think and in opening to you the secret projects of Owen, I shall have to open also my own mind. Not even to you did I ever disclose some opinions in which I never expected to find sympathy, or conceived they could ever form more than a theory. Owen has discovered the means of connecting the theory with practice. One word opened to me a new world, reconciled me with life, and gave me hopes for the human race as high as my former despair had been deep. This is all I can say by letter. I know you will feel convinced I would not write this seriously on a matter of doubtful importance.

This letter contains an allusion to a practice in which Robert Owen was a pioneer—as was Francis Place—but which Owen always went to great lengths to conceal since the subject was so controversial. It was birth control—the *means* as Frances called it, of connecting theory with practice, and which, as she said, reconciled her to life and gave her hope for the human race. Robert Owen's knowledge of it was apparently gained during the visit he made in 1818 to France, the country where very rudimentary methods of contraception had been in quite widespread use since the previous century. Rumour had it that he introduced such methods to New Lanark.

Birth control was Robert Owen's real answer to The Revd Malthus's doctrine that famine would inevitably deal with over-population. For many years Owen insisted in public that production of food could be brought into balance with consumption by the mere fact of organizing society into his Villages of Unity. But privately, as Place remarked to James Mill, Owen was adamant that no Village would become a rabbit warren; population would be regulated.

The fact that Owen did not object on moral or religious grounds to the most powerful means of freeing women from the burden of their sex, was of the greatest importance to Frances Wright who, as we have seen, was emotionally opposed to constraint of any kind, and went so far as to play down the attributes of her own femininity.

Owen's influence was clearly apparent in the so-called Trust Deed of Nashoba which Frances had drawn up at the end of 1826 after fever had warned her that arrangements must be made in case of her death. This Deed altered the character of Nashoba from a purely philanthropic enterprise with a single purpose—the emancipation of slaves—to a complex and visionary scheme similar to the one Owen brought to New Harmony.

Frances ceded all her property, including the slaves, to a number of trustees of which Owen was one, on condition that when their labour should have paid a sum of $6,000 plus 6 per cent interest and expenses, they should be emancipated and colonized. By 'colonization' was meant the removal of newly freed men and women to countries such as Haiti or Sierra Leone, where blacks could enjoy the privileges of citizenship, and where they would not pose a threat to order in the United States. The white members of the Nashoba community, as the farm was called in the Trust Deed, were to be very carefully chosen and to qualify as individuals; husbands might join without their wives, and vice versa. All would live together, holding their goods in common and pursuing their chosen occupations. Those who did not work would be expected to contribute to their keep, a sum which was eventually fixed at $100 a year, which caused Harriet Garnett to scoff that the Wrights had set up a boarding-house.

While Frances undoubtedly remained zealous in her desire to bring freedom to an oppressed race, it seems that after her visit to New Harmony in 1826 she was no longer in any great hurry materially to alter the conditions of those individuals belonging to that race who came under her authority at Nashoba. While awaiting the moment of their emancipation—which she must have known by then would take years— she expected her slaves to perform all those tasks the white members of the Nashoba community would find too hard, or simply uncongenial— 'occupations which their habits render easy, and which to their guides and assistants might be difficult, or unpleasing', as the Deed puts it.

This was some way from the ideal which she expressed in elevated language at the beginning of her enterprise and which had won her the admiration of liberals everywhere.

It is the moral condition of the race of color which engages me—it is to prepare the two colors for the coming change. It is to kill prejudice in the white man by raising the black man to his level. It is by offering not the mere theory but the practice of equality beneath the roof of Nashoba and presenting a first example by union and brotherhood.

Now her attitude to the slaves, as opposed to her ambition on their behalf, seemed to differ but little from that embodied in the Constitution of the Preliminary Society of New Harmony, where blacks were to be admitted, if at all, as 'helpers'.

Beside Robert Owen, the trustees of Nashoba included Robert Dale Owen, William Maclure, and General Lafayette. Among those who expected to live by the Wolf River were Frances herself, Camilla Wright, George Flower, James Richardson, and The Revd Robert Jennings who engaged his services as a teacher by letter, being then in the East. He was to be joined by another young man from Harmony, Richeson Whitby, who had lived in a Shaker community before he became a member of the Preliminary Society when he was superintendent of the department of domestic economy. Lastly Frances named Cadwallader Colden, an old friend and a relation by marriage of Charles Wilkes. Colden was a prominent New York lawyer and politician whose name added weight.

But not enough to reassure the Garnetts or their friends. One of these was J. C. L. Sismondi, the Swiss historian, once a member of Madame de Staël's circle at Coppet, in its day a kind of Société d'Auteuil in exile. Sismondi admired Frances and Camilla Wright, adored the Garnetts, and had met Robert Owen on the cotton master's tour of Switzerland in 1818. In April 1827 Sismondi expressed his regret that Frances was exercising her 'heroic enthusiasm' under the direction of Owen, 'the first intelligent man to come near her for years', but a man 'whose head is so illogical, and who has given himself up to such dangerous dreams about ways of improving mankind instead of studying what it is. If Mr O has been the cause of depriving humanity of the fruits of the sacrifice of these two excellent creatures [the Wrights] he will have done much more ill . . . than by all the writings which scandalized Americans.'

Sismondi believed that one of the attractions of Robert Owen for Frances Wright was the passion with which he attacked religion. Frances herself was madly religious, Sismondi told Julia Garnett; she had made for herself a mysterious system which did not disgust her by its absurdities. She was a new Saint Theresa in whom the love of principle and usefulness operated as the love of God had in the other. Frances detested the forms and practices of established religion, Sismondi decided, because she thought its power fostered slavery. As her autobiography makes clear, Frances believed that all mankind, of whatever colour, was held in thrall by religion. She perceived it as a vast conspiracy, not in a metaphorical but in a real sense—positively shaping men's lives in spite of their desire to act otherwise. She vowed to overcome it.

CHAPTER 13

'CO-OPERATION HAS WELL NIGH KILLED US ALL'

ROBERT Dale Owen was not allowed to kick his heels for long at Harmony after the disintegration of the community. Frances Wright who was there in May 1827 put him under orders as a Trustee of Nashoba to accompany her back to Tennessee. He obeyed, as he put it in his memoirs, in the hope of finding there 'more congenial and cultivated associates than those with whom I had been living for the past 18 months'. One cannot say whether this sweeping statement indicated some offence to Robert Dale by his friends in the Education Society who, if not cultivated in the manner to which he was accustomed, were conspicuously learned. It may be that his memory was at fault concerning them as it evidently was with Frances. However much he found her wanting when he came to write his memoirs, she was certainly congenial at the time; 'sweetest Fanny' was his customary address.

And she was undeniably cultivated. Besides the accomplishments proper to all well brought up young women she had acquired a knowledge of the classics—albeit in translation—and a sympathetic understanding of the ideas that had inspired Robert Owen. The opportunity to teach herself had been provided by her great uncle, James Mylne, Professor of Moral Philosophy in Glasgow College.

Robert Dale Owen deferred to her intellect, envied her vigour, confided himself to her strength. His idealism was revived by her account of Nashoba. He prepared to go there in much the same frame of mind as he imagined Southey, Coleridge, and Wordsworth had enjoyed when, thirty years before, they had resolved to banish worldly cares and selfishness for the wilderness on the banks of the Susquehanna. He was rather put out when at last he saw the land on the Wolf River. It was all second rate and only 100 acres cleared; three or four log houses on it and a few cabins for the slaves: these were the only buildings. The slaves, he thought, were allowed to shirk by Richeson Whitby whose experience in an easy going Shaker village had not fitted him for the more exacting role of plantation overseer. The situation appeared to call for a firmer hand, which he might well have provided, having a good eye for land, a knowledge of the theory of agriculture, and experience in directing workers gained at New Lanark where he had been left in charge during the prolonged absences of his father.

George Flower, who was the obvious candidate, had departed a few weeks earlier, in April, as a result of an unspecified disagreement. He did not return, and made no mention of Frances Wright when he came to write his memoirs. His wife, Eliza, had something to do with the rift, for Camilla, who had begun by praising her, wrote after she had gone that their hopes had not been realized; Eliza was not suited to fill any situation at Nashoba, 'nor does she possess a mind calculated to enter into the views connected with it'.

The puny strength of Nashoba was to be further reduced. A new crisis in Frances's illness seems to have occurred on the way back from Harmony; at Memphis she had to be placed in a hammock slung in a covered wagon to convey her to Nashoba. James Richardson there pronounced her so ill that only a sea voyage could save her. It was therefore decided that she should leave at once for Europe where, having recovered her health, she would recruit suitable members for the new community. Robert Dale elected to accompany her, rejoicing at the approach of a reunion with his sweetheart at New Lanark. Margaret's absence had prevented him from becoming attached to any of the girls at New Harmony, easy though this would have been in the freedom from supervision that they enjoyed, and pleasant to one as bothered by loneliness as he was.

Camilla was to remain at Nashoba since Whitby, on whom the chief responsibility was to fall, argued strenuously that one of the proprietors must remain in order to control the slaves. 'I have left my Camilla with attached friends and good assistants and in a home she loves', Frances assured their relations, having departed with Robert Dale via New Orleans at the end of June. During the voyage to France, which lasted several weeks, she gradually recovered her strength.

The decision to leave her pretty, gentle, and mild-mannered sister struck the Wrights' acquaintances as an act of extreme irresponsibility on Fanny's part. Sismondi had already voiced the general opinion that, as women, they were terrifyingly vulnerable in Tennessee. He comforted himself with the belief that Richardson had fallen in love with Camilla; if he would marry her, things would be much easier.

Professor Mylne was horrified. Camilla, his great niece, was alone with

Negroes and whites 'whose intellect seems to be destroyed'. He had been alerted to the situation in a manner calculated to arouse his anger and apprehension. As a trustee of Nashoba, James Richardson had sent a letter to a Glasgow newspaper describing the principles that governed the conduct of the community there. When he read it the printer took it to Mylne, unwilling to publish without his permission. The Professor recoiled from the contents, which included a reference to unrestricted sexual intercourse, and refused. His anger was fuelled by Robert Owen freshly back in Glasgow from New Harmony. Disingenuous as ever, he 'represented Fanny as having gone to much more extravagant lengths than he himself'. According to Mylne, while Owen had 'very little limit to his extravagances, and ... but a very small share of sense and knowledge,' he had enough to perceive that Frances's folly could not fail to bring ruin upon her project and disgrace to herself. Owen declared that Frances had invited trouble at Nashoba and professed deeply to lament the fact. Mylne asked Julia Garnett if she thought the sun had affected her niece's head. 'Or is it as I rather fear that her excessive passion for notoriety has led to an incipient disorder of the mind? If so how will her intellect sustain the shock when [Nashoba] fails?'

Mylne was the more distressed because he had been very proud of his great nieces when first they came to live with him; two young women he described, with satisfaction, as 'well principle, well refined, elegantly accomplished, fit to take their places among society of every rank, and to be received in it with esteem and respect'.

It was not long before disgrace wholly overtook the Wright sisters. Thwarted in his attempt to publish details of Nashoba in Glasgow, James Richardson found an outlet in the Baltimore paper, the *Genius of Universal Emancipation*, whose Editor, Benjamin Lundy, was a noted abolitionist, and known to Frances Wright. On 25 July 1827 the *Genius* reproduced extracts from a manuscript known as the Nashoba Book. A furious storm was raised.

Shortly after they met Frances described James Richardson as trustworthy, prudent, attentive to business, with a finely cultivated mind and every liberal sentiment. Robert Dale Owen described him, years later, as upright, impractical, and of a mystical turn of mind. Prudent is not the word that suggests itself in reading the extracts he supplied to the newspaper: naïve is more to the point and stupid not inappropriate. Driven by a desire for notoriety as strong as that of Frances Wright, or to put it more charitably perhaps, by the same desire to propagate beliefs which had overexcited him, Richardson blundered into an area that was quicksand in the South; the human contact between white and black.

The first extracts reprinted from the Nashoba Book reveal an uneasy mixture of cajolery and the threat of force in dealing with the slaves, a confusion of attitude and purpose that boded ill for the smooth running of the enterprise. But the cause of the huge uproar that followed publication lay in two particular entries.

Friday, June 1, 1827.

Met the slaves at dinner time—Isabel had laid a complaint against Redrick, for coming during the night of Wednesday to her bedroom, uninvited, and endeavouring without her consent, to take liberties with her person. Our views of the sexual relation had been repeatedly given to the slaves; Camilla Wright again stated it, and informed the slaves that, as the conduct of Redrick, which he did not deny, was a gross infringement of that view, a repetition of such conduct, by him, or by another of the men, ought in her opinion, to be punished by flogging. She repeated that we consider the proper basis of the sexual intercourse to be the unconstrained and unrestrained choice of *both* parties. Nelly having requested a lock for the door of the room in which she and Isabel sleep, with a view of preventing the future uninvited entrance of any man, the lock was refused, as being, in its proposed use, inconsistent with the doctrine just explained; a doctrine which we are determined to enforce, and which will give to every woman a much greater security, than any lock can possibly do.

Sunday Evening, June 17, 1827.

Met the slaves—James Richardson informed them that, last night, Mamselle Josephine and he began to live together; and he took this occasion of repeating to them our views on color and on the sexual relation.

The effect of publication was to fix Nashoba in the public mind as dissolute, its blacks at the mercy of licentious owners just as in any other remote and run down plantation, with the added horror that white women openly connived at what was going on. 'Brothel' was the word that sprang to mind, and it was used. Friends tried to keep the fact of publication from the Wrights' adviser, Charles Wilkes, who, as soon as he was apprised of it, wrote to Camilla asking her to deny it. She did not. Instead she defended it and expressed her

entire disapproval of the marriage tie, which I regard as not only in the utmost degree irrational, in requiring of two individuals to love each other during life, when they have not the control of their affections for one hour, but in the highest degree pernicious in compelling these individuals to continue united, when the feelings which brought them together may not only have changed, but, as I have known in several instances, have turned to utter aversion.

She also viewed marriage, Camilla informed Wilkes in her reply, as one of the most subtle inventions of priestcraft for poisoning human felicity and perpetuating misery and crime.

Wilkes was devastated. 'Such is the issue of the plans of these excellent young women', he wrote to Julia Garnett, 'for excellent and virtuous I still cannot doubt their being. Such is the consequences of their overweening confidence in their own judgments. That such young women should be the dupes and the victims of the wretched sophisms ... of a madman like Owen is truly lamentable.' Wilkes remarked that he could not deny the Wright sisters his assistance but henceforth his house must be closed to them. He blamed Frances for her disregard of the mischief she might do in her attempts to distinguish herself, 'and gratify a paltry ambition'. Professor Mylne also suspended relations with the sisters. Cadwallader Colden found himself seriously embarrassed by the use of his name as a trustee of Nashoba.

Though he remonstrated with Frances about the inadvisability of publishing such views in the present state of society, Lafayette at least stood by her. She was at La Grange for much of the summer of 1827, emaciated and marked by fever which had caused her hair to go grey. The traces of her illness made Julia Garnett tremble for the future; she told Sismondi that he should know what she could not express to anyone else.

I sincerely believe that Frances is incapable of judging for herself. Mr O's system took possession of her mind when under the effect of a brain fever it has never left her and she speaks as one incapable of seeing the consequences of the principles she admires, principles to which her whole life all the feeling of her heart are in direct opposition.

While so many of Frances's friends looked askance at her plans, Robert Dale Owen clung to his trust in her and her vision of the community that was to be established at Nashoba. Some kind of prop was the more necessary since he suffered a cruel blow when, in August, having left Frances convalescent at La Grange, he went home to Scotland to be reunited with Margaret. He found her more beautiful and interesting than he had remembered, or could have expected. Yet, though he was convinced that if he proposed she would accept, something went wrong between them that caused him to hesitate. Apparently she deceived him in some small matter—or she may just have laughed at him. In any case he pronounced her not 'sincere', and postponed his intention of making her his wife.

In his memoirs he put the onus on his mother; she is represented as begging him to wait three years until it was clear that Margaret's character compensated for her humble origin, and was suited to the very great privilege of becoming his wife. Although at the time he was 26 years old, Robert Dale did not find the strength to dismiss the pain lightly. Margaret's insincerity provoked a lasting resentment in him, a grudge that he allowed to fester ever afterwards.

That summer was altogether a sad time for Robert Dale. His mother was obviously very ill, and distressed at Robert Owen's intention of taking their two younger sons, David Dale aged 19 and Richard 17, back with him to Harmony, which in the aftermath of the Declaration she could no longer view with approval. And it was the last time he was to see the beloved house where his childhood had been spent, for Braxfield was to be given up on grounds of expense, and Mrs Owen and her daughters moved to a far less imposing lodging in Glasgow. 'The more I see of the Old World the less I feel inclined to remain in it', Robert Dale wrote to Frances Wright at the end of August. 'But I should like to rescue out of it a few rational beings who are too good for it and would be much happier in the woods.'

Among these few he numbered, surprisingly, Henry Leigh Hunt, Editor of the radical London paper, the *Examiner*. Robert Dale had corresponded with him while living at Harmony and now described him to Frances as an excellent amiable liberal young man with a 'sincere' and pretty wife who shared his views. The Hunts introduced him to another person he considered a candidate for Nashoba, Mary, the 29-year-old widow of Percy Bysshe Shelley. In 1827 she was living in seclusion at Arundel, near Brighton, having returned to England from Italy after Shelley's death in 1822.

In his memoirs Robert Dale wrote that if fate had thrown him and Mary Shelley together at that period in his life instead of bringing him into contact with Frances Wright, her influence would have been much more salutary. 'I required to be restrained, not urged; needed not the spur but the guiding rein.' Mrs Shelley who, according to Robert Dale, was genial, gentle, sympathetic, thoughtful, mature in judgement beyond her years, and above all 'womanly', would have given him different advice from Frances Wright. At the time Robert Dale believed her eager to go to Nashoba, an impression that Frances, who descended on Mary at Arundel in September, also allowed herself to entertain, rejoicing in the fact that the daughter of William Godwin and Mary Wollstonecraft approved the principles that had inspired Nashoba.

Mary Shelley received Frances with affecting warmth and respect. But she had no intention of burying herself in the backwoods of Tennessee.

America, she wrote later, appeared to her so remote as to be altogether cut off from human intercourse. Neither she nor the Hunts would have been of practical use at Nashoba, having already displayed lively distaste for roughing it in the successive ramshackle *palazzos* and *villinos* they had occupied with Shelley in Italy.

But in spite of her resistance to emigrating, Mary Shelley took a keen interest in the Nashobites, as she called them, and urged Robert Dale to take the greatest care of Frances, whom she contrived to see as not only sensitive but essentially feminine. 'Now then practise yourself in such lessons as may make you loveable ... and therefore more likely to make a favourable impression', she wrote.

Nothing is better calculated to instil sweetness of disposition, and that best and most endearing of qualities, tenderness, than constant attention to a woman with whom you are not in love, yet for whom you have affection and kindness. Study to please Frances in all minutiae, divine her uneasiness, and be ever ready at her side with brotherly protection.

Such conduct with regard to Fanny would assure Robert Dale that when the time came he was capable of inspiring a lofty-minded, sensitive, and talented woman with love for himself. Mary Shelley, it seems, was disposed to mother Robert Dale much as Marie Fretageot was.

The duty of caring for Frances on the return voyage to the United States in the autumn of 1827 devolved, however, not on Robert Dale, who was detained by his father in Scotland and followed later, but upon a female friend. Like many other women in Frances Wright's life this friend was seized by a passion for her that can only be described in terms of a schoolgirl crush. The victim, this time, was Frances Trollope, wife of a London barrister called Thomas Trollope, and mother of seven children, including Anthony, the novelist. In 1827 he was still a boy at school, and the fact that his mother abandoned him together with her husband and most of the rest of the family in a dash for the ship taking Frances Wright to New Orleans, was yet another cause for exclamation in the Garnett correspondence.

In 1827 Frances Trollope was a woman of 48 whose life almost up to that point had been spent in uneventful if not entirely tranquil domesticity. She was a lively, gossiping, observant, and socially ambitious woman who filled the pleasant country house her husband had had built near Harrow with a constant stream of visitors. The Garnett sisters had been known to her for most of her life, for her father, a clergyman with a living near Bristol, had been an intimate friend of John Garnett. His

widow's move to Paris with her daughters brought Frances Trollope
with her husband to visit them. It was in 1823 that they made the
acquaintance of Frances and Camilla Wright, and were invited by
Lafayette to stay at La Grange. Frances Trollope's head was turned. She
became infatuated with Frances Wright, and obsessed by her unusual
relationship with the illustrious General. She kept abreast of the doings
of her 'sweet Fanny' by means of Julia and Harriet Garnett.

At the same time her own life became increasingly difficult and sad.
'Trollope', as the Garnetts abruptly termed her husband, became
unbearably irascible; to be with him was a penance—the reason, it has
been suggested, an undiagnosed brain tumour. Financial troubles
crowded in upon his wife who was desperate to discover ways of meeting
the school fees of her sons who were either at, or destined for,
Winchester. Henry, the second son, did so badly there that his father
withdrew him, sending him instead to a counting-house in Paris. His
mother visited him in the summer of 1827 and was therefore on hand to
listen to 'dear noble single hearted Fanny' extol the benefits of Nashoba,
and to suggest that Mrs Trollope, with Henry, should join her there. As
the time of her idol's departure drew near Frances Trollope became
increasingly disturbed. 'My dearest Harriet', she wrote, 'will it be
possible to let this "angel" (yes Harriet you are right she *is* an angel) will it
be possible to let her depart without vowing to follow her? I think not . . .
The more I see of her, the more I listen to her, the more I feel convinced
that *all* her notions are right.'

On her return to Harrow 'Trollope' told his wife that they must let
their house in order to retrench upon their expenses 'at which my heart
sickened', Frances Trollope explained to the Garnetts, 'and I used all my
power to persuade him that a year or two passed at Nashoba would
repair our affairs'. Whether he agreed or not—the Garnetts were doubtful
on that point—on 4 November 1827 Frances Trollope with Henry and
two of her daughters sailed with Frances Wright on board the *Edward* for
New Orleans, having told no one of their intention. Harriet Garnett was
both alarmed by her friend's decision to throw in her lot with one who
had become the target of vituperation, and exhilarated by the drama of it
all. 'The gates of the most rigid convent are not so unsurmountable a
barrier betwixt the world and the nun they enclose as public scorn makes
against a woman who has joined such a community as Nashoba', she
declaimed.

But it was anger rather than scorn that Frances Trollope eventually
provoked in the public mind, for she wrote a celebrated book about the

experience that began with her going to Nashoba in the company of
Frances Wright. *Domestic Manners of the Americans* was odious to its
subjects for Mrs Trollope—'Madame Vinegar'—perhaps unconscious of
the effect of her strictures, hit out all round in her description of the
boorishness of the natives, the discomfort and ugliness of the surround-
ings, and the flat monotony of the country she encountered on her way
up the Mississippi. It has been said in her defence that the starkness of the
picture she presented was largely due to the fact that, by landing at New
Orleans, she was immediately confronted with all that was most raw and
crude in a developing country: unlike Frances Wright, Mrs Trollope
first entered the United States by the back door.

She was certainly tart in dealing with the people she encountered,
among whom was William Maclure who was at New Orleans when her
party disembarked. She depicted him as an old man, spouting aphorisms,
and chided him for his periodic absences from New Harmony. She also
contrived to suggest that Marie Fretageot had been his mistress, that the
boy Achille who passed as her son at New Harmony, was their
illegitimate child, and the Madame was feathering her nest through the
hard work of the pupils at the school of industry at Harmony while
neglecting their education. Henry Trollope may have been responsible
for this unflattering picture for he spent some time at New Harmony and
wrote home to England complaining about the menial work he, as a
pupil, was required to do.

Domestic Manners gave a rather more charitable picture of Frances
Wright's motives in founding Nashoba, though the place itself was
dismissed in one word—desolation. As author Mrs Trollope needed to
say no more, for the book contained a drawing of the place by Auguste
Hervieu, a French artist who had been a member of Mrs Trollope's
household at Harrow, and accompanied her to the United States. He
represented Nashoba as a small clearing in a dark forest with a few square
buildings inside a split rail fence; black and spiky lines conveyed a sense
of punishing effort as well as bleak despair. Of Frances Wright, Mrs
Trollope remarked that her mind was so occupied by the object in view
that all things else were indifferent to her.

Privately to the Garnetts she expressed the alarm and fear that
overtook her on board ship, after setting out, as she said, 'in confidence
of being happy and ready to endure privations of many kinds'.

I was a very poor creature during the voyage and persuaded myself repeatedly
that it was my weakness of mind and body that made me deem Fanny too
eccentric when I saw her sitting on a coil of rope in the steerage reading to a sailor

occupied in patching his breeches ... some of the wildest doctrines of equality
and concubinage that were ever traced on paper—writing such and reading them
aloud was her chief occupation during the voyage and I often recurred to the idea
that had tormented us at Paris that she was not in her right senses. But I have
since quite abandoned this mode of accounting for what is extraordinary in her
conduct. *Something*, I know not what, *must* have befallen her when she followed
Lafayette to America which totally unsettled all her views and plans of life ... it is
said without scruple that she has had a connection with George Flower—and that
Camilla lived with her husband five months before she married him. Fanny's
connection with George Flower is said to have taken place before she purchased
Nashoba. He brought his wife and children to reside there and they continued to
do so till the jealousy of the wife made it impossible to continue together.

Mrs Trollope did not vouch for the truth of these remarks but reported
them as widespread.

On reaching Nashoba, [she continued] I found it so infinitely more dreadful than
I ever imagined that I almost immediatly decided upon not suffering my children
to breathe the pestilential atmosphere more than a day or two. It is impossible to
give you an idea of their miserable and melancholy mode of life while I was there.
Whitby and his wife [Camilla] both looking like spectres from fever and ague ...
The food was scanty and far from wholesome—no milk or butter bad water very
little bread and no meat but Pork—in short I left them in ten days and from that
time have never ceased to hear the most violent abuse of these unfortunate sisters.

The marriage of Camilla Wright to Richeson Whitby referred to
above, took place before Frances Wright, with Frances Trollope,
returned to Nashoba. After her vehement opposition to the whole idea of
marriage—her 'phillipic' (*sic*), Camilla called it—there was naturally
furious speculation as to the reason for it. Mrs Trollope represented
Whitby as a brute and, though Camilla protested to her that she was
happy, suspected that she was merely putting a good face on things. In
consequence some writers have variously concluded that marriage was
forced on Camilla as a result of Whitby raping her, or that she resorted to
him as a protection from the attentions of other white men in the vicinity
of Nashoba. But by those who knew him well Whitby is represented as a
decent man. Moreover the Wright papers refer to a 'secret' connected
with the marriage.

Camilla herself told Harriet Garnett that the circumstances which
induced her to conform to the legal ceremony of marriage were 'of a very
peculiar nature and such as it were impossible to explain by letter'. As
their adviser, Charles Wilkes had sight of a document signed by Whitby
by which he renounced his right as her husband to any of Camilla's
property, which caused Wilkes to remark that Whitby at least had not
married her for her money. The evidence, therefore, points not to an act

of last resort intended to rescue Camilla from an unpleasant situation, but a carefully prepared arrangement, made, one must conclude, in the expectation of a child.

Camilla conceived in May 1828 and bore a son at the end of January 1829. He was christened Francis and his short existence was passed, not in the company of his father, but with his maternal aunt and namesake, Frances Wright. According to Amos Gilbert, a Quaker printer who was closely associated with the sisters after they went back East, Camilla was induced by Frances to marry, 'that there might be a child in the family'.

Shortly after Frances returned to the clearing by the Wolf River a remarkable document was issued to a number of newspapers. Its title was *Explanatory Notes, respecting the Nature and Object of the Institution at Nashoba, and of the principles upon which it is founded: Addressed to the Friends of Human Improvement, in all Countries and all Nations.* Frances explained that it was now her purpose to put into effect a number of principles essential to the progress of the human race, for which she believed herself to have the necessary mental courage and passion for reform. She represented men as less free than they might be, as under the control of repressive religious and political institutions which imposed class divison and forced them to labour to create false wealth. Public opinion was to blame in perpetuating this state of affairs, particularly among women. 'In what class do we find the largest proportion of childless females, and devoted victims to unnatural restraints', Frances demanded; she found it 'among the cultivated, talented and independent women who . . . shrink equally from the servitude of marriage and from opprobrium stamped upon unlegalized connections'. Frances urged that moral liberty was essential in order to question existing restraint, and to make people equal without regard to sex, class, race, or colour. Moral liberty was in her gift, to pass onto those who came to live at Nashoba.

With regard to her original plan, for the slaves to emancipate themselves through co-operative labour, experience had taught her by then that, in their existing state of mind, having known nothing but servitude, they would never achieve the voluntary effort to make it possible. It was, therefore, decided to restrict the number of slaves to those originally purchased, and concentrate instead on admitting 'respectable' free Negroes to live on terms of absolute equality at Nashoba, and to have their children educated there. In this way would they gradually attain the same mental and moral level as whites.

Frances insisted that amalgamation of the black and white races was her eventual aim.

The only question is, whether it shall take place in good taste and good feeling, and be made at once the means of sealing the tranquillity and perpetuating the liberty of the country, and of peopling it with a race more suited to its southern climate, than the pure European,—or whether it shall proceed, as it now does, viciously and degradingly, mingling hatred and fear with ties of blood—denied, indeed, but stamped by nature on the skin.

This was anathema to the South, a call that even Robert Dale Owen felt unable to defend, a statement which provoked further great anxiety among her friends. Frances was alone at Nashoba when the *Explanatory Notes* came out. Frances Trollope departed after only ten days and, leaving Henry at New Harmony, took refuge at Cincinnati. In April Camilla and her husband were also driven to retreat to Harmony where they hoped to recuperate from fever. Richardson had already gone, full of remorse at the disaster his hasty publication of extracts from the Nashoba Book had brought upon the place. Even Robert Dale Owen spent only a few days with her, for a crisis had developed on the Wabash which demanded his immediate attention.

Writs had been issued against Robert Owen the previous summer for the non-payment of goods delivered to the New Harmony store. In his absence from the country the autumn session of the circuit court had authorized attachment of his property. Now the spring session was to hear these and other claims, and counter-claims by Owen. He was plaintiff and defendant in more than a dozen cases. A stream of orders couched in ancient legal language went forth to perplex the farmers and storekeepers of Posey County, Indiana, and though Robert Owen petitioned for the cases to be removed to a place where he might secure a fairer hearing, were duly aired. The matter was complicated by the fact that William G. Taylor claimed that Owen had charged him money for writing a monopoly of trade in Harmony into his lease, but had subsequently allowed others to open stores in the town. He sued for breach of contract, lost, and appealed; at which the whole vexed question of monopoly was opened to public debate.

The 'tangled web', as Camilla called it, of their pecuniary affairs at New Harmony now threatened to ruin the entire Owen family. To meet the demands of Taylor and other creditors Robert Owen was obliged to sell his shares in the New Lanark Company, as did Robert Dale and William Owen, thus severing a connection that had begun in 1799. Of the money realized £6,000 had to be devoted to the support of Ann Caroline Owen and her daughters, leaving very little in their hands but the estate of Harmony.

It was therefore with dismay that Robert Dale discovered that the *New Harmony Gazette* was about to founder. He knew that in the existing state of his father's affairs he could not rescue it. Camilla explained, 'in this dilemma I went to Fanny, then alone at Nashoba, entreating her to come up to Harmony and discuss with us the measures to be pursued under such an accumulation of difficulties'. The upshot was that Frances Wright advanced the money to save the *Gazette*, and become co-editor with Robert Dale Owen. Their collaboration appeared to herald a new beginning at Harmony, an impression which was underlined in June by the seasonal departure for Europe of Robert Owen, 'leaving Robert [Dale] to fight his battles', as Camilla said.

In August The Revd Robert Jennings reappeared at Harmony. He had been on his way to Nashoba for some time but was impeded by his wife and family whom Frances was far from anxious to receive. Jennings was involved by Robert Dale in a new plan to promote a school at Harmony, separate from that under the control of the Education Society. Jennings proposed to Frances that she should return with him to Cincinnati and, while he gathered his family to return with him to Harmony, give a series of lectures to promote their ideas, and to acquire badly needed new subscribers for the *Gazette*.

It was an unheard of exploit for a woman to speak in public, and few people came to the first lecture. But when Frances persevered, 'even her most violent opposers expressed their admiration and wonder at her transcendent talents as a public speaker & almost admitted her eloquence to be irresistable'—there spoke a proud Camilla. At Louisville and Vincennes where Frances also spoke on her way back to Harmony, crowds flocked to hear her. Their attention was both soothing and exhilarating to Frances. In contemplating them a tide in her mind began to ebb, exposing the reality of Nashoba; heat, loneliness, exhausting physical labour that brought very little reward, the constant threat of fever, the intractability of the slaves. 'My dear Jennings', Frances wrote in a letter which, to the delight of her opponents, got into the newspapers, 'co-operation has well nigh killed us all'. A new mission beckoned; to edit the *Gazette* and to reinforce its liberal message with another course of lectures. Her friends at Harmony urged it upon her, the question was whether to work from there, or to remove to the East. Richeson Whitby was dispatched to see to matters at Nashoba. There, as Camilla told the Garnetts, all hope of an association was at an end; 'she thought it would be a poor appropriation of her talents to sit down and devote herself to the emancipation of a few slaves'.

PART IV

POSITIVE KNOWLEDGE

CHAPTER 14

'THIS PRESIDING SPIRIT OF OUR FORESTS'

In the summer of 1828, when Frances Wright and Robert Dale Owen took over the *New Harmony Gazette* the town was unique among frontier settlements. It still sheltered a number of very gifted people whose imagination drew upon their special knowledge and was sustained by skill, and the habit of consistent work. Though the manner in which it had ended was universally deplored, for those who had remained the disintegration of the Community of Equality was not in itself a disaster. The departure of a large number of the participants enabled them to live in a more reasonable, if precarious, degree of comfort.

Much was achieved that was remarkable if only for the fact that the place was still desperately remote. Though by that time roads were being driven through the Indiana forest, as one English traveller who endured the journey to Harmony by Dearborn carriage observed, the most the contractors undertook to provide was a certain width, with no stumps higher than 15 inches in the actual middle of the road. Other bone-jolting, tooth-loosening encounters were with the 'corduroy'—wooden rails laid side by side for crossing swampy ground, and 'republicans'—projecting roots of trees so-called from the tenacity with which they clung to the ground they grew in. By day one could see no further than 10 yards into the forest, at night nothing, so that horses balked at going on and had to be closely led. To stray beyond the blazes was likely to be costly, for the carriage might drive in to a cul-de-sac of trees which had to be felled before it could be turned.

And, just as in the Rappites' time, the same traveller noted that cash was extremely scarce; pork, lard, flour, and anything else that came to hand had to be shipped on down to New Orleans where the price they fetched depended on the rapidly fluctuating state of the market in such commodities, and the condition in which they arrived.

Yet the town which had to be sustained in this strenuous way possessed much treasure; things that were scarcer than gold in the western country, and in their own right, splendid. Foremost among them was Maclure's library, consisting of more than 2,000 books, many of them rare. Book-buying had always been a passion with him, as it was with his friends; George Erving, who was commissioned by Thomas Jefferson to buy for him in Europe, as, later, he was by the Library of Congress itself; and the dealer, Obadiah Rich, whose list was particularly strong in Spanish works. Maclure's own library contained a very fine selection of books on natural history, together with the plates originally made to illustrate François-André Michaux's *North American Sylva*. Maclure had bought these in Paris in the hope that, once its printing press had become established, this magnificent and famous description of American trees might be profitably reproduced at New Harmony. Books apart, there were Maclure's own gleanings from the Alps, the Apennines, the Spanish Pyrenees; fossils and rocks picked up years before, lately retrieved from the cellars of the Academy of Natural Sciences, packed, and dispatched at great expense to the Wabash via New Orleans.

Perhaps the rarest and least known treasure at New Harmony was in the care of Charles Alexandre Lesueur. Among his scanty personal belongings he had papers of his late friend and colleague, François Péron. These, together with his own portfolios of drawings of animals, birds, plants, and fish, constituted an amazing record of Baudin's great voyage to Terra Australis in 1800.

As long as he lived in Harmony, Lesueur kept in touch with his scientific colleagues at the *Muséum* in Paris, and the *Jardin des Plantes*; more particularly with Georges Cuvier who, among his manifold pursuits, shared his knowledge of, and passion for, ichthyology.

Beginning in 1828, Lesueur made a yearly journey to New Orleans, partly to confirm his continued existence before the French Consul so that the small pension granted for his work on Baudin's voyage might continue to be paid, partly to satisfy his hunger for new things and creatures to observe. If left in one place for too long Lesueur grew fretful. In the first years at Harmony he and Gerard Troost, with whom he shared a common past and friends at the *Muséum*, often escaped on long journeys of exploration up and down the rivers. At New Orleans, Lesueur found a congenial companion in Joseph Barrabino. He was by origin Italian, but a polyglot; from the portrait painted by Lesueur, he appears a swarthy, vigorous, swashbuckling man. He was a druggist and an ardent naturalist in whose shop a crowd of like minded enthusiasts was always to be found.

It is unfortunate that when so much was written and has survived concerning the days of George Rapp and of Robert Owen at New

Harmony, Lesueur was incapable of expressing himself except through the medium of drawing. His letters, clumsily composed, at times almost incoherent, rarely explain the detail of his life, confining themselves to scientific matters, often obscure. However, one of them addressed to colleagues at the *Muséum* in Paris laments the departure, which Lesueur described as 'forced', of all the people of talent who might have assured the success of the enterprise, as he believed it to have been conceived by Robert Owen and William Maclure. Among those who left quite early on was 'l'ami, Troost' who went to take up the post of Professor of Chemistry and Mineralogy at the new University of Nashville, Tennessee.

Blame for the break up of *la belle réunion* of like-minded people at New Harmony was laid, by Lesueur and others, on Robert Owen, as Simon Ferrall found on visiting the town. He was a London barrister, an expert on constitutional law, who came to visit a friend living at Harmony. He was already *au fait* with Robert Owen's career, and with his behaviour on returning to England from Indiana after the disintegration of his scheme. Ferrall's assessment was the result of a fortnight's sojourn in the town, during which he cross-examined most of its inhabitants on the cause of the débâcle. Three years later, in 1832, his letters—whether expurgated or not is unclear—were published as a book, *A ramble of 6,000 miles through the United States of America*.

Ferrall reported that there were as many reasons advanced for the collapse of the Community of Equality as persons questioned. Some called Robert Owen a fool, others worse. The only charge he proposed to notice (presumably because he thought it the most likely), was that Owen invited people to throw up their establishments in other parts of America and come to Harmony, 'conscious at the same time that the community could not succeed, and, indeed, not caring much about its success, having ultimately in view the increase of the value of his purchase, by collecting a number of persons together, and thus making a town—a common speculation in America'.

As to Robert Owen's public statements, Ferrall remarked upon the difference between reality and his assertion that the New Harmony experiment had succeeded 'beyond his wildest dreams'. Then to say that he had been informed that the people of America were capable of governing themselves and that he tried the experiment and found it was not so; and that 'the place having been purchased it was necessary to get persons to occupy it', constituted but an imperfect excuse for having ordained the separation of families, caused many thriving establishments to be broken up, and even the ruin of some few individuals who threw their all into the common stock. These persons advanced so many facts that Ferrall, visited by the same reluctance that afflicted Robert Torrens, Robert Southey, James Mill, and many others, was yet forced to conclude: 'one must be blinded by that partiality—which so known a philanthropist necessarily inspires, not to be convinced that however competent he may be to preach the doctrines of co-operation, he is totally incompetent to carry them into effect'.

Some of Owen's friends in London said all went well until he gave up the management. Yet Owen himself said he only interfered when things went wrong, Ferrall reported. All at New Harmony were agreed that Owen interfered from first to last. 'Very little experience of a residence in the back-woods convinced Mr Owen that he was not in the situation most consonant with his feelings. He had been when in Europe surrounded by people who regarded him as an oracle, and received his *ipse dixit* as sufficient solution for every difficulty.' At Harmony it was quite different, for most of those who came had been accustomed to exercise their own judgement in matters of practice, 'and this Mr Owen is said not to have been able to endure'. Owen's mind was warped by the constant contemplation of his Utopias, Ferrall decided. Owen's merit— and it was no small merit, Ferrall remarked—lay in the fact of his having collected together the ideas of Rousseau, Voltaire, Plato, Condorcet, Sir Thomas More, and others, arranged them in an intelligible manner, and devoted time and money to assist in their dissemination.

For the rest of his life all Robert Owen's scanty resources were to be devoted to this aim. But first he had to extricate himself from the unhappy tangle of affairs in Indiana. Disaster was only averted in the summer of 1828 through the help of Frances Wright and William Maclure. Maclure told Marie Fretageot in January 1829 that Owen was about to return to Harmony bringing with him money enough to settle his debts. '(He) says he has sold all his own as well as his sons' shares in the cotton mills at New Lanark for a good price and has given orders to Robert Dale to draw for and pay off, our mortgage and Miss Wright'.

In 1829 Owen did return to New Harmony but by a route that no one else would have contemplated. With the charred remains of hope on the banks of the Wabash yet to be disposed of, he already had in his mind's eye another scheme, a perfect reproduction of those that went before, but on an enormous scale. Marie Fretageot warned Maclure, who was then in his winter quarters in Mexico, that he would see Owen before she did. Robert Dale had come to her with a letter from his father informing him that Messrs Rothschild and Baring, being owners of a huge tract of land in the territory of Texas, had entrusted him with the power of forming a Community there, and had 'directed' him to Mexico City for consultations with the government about it. In spite of her recent experience, Madame's desire for the success of such an enterprise was still strong though, as her letter shows, she had grown wary of Robert Owen. Whatever happened it would at least provide settlers in a country much in need of them and if the management was not good enough to ensure its success, yet the principle might remain in the minds of those who would be collected there, should the undertaking be attempted. She hoped Maclure would not do anything to prevent it, if only for the sake of public interest. For her own part she would not be sorry to know that Robert Owen was busily engaged some hundreds of miles away from New Harmony.

Owen's interest in Texas, in those days thinly populated, and remote from the control of government in Mexico City, may have been aroused by his old friend, John Dunn Hunter. He had not returned to Harmony in 1825 but, from New Orleans, gone on to ask the Mexican government for a grant of land in Texas where Indians might live in safety and comparative prosperity. Disgusted by the refusal of the Mexicans to enable him to realize the vision that obsessed him, Hunter became embroiled in an attempt by Americans to set up an independent republic on Texan soil. According to a newspaper cutting preserved among the papers of Francis Place, Hunter was killed in mysterious circumstances near Nagadoches in 1827. The writer of this described him as a highly intelligent and talented man of sturdy appearance and simple manners, whose grave aspect was only disturbed when speaking of the Indians, when he always became agitated.

Though expressed in diplomatic language, the message delivered to Robert Owen by the Mexican Minister in London was perfectly clear: his government, beset by chronic civil war, had no desire to receive him. It was a rebuff that Owen represented otherwise, not only to himself, but apparently to those Englishmen to whom he applied for letters of recommendation for use in Mexico, letters which, when he saw them, astonished William Maclure by the eminence of their authors, and of those persons to whom they were addressed. 'He was particularly recommended to the Bishops', Maclure exclaimed to Marie in disbelief, 'who from his services as he says with those of England he has great hopes of convincing them that it is in their interest to patronize and support the new order of things he wishes to introduce, founded on the divine law of nature that man is the child of circumstances'.

Maclure met Owen at Jalapa towards the end of January 1829, before he set out for Mexico City, unsure of what his former colleague proposed to do. 'So long as he stops at theory all will be well', he told Marie Fretageot, 'but should he attempt practice, the second edition of New Harmony will be published to the world confounding his theories and bringing loss and disappointment on all that have placed faith and confidence in him.'

As things turned out, Maclure need not have worried. Owen was in an unusually passive mood, soothed by the clear and bracing air of the high plateau and its distant views. He was almost happy, ready to look at the world about him without preaching about what it ought to be. The narrative he published shortly after he left Mexico is unusual among his writings for describing these personal impressions. It was normally his rule, even in private letters, after scrupulously observing the forms of politeness, to pass at once to business and then to the reiteration of his one idea. There was no time, or call, he felt, for anything else.

Yet, in one crucial aspect the essential Owen reappeared. Maclure noticed that, whereas the Mexican bishop and other leaders, including the victorious general Santa Anna, to whom Owen explained his Texan plan, were polite enough not to contradict him, Owen as usual took their attitude for definite encouragement. And, in this, the very architecture of the capital was made to play a part. Pacing out the great central square of Mexico City, Owen was pleased to find it measured 1,070 by 870 feet. Squares for the residence of the population of all countries under his new system would extend to 1,000 feet on each side, he remarked; of course, unlike the great square of Mexico, in his utopian city there would be no streets, no lanes, no alleys, no courts, leading off the centre: 'these form vicious and unfavourable circumstances, too prejudicial to happiness to be admitted into an improved state'.

Owen's account of this visit to Mexico let it be understood that nothing stood between his plan and its realization but the small matter of legislation to sanction it. He could not wait for this, he said; he was called to higher things, namely to a debate at Cincinnati in April. It had been arranged the previous year, as a result of a challenge by Owen to all comers to dispute with him that Christianity was a fraud. He therefore went by Vera Cruz, and New Orleans, to Harmony, where he spent five days and did not find time to pay off the mortgage held by Madame Fretageot on behalf of William Maclure.

At Cincinnati, his opponent was the celebrated revivalist, The Revd Alexander Campbell, who was head of his own religious sect. In her *Domestic Manners of the Americans*, Frances Trollope described the encounter, which became notorious. It was held before a large audience crowded into a Methodist hall, and was produced like a melodrama. It ran for fifteen sessions on succeeding days. Mrs Trollope concluded that, though remarkable, it was an experience not to be commended nor, she hoped, repeated. Judging by the applause he received The Revd Campbell won hands down. Owen, she said, practised the *suaviter in modo* to perfect effect. His gentle voice, his manner, sometimes playful, never ironic, his affectionate interest in the whole human family, the air of candour with which he expressed his wish to be convinced he was wrong, his kind smile, the mild expression of his eyes, won an astonishing degree of tolerance for sentiments odious to the majority of his hearers. This was his last appearance; shortly after it he left for Europe and, though all his surviving children were soon to settle permanently at New Harmony, he did not return for many years.

During 1828 a new alignment came into being in the town. Robert Dale Owen and his three younger brothers, William, David Dale, and Richard, shared Community Number One with Frances Wright, Camilla and her husband, Richeson Whitby, The Revd Mr Jennings, and a Dr Chase, with whose very pretty wife, Martha, the three youngest Owens were very much in love. To them were added Phiquepal and his boy pupils; he had abandoned the School Society after friction with Madame had culminated in a terminal quarrel with Maclure. According to his version, Phiquepal did not pay nearly enough attention to the all-important subject of natural science, and was ruining books from his library by tearing out the prints. Phiquepal and his boys occupied themselves printing the *New Harmony Gazette* and another Journal which Maclure intended for a wide circulation among scientists. Its antecedents might be traced to the bulletin produced in the early days of the *idéologues*; it was called the *Disseminator*.

Camilla was a frequent visitor to Marie Fretageot at this period, passing the fence that separated Community Number One from the School Society in order to relate the upsets that frequently took place; especially those to do with Martha Chase. Meanwhile, Robert Dale Owen was struggling to hold on to what the Owen family now referred to as the 'estate' of Harmony, while publishing the newspaper which had acquired a new and longer name, *The New Harmony and Nashoba Gazette and Free Enquirer*. His steadiness under trying circumstances was saluted by Madame.

Frances Wright, having been accorded the great distinction of delivering the Fourth of July oration at New Harmony, spent the rest of the summer fighting battles elsewhere. She had detected a conspiracy which she believed threatened the very foundation of the Republic. She chose as her ground the entire Ohio Valley, upon which she inflicted a series of public lectures. The cause roused all her former energy and quickly dispelled any inclination she may have had to return to a useful, but necessarily retired, existence at New Harmony. There was an evident attempt, she said,

through the influence of the clergy over the female mind—until this hour lamentably neglected in the United States—to affect a union of Church and State, and with it a lasting union of Bank and State: and thus effectually to prostrate the independence of the people, and the institutions of the country. . . . Frances Wright determined to arouse the whole American people to meet [the threat] at whatever cost to herself.'

That summer's appearances in the public halls of Cincinnati convinced Frances and her colleagues that she had found the role she was best suited to play. Her voice, her manner, joined to qualities of courage, composure, imagination, backed by intellect and learning; all these went to enhance the piquancy of a situation in which a woman raised questions and proclaimed support for views that no other female, and few enough men, had called into play against the dead weight of orthodox opinion.

Almost immediately she became the acknowledged leader of free thought in the United States, and joined to that belief a call for a liberal system of public education, better conditions for working people, and fair treatment under the law for all members of her sex, but particularly married women. Birth control formed part of this programme; free love did not, but its practice was inevitably ascribed to her.

Frances could no longer remain based at Harmony; her fame, her mission, imposed responsibilities she could not shirk. By January 1829 Madame Fretageot was in a positon to report positively to William Maclure.

Our little place furnishes some news that you must hear. Frances Wright has made wonders in her preaching at Baltimore, Philadelphia, and especially New York. It is decided that they will transport their establishment in that last town. Robert Dale is going there for helping an institution on the plan of Epicurus in

Athens, as well as the continuation of his paper under the title, *The Free enquirer*. Thus we lose them all, and if I am not mistaken it will prove beneficial to our establishment in removing the public opinion from our place.

By this she meant adverse public opinion. And, taking a very long view, Madame added, 'the spreading of liberal principles abroad will smoothe our ways'.

Phiquepal and his little boys also made their way to New York where they continued with the printing of the *Free Enquirer*. Together with Robert Dale and his brothers, Richard and David Dale, they all lived together in a commodious house rented by Frances Wright some five miles from the centre of New York. In the spring of 1829 they were joined there by Camilla with her infant son, Francis.

The adventures of the group which departed to New York are relevant to this narrative in so far as whatever Frances Wright and Robert Dale Owen did, or said, or published in the *Free Enquirer* was irrevocably connected with the place they came from.

Robert Dale Owen was continually harassed by problems left behind at Harmony where his brother, William was supposed to be in charge. Having born the brunt of setting up the enterprise—and incurred reproach for allowing Rapp to take advantage of him in the process—William now had the thankless task of clearing up after everyone else. This involved him in taking over debts at the store amounting to some $20,000. Hoping to sell its cargo for whatever it would fetch, he took a flatboat loaded with the inevitable pork, lard, and flour, down river to New Orleans where it was seized by creditors and William himself narrowly escaped jail. Robert Dale eventually rescued his brother with the help of another loan for $10,000 from Frances and Camilla, apparently the last of their disposable funds. From 1828 to 1831 Madame Fretageot was the only force that held New Harmony together, a worthy successor to the Rapps. It was not an enviable position, though it attracted envy, for many did not understand the difficulties she faced. Foremost among these was the fact that although Maclure was still regarded as a very wealthy man, by his own account he had lost more than $100,000 as a result of his association with Robert Owen. Now he was determined to hold on to the remainder of his fortune in order to promote his own ideas. As he approached seventy, he felt that time was running short.

Every natural resource at Harmony was squeezed by Madame to its full extent; so that apple trees, for example, provided not only fruit, but also cider, brandy, and vinegar. Meat was not a problem; apart from the venturesome hogs, they lived on venison, ducks, geese, and squirrels, mostly shot by the boys of the school.

Madame Fretageot longed to discover some lucrative activity that would please her boys better than farming. At various times she suggested to Maclure that they start a cotton-spinning factory at Harmony; or raise silk worms; even purchase a small steam-boat to be hired out at profit. One scheme she put into effect had two of the most reliable boys hawking prints on a wagon round the settlements of Indiana, Kentucky, and Illinois; it produced a profit of eleven dollars. Maclure poured cold water on most of her proposals, as he did on Dr Chase's efforts to raise poppies for opium, and manufacture white lead at Harmony.

By 1830 Maclure had grown doubtful about the wisdom of continuing his enterprise at Harmony; he toyed with the idea of returning to Europe. As a result of the adverse publicity generated by Robert Owen the schools at New Harmony were condemned to a perpetual lack of pupils. Maclure tried for a time to recruit orphans—good material, unspoilt by parental interference. He looked for them at New Orleans, supposing it to be the scene of continual disasters and, therefore, productive of destitute children. He did not find them.

It is difficult to assess what standard of education was achieved by the School Society's efforts at New Harmony. Marie Fretageot was the target of hostile comment which extended to her performance as a teacher; her own brother who arrived on the Wabash in 1832 accusing her of negligence with regard to his sons, Peter and Victor Duclos. As for the boy Achille, Maclure complained furiously about his lack of progress after taking him on a journey to Philadelphia. He could neither write nor spell in English, could not tell the Pole from the Equator and though endowed with a good deal of sense was 'deficient in the foundation of intellectual cogitation'. Maclure placed the blame for this on Phiquepal who had had Achille in his charge ever since they had left Paris in 1823. He was always unreliable and seemed at times to be possessed by a kind of frenzy.

Among her responsibilities at Harmony, Marie Fretageot had charge of all the buildings on Maclure's land which, like those belonging to the Owens, had become a matter of concern. By 1829 it was clear that a considerable amount of money would have to be spent on them. The Harmonists had built without foundations and some houses were on the point of collapse. The only thing that relieved her mind, Marie told Maclure, was 'to go about the town inspecting everything'.

This energetic watchfulness coupled with a characteristically decisive manner seemed to many of those subjected to it, unbearably imperious. It was held to be the reason why many of the people within the orbit of the School Society had left New Harmony, a fact that was conveyed to Maclure when he went East. As a woman doing a man's job in a wholly masculine-orientated country, and as representative of an absentee landlord, Marie was in a position guaranteed to make her unpopular.

This was understandable. Yet the sheer number of antagonists argues a certain bias towards dispute on the part of Madame. She sustained a long drawn out quarrel with the Neefs, whose lack of competence at teaching she derided. She was often at cross purposes with Lucy, the girl who had been her favourite pupil at her Philadelphia boarding school. Lucy was the daughter of Mrs Sistare of New York and came to Harmony with her two sisters on board *Philanthropist*. In 1827 she married Thomas Say.

As time went by, even Madame's fierce spirit began to falter. She was too often ill from the fever that had not yet departed the place: 'sick, flat in bed' for days at a time. It was both tedious and difficult to settle matters requiring Maclure's assent when to seek and receive it took as long as four months. The burden of her responsibility weighed so heavily on her that she took to getting up at 4 a.m. in order to have time alone before the business of the day began. Then something worse than fever took possession of her, body and mind. She put on more than twenty pounds in weight and at the same time suffered from a sudden access of doubt that was very disturbing to her. She felt obliged to confide in Maclure, explaining more than once that she approached the age that every woman feared (as far as is known, in 1830, she was about fifty). 'Ho, do come' she begged him, desperate for his advice and company.

He would not budge from Mexico, fearing exposure to recrimination if he showed his face at New Harmony, and as he explained to Madame, finding himself morally and physically well placed in a country whose recent revolution provided him with much material for the creation of new axioms. And the warm winter climate was exactly to his taste. He was not only growing self-indulgent but testy and suspicious. In a hand reduced to almost total illegibility by his desire to expound at length while sparing paper—'my minimum writing' he called it—he unreeled great lengths of closely woven thought destined for the *Disseminator*. Woe betide Madame if, when he received a copy, the text was inaccurately reproduced, or cut. He chided her for this and other alleged offences, including the failure to obtain a decent order for the *Sylva*, the great work on trees. No wonder both of them began to cast about for a means to get rid of the property.

As in the days of the Harmony Society, it was difficult to imagine who, or what organization, might pay a suitable price for the peculiar establishment beside the Wabash which was now visibly run down. Yet, in 1831 Madame Fretageot was alerted to the presence at Economy of someone who she thought might buy, and to whom Maclure announced himself willing to sell. He was a most strange person; wonderful even, to the members of the Harmony Society who met him when he came among them announcing the millennium. He called himself Archduke Maximilian of the Stem of Judah and the Root of David—and travelled *incognito* as Count Leon. He claimed to have come from a background in Germany that was as Gothic and fantastic as the scenes described by the Brothers Grimm.

The reality was hardly less strange, for the antecedents of Bernhard Muller, as he was in real life, were not dissimilar to those of Father Rapp. His belief in the millennium was just as profound; his desire to influence events as strong, and his presence even more commanding, with the added advantage of a mysterious origin—so that his appearance at Economy caused a famous schism. Members of the Harmony Society had become increasingly disaffected by the strict rule of their own patriarch, took him at his word, and greeted Leon as the fulfilment of a promise that Father Rapp had made to them many years ago. They transferred their allegiance to Leon who was preparing to form his own religious community. It was as a result of hearing reports of these events that Madame and Maclure entertained the hope (which was not fulfilled) of handing Harmony back to something like its original purpose.

Leon's presence at Economy was made known to Marie Fretageot at the end of November 1831; it was a measure of her devotion to Maclure's interest that on hearing of it at the Ohio landing where she was about to board a departing boat, she made to turn back to Harmony in order to be able to treat. The violent objection to her change of plan which Thomas Say, who was bidding farewell to her, could not conceal, not only shocked Marie but convinced her that after all she should proceed to France. Her departure from Harmony was almost a flight; in recent months she had begun to suspect that its inhabitants wished her ill.

Paris rapidly restored her spirits. Returning in December 1831, after an absence of nearly ten years, she rejoiced in everything; the water of the Seine, the wine of Burgundy, the fine light bread, the welcome of her friends. She was also much encouraged by a change of attitude in

Maclure, whose 'disaprobation' regarding her conduct of affairs at Harmony had caused her much anguish. Obviously worried that he might lose her services, he wrote to her at Paris soothingly, and sent generous amounts of money.

This was to enable her to buy books for Indiana, second hand as well as new, and to this end Maclure gave her tips on how to get the better of the Paris dealers. She was provided with a list drawn up by Thomas Say of works to form the nucleus of a natural history library for New Harmony. Maclure had abandoned hope that the schools would ever flourish there and decided to concentrate his efforts on improving access to knowledge; 'the millions will educate the millions', he explained. He asked for runs of periodicals, and scientific journals whose contents could be extracted and cheaply reprinted. He hoped that Madame would be encouraged to return to Harmony and do her best for the place. 'Europe will not suit you', he wrote hopefully, 'after so active a life in such a different part of Society as New Harmony.' Thomas Say also wrote from Indiana to persuade her to return; life as Maclure's agent did not suit him; he fretted for his insects.

In the spring of 1832 a catastrophe threatened to forestall her. Cholera originating in the Far East was sweeping across Europe. 'If I die it will not be of fear,' Marie assured Maclure. When she too was seized by the fearful chill that announced the onset of the disease Madame retired to bed, summoned a strong woman to massage her all over, and drank iced water until a 'light perspiration' was induced. Whether she had caught cholera or not, she escaped and sent Maclure a detailed account of her precautions, because she was afraid that the sickness would soon reach Mexico. After the illness relaxed its grip, Madame found herself too weak to think of leaving France for some time.

Eventually at the end of 1832 she decided to take ship for Mexico before returning to Harmony: she had to come to proper terms with her much loved, much respected but cantankerous and elusive patron. It is to be hoped they met, but if they did, Madame's long-delayed happiness must have been brief for shortly after landing she again contracted cholera. This time it killed her.

The supervision of Maclure's property at New Harmony now fell entirely upon Thomas Say; it was too heavy a burden for him, whose sojourn on the Wabash was already regarded by his friends and scientific colleagues as a form of exile. Ever since the departure of Say and Lesueur for Indiana in 1825, certain members of the Academy had campaigned for their return to Philadelphia, deploring the waste of their talent at New

Harmony, and accusing Maclure, as author of the move, of wilful damage to the cause of science in America.

Work at New Harmony was carried out in the face of great difficulties—the remoteness of the town, the constant search for suitable paper for printing; the lack of current reference books. Say persevered while he lived there contributing dozens of articles to scientific journals, many of which appeared in the *Disseminator* published in the town, while labouring to complete his two great works, *American Conchology*, and the *Entomology*. The *Conchology* appeared in six volumes, printed at New Harmony, with plates beautifully engraved and coloured by his wife, Lucy, who learned her skill from necessity, the engraver having died. Three parts of the *Entomology* had been completed by the time Madame Fretageot went to Paris where she brought it to the attention of the scientists at the *Muséum*. Besides these works the New Harmony press also printed the collection known as *Opinions on various subjects* by William Maclure. And it produced a prospectus, with illustrations, of Lesueur's projected work on the fishes of America. Further than that he would not go while he remained at New Harmony and made it plain to his scientific colleagues in Paris that serious work on it must wait until he returned to Europe.

Ill health was the greatest threat to achievement at New Harmony. Say suffered most. In a letter to his dear friend Charles Buonaparte, written in the summer of 1830, he deplored the lack of time imposed by a recurring bilious complaint. 'Great industry is requisite in this remote region to compensate for the disadvantages under which a naturalist must labour', he complained to the Prince, 'the partial distribution of books, the want of Museums, the want of stimulating intellects'. He was apt to relapse into a state of apathy, prone to that carelessness and indifference characteristic of the backwoodsmen. 'That I have partaken of this presiding spirit of our forests in some degree cannot be denied', Say confessed. 'If you ask me what I have achieved in Natural History my almost constant ill health and the aforesaid circumstances will prevent me from giving a satisfactory answer.'

The low and confined situation of the town produced a feeling of constraint—the Harmonyphobia that afflicted Applegarth, Phiquepal, and others. By 1831 Say's letters were using words like 'gloom', 'dark', and 'oppressive' to describe his feelings. The collapse of the Community of Equality was an especial blow to him; it made him uncharacteristically bitter. To George Ord in Paris Say complained: 'since the gilded projects of Mr Owen have evaporated into thin air our town presents no striking distinctive character, it has become specifically identical with any other backwoods country town'. Communication with the outside world was solely through the post office, and should a stranger walk into New Harmony he would be in danger of exorcism as a ghost. To Charles Buonaparte he suggested that, without letters, he would be 'annihilated', and begged him to continue to provide a loophole through which he might peer at the scientific world. Even the conversion of a small clearing to a cornfield distressed him, since he could no longer use it to botanize; the nearest open prairie was at Wanborough where, he said surprisingly, he had never been.

His depression was increased by a sense of poverty; he told a friend that he and Lucy did not want children until they could afford to support them better. He was reduced to asking that extracts copied from books at the Academy might be sent on single sheets of paper to save postage. He grew thinner than ever, pale, and stooping, alarming the friends who saw him when he paid a brief visit to Philadelphia in 1832. They cast about for ways to deliver him but he was detained on the Wabash by Maclure, who felt he was better there, and wanted him to supervise his plans. It was too much. In 1834 he died, and his death was viewed as a tragedy, a matter of reproach to William Maclure.

It was a heavy blow to Lesueur, and it was followed in the same year by that of Barrabino when the cholera reached New Orleans. The loss of Say and of Madame Fretageot seems to have inclined Maclure to abandon New Harmony: in 1834 he gave instructions for his library to be moved back to Philadelphia. It must have seemed another signal to Lesueur. There are traces of a bitter dispute concerning the compensation Maclure should pay Lesueur for years spent on the Wabash, which the latter had come to regard as wasted. Nothing was resolved until 1837 when Lesueur returned to Paris where George Ord, who remained his close friend, fulminated over the conduct of Maclure, the 'boasted Maecenas'.

I never would forgive this man for the insuperable injury which he did to Science in dragging away with him from Philadelphia our worthy friend Say, the sacrifice of whose life all the good deeds of the former never can compensate. What think you [of Lesueur's] reward for twenty years' of humble service under the fostering care of his liberal patron? $100 per annum. But methinks I hear you say, did he not give him a large collection of Engravings and another of Minerals, books etc? He did; but one day under pretence of wanting something in the cabinets, he borrowed the keys, which he unceremoniously put in his pocket saying [to Lesueur] I have no further need of your services, Sir.

In the end Lesueur went home to Normandy. He was invited to look after the Museum of Natural History at Le Havre to which he brought a share of the treasure collected in the course of his long and adventurous life; the rest went to the Paris *Muséum*. He had a house at St Addresse, in a valley near the sea, from which he had been parted for so long. In 1846 he died, aged 68.

That is to anticipate. What of New Harmony following the dispersal? When the tribunes departed did the Dark Ages begin? The answer is that, just as the native British went on ploughing around the pavements of the Roman villas, so the settlers on the Wabash made what use they pleased of the alien buildings in their midst. In due course New Harmony became like the rest of Posey County, Indiana, a place to serve the needs of farmers who brought a pleasing order to the land; so that great stands of trees, and fields of wheat, and beans, and Indian corn, and vines and open grazing ground fell into a harmonious and productive pattern that George Rapp would have approved, no different from the country that surrounded it.

Likewise the descendants of Robert Owen who, obliged to shape their lives according to the circumstances prevailing at New Harmony, became in the process little different from their neighbours. But their first return, in 1833, was to fulfil what they saw as a particular duty, while hoping to establish yet another special way of life.

CHAPTER 15

AFTERGLOW

WHEN Robert Dale Owen paid a brief visit of inspection to New Harmony in 1831 he was shocked by its unkempt appearance; the streets were dirty, the fences broken and gardens overgrown, while the Rappite houses which he confessed he had never found comfortable, now added the infirmities of old age to the defects of their first construction. But more disturbing to him than material signs of decay, was his inability to detect any desire for improvement among its inhabitants, and a hint of what he called 'that aristocratical spirit of class which is so ludicrous, yet so often found in country villages'. He laid the blame for permitting this upon his brother Richard's wife. She was pretty, flighty Martha Chase who had abandoned the doctor to marry the youngest of the Proprietor's sons. As William, the only other brother in residence at the time, was not married, it fell to Martha, as the only Owen lady, to perform those duties of protocol on which Robert Dale set great store.

Martha seldom associated with the villagers, and when she did it was not to their advantage, Robert Dale complained; she had not force of character enough to put down the thousand petty jealousies that hampered uncultivated minds. It was a situation he proposed to remedy by taking a wife himself before he returned, as he knew he must, to settle permanently in New Harmony.

His conscience moved him to this course. William and Richard appeared incapable by themselves of promoting that measure of prosperity which the interest of the people his father had attracted to the town seemed to Robert Dale to demand, while he was himself under a direct obligation to repay the $10,000 advanced by Frances Wright. His only resource in this was the land at Harmony which, beside supporting him, must be made to produce a surplus. He knew that the enterprise would be very hard, but comforted himself with the thought that, living there, he might pursue a literary career while indulging his passion for rearing horses. With a few congenial companions whom he hoped to persuade to join him, Robert Dale envisaged a decent, if frugal, existence on the banks of the Wabash.

With an eye to his forthcoming duties as squire, he devoted much thought to the qualities essential to a chatelaine, and discussed them at length, and intimately, in the correspondence he had been conducting over the past three years with a man he had not yet met. Robert Dale had become acquainted with Nicholas Trist, a grandson-in-law of Thomas Jefferson, and a favourite of the old man, when Trist wrote to express his admiration for the *Free Enquirer*, and his sympathy with its ultra liberal stance. But Trist, who in 1829 became private secretary to the President, Andrew Jackson, could not afford to let Washington know of his connection with the notorious free thinker from New Harmony, and so a friendship by letter was begun, on which Robert Dale came greatly to rely.

He used his letters to Trist to explore his own personality; though he was now over thirty the shortcomings he thought he detected unduly agitated him. The all important question of his marriage, and the education of his children, played a large part in his thoughts, for *his* descendants had to be out of the ordinary and certainly not the product of unreasoning inclination. From London his father had made some kind of suggestion to him that implied he was bound to the mill worker's daughter, Margaret. The outburst this provoked was extraordinary. Robert Dale acknowledged his continuing love for Margaret, but insisted that, while his feelings were engaged, his judgement most certainly was not. 'I fear, I very much fear she is not *perfectly* sincere. You [Robert Owen] will say how could she be so? But *if* she is not so it matters not that we can explain *how* that trait in her character was formed. I cannot trust my happiness for life in the hands of one in whose sincerity I have not perfect confidence.' But in order that the time and effort spent in improving Margaret might not be wasted, Robert Dale suggested that William might take her instead. 'He does not, like me, look for all but perfection in a woman. He has not seen, I know, as much of female intellect as I. His standard is fixed far lower.'

The pattern of female intellect to which Robert Dale referred, of course, was Frances Wright with whom he had sustained a close and affectionate relationship while they were jointly editing the *Free Enquirer*. Though, years later, he declared that he had never been in love with her, his attitude towards her at this time verged upon the proprietary. The bond was strengthened by adversity for, shortly after moving to New York, the paper had captured the dangerously exposed ground in the forefront of a bitterly contested battle to enlarge working men's rights. But at the height of this battle, Frances as General, had deserted, leaving Robert Dale to struggle on alone.

Her first defection occurred in the autumn of 1829 and lasted eight months while she went to the rescue of the Nashoba slaves. Camilla's husband, Richeson Whitby, had proved less than effective in running the establishment on the Wolf River, and Frances was warned that the land was reverting to waste. On hearing this she appealed to Lafayette who, from Paris, sent letters of recommendation to an old political acquaintance, President Boyer of Haiti. It was to his Republic that she proposed to remove her slaves (about 30 of them), thus honouring the undertaking she gave at the outset of the Nashoba enterprise, that she would never free Negroes to live in the United States. The obvious choice to conduct the slaves to Haiti was George Flower whose journey to settle his own Negroes in the black Republic in 1823 had first awakened official interest in the traffic. But he did not come forward; being either unable, or more likely, unwilling to become again involved with Frances Wright.

With characteristic boldness, therefore, she proposed to go herself. Although to reappear at New Orleans en route for Port-au-Prince after her remarks advocating miscegenation was extremely risky, she did not hesitate. But in the emergency she accepted the offer to accompany her of William S. Phiquepal who insisted that his young pupils could print the *Free Enquirer* without his supervision.

Their mission was successful in that the Nashoba slaves were received as citizens in Haiti, and given land on which to settle. When it was completed Phiquepal went directly to France with the intention of fulfilling a long-standing ambition to learn the art of lithography. In May 1830 Frances returned to New York, where she found Robert Dale greatly in need of her support in the forthcoming electoral campaign in which the *Free Enquirer* was vigorously campaigning on behalf of the newly emergent Working Men's Party.

But after only six weeks, during which she resumed her public lectures, Frances again deserted him on the grounds that as she had become the subject of vituperation in the newspapers, her presence would prejudice the workers' chances of gaining votes. She also pleaded that Camilla needed her. She had lost her baby son the previous August and now must have a change of scene. On 1 July the Wright sisters sailed for Europe.

Camilla was indeed desolate. She was the greater loser as a result of the adventures in Tennessee. Her name was more directly linked than her sister's with the scandal over relations between white and black at Nashoba; she suffered more ostracization of their former friends; unlike Frances she was not sustained by work, or borne up on a pleasing tide of notoriety. Only the baby had brought comfort and when it died her grief was extreme. On arriving in France she appears to have gone off by herself. In the winter of 1831 she fell gravely ill, of inflammation of the lungs: on 8 February in Paris, at the age of 34, she died.

Frances wrote to Robert Dale to say that grief at Camilla's death would prevent her expected return to New York. But there was another reason to keep her in France which she did not tell him. She was living with Phiquepal and had a child. What prompted her to this course is a mystery. Phiquepal was 18 years older than she. He was a difficult man, who required patience beyond the endurance of most people; almost a buffoon, he was a figure from whom society withheld the kind of respect Frances's other male acquaintances had effortlessly commanded. As if for that reason their liaison was kept secret for as long as possible. Harriet Garnett only succeeded after strenuous efforts in getting in touch with Frances; she met with a stony response and had to accept that Frances wanted to be left alone. Lafayette too regretfully acknowledged that their former intimacy would not be renewed. When, on her arrival from New Harmony, Marie Fretageot persisted in tracking her down, she was appalled at the disorder and poverty of Frances's lodgings, and by her silence and chilly behaviour. There were rumours that she called herself d'Arusmont, Madame reported to Maclure; that was a name she associated with Phiquepal; could they be married? 'Poor Frances ... better if she had drowned herself', Marie wrote.

On Robert Dale, who had believed himself to be in Frances's perfect confidence, the unexpected news of her connection with Phiquepal had a profound effect. It was in some measure a betrayal of his trust; like Margaret, Frances had proved herself less than sincere. It affected his decision to settle in Indiana. He could not support the expense of the *Free Enquirer* by himself, or carry indefinitely the burden of being sole editor. In these circumstances the steady attendance at the lectures in the Hall of Science in New York, where he deputized for Frances Wright, of a young woman who evidently admired his person as much as his words, was of some solace to Robert Dale.

Her name was Mary Jane Robinson. As he explained to Nicholas Trist, she was the daughter of a moderately wealthy man who had risen from humble circumstances, and was now a generous supporter of the Working Men's Party. Although very young—she was born in 1813 and was almost the same age as Margaret—Mary Jane had given early evidence of a rare determination, application, and a particularly practical turn of mind. At 16, believing that women ought to be capable of following a trade, she apprenticed herself to a mantua maker, and worked until she considered herself proficient. After reading Shelley's *Queen Mab* she turned vegetarian, a course which commended itself to Robert Dale who, under the stress of loneliness and overwork in Frances's absence, had put himself on a diet of milk, bread, barley, and the occasional biscuit.

As it emerges from his letters to Trist, Robert Dale's view of Mary Jane was remarkably detached. He said that he had been careful not to propose to her before he had observed her behaviour with children. Finding this admirably 'rational', he put the question and was immediately accepted, though their acquaintance was very slight. For Mary Jane's part, as soon as she saw Robert Dale, she was said to have declared that she would have him for a husband, or no other. They were married in April 1832, on which occasion Robert Dale drew up a statement protesting against the unjust laws that now gave him rights over the person and property of his wife, and 'morally' renouncing them.

He was frank in his description of his 19-year-old bride, telling Trist that she was a little woman, not pretty, at first sight scarcely interesting looking, without much refinement of manner, with little of European accomplishment, having had few advantages of society, and but an indifferent literary education. Yet, he concluded, there must be something sterling about her to fix his choice. Other men might have been suspected of false modesty in such an account of the woman they had chosen. Proof that Robert Dale was absolutely serious emerges from the fact that these reservations were not concealed from Mary Jane for fear of wounding her, but after their marriage tenderly enumerated as part of the process of educating her for her position as his wife. She acquiesced in this, being unreservedly in love with him, conscious of his greater experience, and a realist. She was also by nature modest.

He was very soon in her debt, for she spoke up stoutly for his *Moral Physiology*, a pamphlet published in 1830, about which he was very much on the defensive. It was the first treatise in favour of birth control to appear in the United States, where the attitude to the practice, then and for many years to come, was prudish and condemnatory. At New Harmony a prospectus for *Every Woman's Book; or, what is love?* by the Englishman, Richard Carlile, one of the first to advocate the practice in that country, had been printed on Owen's press without his consent. Urged to publish the whole work which was known to be in his possession, Robert Dale refused on the perfectly truthful, but somewhat bizarre grounds, that his printers were little boys. Challenged again in

New York, where the *Free Enquirer* advocated birth control as part of the move to emancipate women, he wrote *Moral Physiology* and, against the advice of all his friends, bravely published it. It made no case on neo-Malthusian grounds, but argued for women to be free to enjoy their natural physical desires without fear of the consequences. The argument of the soberly written work seems strange to the modern reader in only one respect—Robert Dale's quaint conviction that in France, which he held up as the most enlightened country, no self-respecting man ever failed to take precautions.

Before they settled permanently in Indiana, Robert Dale took Mary Jane to Europe, partly in search of candidates for the society planned for New Harmony, which Nicholas Trist, whom they had met at last in Washington after their wedding, had agreed to join. It was essential to his sense of well-being to be with good people rather than good-for-nothing people, Robert Dale explained to his wife, 'hence the importance of assembling round myself a few of the choice spirits of the earth'.

He had also to introduce her to what remained of his family. While he had been in New York death had deprived him of his mother, and of two of his three sisters. Great distress had come upon the women of the Owen family after the purchase of Harmony and their departure from Braxfield House. The move occurred some time before the autumn of 1826 when their letters were dated from lodgings in Glasgow. Difficult decisions had to be made—where to look for a suitable permanent residence and which servants might be kept on in their greatly reduced household. Though only in her late forties, Ann Caroline Owen was by then a chronic invalid and most of the responsibility fell to her youngest daughter, Jane. In 1828 the eldest daughter, Anne, succumbed to a nervous affliction that gave rise to bouts of acute delirium, and ended in death. Mrs Owen followed her in 1830, and Mary, the middle daughter, in 1831. She too took leave of her senses before the end.

Mentally and physically exhausted by the long ordeal of nursing them, early in 1832 Jane Dale Owen found herself with no alternative but to join her father in London. He had taken up residence there after his last return from New Harmony in 1829. Their household also included David Dale, the third of his sons who, after a brief sojourn at Harmony and at New York in the heyday of the *Free Enquirer*, had returned to England to continue his studies in science, a subject to which he was passionately devoted.

When in the summer of 1832 Robert Dale and his new wife came to visit Robert Owen in London, they found him caught up in a very

different way of life from that which had been his before the venture to
New Harmony. All connection with the cotton spinning village at New
Lanark was at an end; even Scotland was behind him. Almost against his
will, Robert Owen had been propelled into a more equal association with
members of the working class.

As a result of his various publications and of the New Harmony
experiment—the unfortunate end of which was blamed upon its inhabitants rather than upon its author—Owen's name was honoured as one of
the founders of the co-operative idea. The revelation, by virtue of which
he had claimed attention from the rulers of English society, was now
acknowledged by the people to be his, and he found that the position of
prophet of a powerful new faith was suddenly on offer. He was still
obsessed by the threat of violence, which he feared would arise in a
society divided into opposing factions. On the one hand, there were
workers whose labour produced all wealth; on the other, the non-
producers and administrators who enjoyed it. He expressed these fears in
a penny journal which he began to publish in April 1832 and which he
called *The Crisis*.

He was also furiously busy with a new experiment aimed at reaching a
fairer balance between the work men did, and what they were paid. It was
called the National Equitable Labour Exchange and was an attempt to
reproduce the system tried out at New Harmony, without much success,
whereby the value of goods received would match the amount of labour
performed.

He appealed to Robert Dale to take over the editorship of *The Crisis*
while the Labour Exchange got safely under way. The prospect of an
occupation during the next few months was the more welcome to Robert
Dale since he had determined to send Mary Jane away from him for a
time in order to acquire a European polish to her manners and
appearance. He accompanied her to France and left her with Frances and
Phiquepal who were living at Passy, a suburb of Paris. They had been
formally married the previous year and had another child, a daughter,
Sylva. At Frances's special request they had reverted to the name
d'Arusmont. Though she appeared devoted to her family, Robert Dale
was uneasy when, after so long, he again confronted her. There was a
restlessness about her even in the midst of her domestic preoccupations;
he decided she was still feeling the effect of Camilla's death from which
she might never recover.

Left in Passy while Robert Dale returned to London Mary Jane was
miserable at the separation. Dutifully she set herself to learn French, to

visit places of educational interest, and to watch Frances when she
entertained guests. Patiently she submitted to being 'starched up' into a
special corset designed to correct the fact that she carried one shoulder
higher than the other.

Though often tempted to stay in Europe, in the end Robert Dale
decided that he must not shirk his duty to New Harmony. He was not
convinced that he and Robert Owen could work peacefully together
and he was not in sympathy with the doctrine that was increasingly
referred to by the name of socialism. 'Harmony will suit both you and me
(at least during my father's lifetime) better than London', he wrote to
Mary Jane. 'We can be more independent there and we shall have much
to interest us. The prosperity of the whole country round will in a
measure depend upon our exertion.'

The question was settled when Robert Owen proposed to hand over
all his American property in trust to his four sons. If he ever returned to
Indiana to make another 'experiment' he would require the land back. If
his present enterprise should meet with failure, which according to
Robert Dale he thought 'nearly an impossibility' (but it soon did), he
would ask his sons to send him £300 a year from the estate, a sum that no
English creditor would be able to touch. The creation of the trust was
labelled the noble deed of an affectionate and confiding parent by Robert
Dale, but Mary Jane did not feel so sanguine. In the course of their
correspondence while she was at Passy she had come to know her
husband better. Now she was doubtful whether New Harmony would
content him as a permanent residence for very long. By taste and
education and pride in family, she shrewdly observed, her husband was
unsuited to the circumstances he would have to face in the backwoods of
Indiana.

Mary Jane herself would do her duty but in the summer of 1833, as she
prepared simultaneously for the removal to the Wabash and the birth of
her first child, she foresaw that she might have to undertake a heavier
responsibility than she had anticipated. The hope that she had entertained, of sharing equally in everything that concerned her marriage, was
shattered beyond repair by the fact that, barely a year after their
marriage, she had discovered that he would never return the unqualified
love that she had offered him. In a brave attempt to salvage what she
could of her pride she informed Robert Dale, who had preceded her to
New Harmony, that while she knew they could not be happy, she would
try to be content. 'I have made up my mind to be useful rather than
agreeable to you', she explained.

This bleak frame of mind had been induced by Robert Dale's letters to her while she was in Passy. These began by chiding her for jokes in bad taste, for 'dryness' towards strangers which they took amiss, for unrefined habits, and for a general gaucheness. They went on to represent these imperfections as moral failings which diminished Robert Dale's physical desire for her. Though these were chilling words for a girl of 19 who was not only not pretty, but slightly misshapen, her response was restrained. Gently she tried to make him see how cruel his charge was: 'You have put me, dearest, in a sort of terror of your criticism when I see the effect on your feelings is so serious.'

Worse was to come. Fascinated by the opportunity for introspection which the correspondence seemed to him to afford, Robert Dale recounted the whole episode of Margaret to Mary Jane, making it plain that he was still in love with the mill-worker's daughter. His candour was prompted by the lasting resentment Margaret's behaviour had induced in him, and fostered by a terrifying naïvety. Mary Jane's response was to wonder how Robert Dale supported her at all; 'my person is too little and crooked and I can't "put on" manners'. When they arrived at Harmony, Robert Dale's first care was to survey the resources at his disposal. 'It is a noble estate this, in disorder, neglected ... but capable of becoming as beautiful and valuable a property as any in the whole extent of this great valley. It wants but men—honest, enlightened citizens and those I shall strive to obtain'. So he informed Nicholas Trist when their correspondence was resumed, for Trist could not fulfil his intention of settling at Harmony, having been appointed US Consul at Havana.

The d'Arusmonts did not remove to Indiana either, for Frances feared the effect of the climate on the baby. Robert Dale thought her caution exaggerated; Harmony was not as healthy as many parts of Europe but not nearly so unhealthy as Frances imagined, he told his wife. But on reflection, he doubted whether Frances or Phiquepal would be happy or satisfied at Harmony—'or if they would be *quite* satisfied anywhere'. Frances's character was nearly a noble one, he now remarked, and with proper management would be capable of much. But, in a reference to her marriage, he feared that, situated as she was, she might degenerate into a trifler.

The decisive break in their relationship which had once been so close was brought about by Phiquepal. Shortly after Robert Dale's return to Harmony the Frenchman appeared demanding repayment of the $10,000 Frances had advanced to rescue the Owen brothers from the financial morass created by their father. Phiquepal's manner was peremptory, his action drastic; he threatened to sue. Robert Dale and William had counted on raising a mortgage on the land their father had handed over to them but found they could not because it was in trust. The settlement they were eventually obliged to make with Phiquepal involved the repayment of capital over a period of fifteen years at a swingeing rate of interest.

As for Frances d'Arusmont, the restlessness which Robert Dale detected in her at Passy—the last time he saw her—was a prelude to a great and enduring unhappiness. It soon provoked her into returning to the American lecture halls where she was so much less effective than before that her admirers were dismayed. According to the writer and preacher, Orestes Brownson, who briefly contributed to the *Free Enquirer*, after her marriage to Phiquepal, whom he accused of treating her with great unkindness, Frances's 'charm was broken and her strength departed'.

The separation from her family that Frances's career imposed was very much against Phiquepal's wish. Like her he was obsessively devoted to their daughter whom he wanted to be brought up in France. Sylva became the object of passionate contention between her parents. As she grew older Frances gave way to that inclination to suspect conspiracy where it did not exist which she had already displayed in her youth. Eventually she turned against Phiquepal, accusing him of exploiting the law concerning married women's property in order to deprive her of her money, and of the lands at Nashoba which she still owned. His defence was that her extravagant expenditure on visionary schemes made it imperative for him to salvage something on which to live. In 1850 they were divorced. Though Sylva was sympathetic to her mother, Frances's suspicious, and often overwrought behaviour drove her daughter away. A solitary, somewhat garish, but still defiant figure, Frances came in the end to Cincinnati—'the wreck of what she was in the days when I knew and admired her', Orestes Brownson said. In 1852 at the age of 57 and quite alone, she died. Phiquepal followed in 1855, and Sylva, who inherited Nashoba, went to live in Tennessee.

The non-appearance of the d'Arusmonts and Nicholas Trist at New Harmony meant that the plans Robert Dale had made for a new kind of society beside the Wabash must entirely depend on members of his own family. By 1834 with the arrival from London of Jane and David Dale, the surviving children of Robert Owen had committed themselves to becoming American citizens, and all but Richard who departed for a time after the sudden death of his young wife, Martha, were living in the town.

Life in the huge frame house on the edge of New Harmony more nearly resembled their childhod at New Lanark than anything they had known in the intervening years.

In 1835 Jane Owen whose dark hair, delicate features and volatile temperament betrayed the Celtic origin of the family, married Robert Fauntleroy, a civil engineer who settled in New Harmony. In 1837 at a ceremony referred to ever afterwards as The Triple Wedding, William married Mary Bolton, daughter of one of the members of the Preliminary Society, at the same time as David and Richard (as his second wife) married sisters, the daughters of Joseph Neef. Having been driven away from New Harmony by his passionate opposition to Robert Owen's conduct, Neef was persuaded to return a few years later by the offer of another teaching post. Writing to his father who was living by himself in London, Robert Dale described his new sisters-in-law.

William's wife is the least and the cleverest; Dale's is the most steady and quiet; and Richard's is the loveliest and prettiest . . . They are not what would be called in England accomplished . . . though they all sing; all dance beautifully and two of them play well on the piano; but their manners are good; for the backwoods particularly good.

The ambition Robert Dale cherished of seeing Harmony become a place where literary effort, decorum, and sociability would shine out upon the surrounding darkness depended to a great extent upon the efforts of the ladies of his family, as he freely acknowledged. Writing to Trist he described the atmosphere as it seemed to him to have been changed.

My wife and sister appreciated and seconded my wishes that they should become acquainted with all the more respectable inhabitants and how easy it is when every advance it considered an honor, to exert a powerful beneficial influence. Our ladies associated freely with all who bore a character for integrity and good conduct and the example they set others insensibly followed.

Just over 600 people were living in the town on Robert Dale's return. Beside a number of incoming farmers, the Owens' neighbours included not a few of the original members of the Preliminary Society as well as some who had arrived on board *Philanthropist*. Thomas and Lucy Say were there during the first year, and Lesueur for another four years. The Neefs remained for the rest of their lives, as did Achille Fretageot and others of the boys who had been in Phiquepal's charge in 1826. However anxious Robert Dale was to convey to Trist the pre-eminence of the Owen family in New Harmony, a rival and at least an equal authority occupied the very centre of the town. Anna and Alexander Maclure were living in George Rapp's imposing house from which they supervised the management of their eldest brother's extensive property. Although William Maclure carped at their shortcomings he would not leave Mexico to deal with his own affairs.

Robert Dale made a conscious effort to draw all these people into a new community by means of devices employed in the old. Public dances were begun again and an Institution for Mutual Instruction founded for lectures and debates and public readings. But it was the five young married women of the Owen family, who lived together in the same house, who created the atmosphere of liveliness and warmth for which New Harmony became famous and which was far removed from the stiff formality of Robert Dale. Alexander Maclure gave a hint of what life was like in Harmony in the mid-1830s when writing to his brother William, still in self-imposed exile.

The whole town is agog in getting up the play of William Tell. R. D. Owen is much Interested in it as if the fate of the Republic depended on it and everything is ransacted to find the proper costumes of bygone days. Mrs Owen, Jane and William and all are to take part. Rehearsal has been taking place at the Hall and at R. D. Owen's house for nearly a month past . . . Mr Lesueur has been engaged and is still in Painting some new Scenery for the occasion The people from far and near are coming They are trying to get Mr Neef into the orcastra . . .

Schiller's *William Tell* was translated from the German by Robert Dale. He tried to keep up the habit of unremitting literary effort at New Harmony but found it difficult to bring any of his ideas to fruition. The only one that saw the light in those years was a deeply serious poetical drama, painstakingly researched, on the subject of the Indian Princess Pocahontas.

In the more serious business of getting a living, however, Robert Dale and his brothers were as unskilful as they were unlucky. The annual income from rents at New Harmony habitually fell below the cost of maintenance. The repayments to the D'Arusmonts, and the £300 due annually to Robert Owen, were an unwelcome charge on their slender resources; they had to look about for ready cash. William went on trading in commodities; Robert Dale opened a general store in partnership with his brother-in-law, Robert Fauntleroy. Hoping to sell off land he advertised in English as well as American newspapers inviting settlers to New Harmony. His efforts were largely unsuccessful. As the frontier moved on West the town was caught in a backwater.

The adverse reputation it had acquired during the Community period now in some respects hindered the development of New Harmony. For instance Robert Dale Owen was anxious that a publicly financed school should be established in the town and offered the State land for a site. This was turned down on the grounds that the land in question was encumbered by the Owen trust, an excuse which concealed a general reluctance to co-operate with 'aristocratic' landowners, as both Robert Owen and William Maclure were considered to be. When in 1836 the State embarked upon a planned development of roads, bridges, canals, and other public works, it seemed possible that a waterway might link the Wabash at New Harmony with the Ohio. Robert Dale bought up land along its supposed route and lost heavily when it went elsewhere. It began to dawn upon the citizens of New Harmony that all they would see of profitable schemes would be a demand for taxes which they could ill afford.

It was as a protest against this unfair treatment, and in a bid to help his neighbours, that in 1836 Robert Dale sought the Democratic nomination to the State Legislature at Indianapolis and was elected. The move was to alter the whole direction of his life. For the next seventeen years he was at the disposal of the leaders of his party and away from home at least half the time; political business occupied the winter months and campaigning much of the summer. He went to the Legislature 'by bridle paths, on horseback, fording rivers, occasionally finding a canoe, dumping the saddles in it and swimming the horses behind'.

In 1842 he was elected to the House of Representatives in Washington where he lived a bachelor existence, messing with a small, close knit group of party members; it was not unlike being back at Hofwyl. Mary Jane was left at home to bring up the children and see to the running of the 'estate'.

In all the Owens had six children; two of them died young, the eldest before she was a year old. As her letters show, Mary Jane was oppressed and frightened by the emptiness of the country around New Harmony, but set herself to make the best of things The work was hard. Her daughter, Rosamond, remembered her churning butter at 5 a.m., milking, curing ham, and making all the children's clothes. In bloomers and a sun hat she wheeled a barrow round the vacant lots in the town where she grew vegetables for sale. Her organizing skill made of the crowded Owen family house a community in itself with a rota for domestic tasks and its own school. As long as the Institution for Mutual Instruction lasted Mary Jane gave lectures and took part in debates. She told her children that

Robert Owen's community had failed because the working men refused to labour when they found that all their wants would be provided. Manual work fell to the 'ladies and gentlemen' whose 'mental responsibilities' had in consequence to be neglected.

As to her position as Robert Dale's wife, their daughter, Rosamond, insisted that far from neglecting Mary Jane, as he was accused of doing, Robert Dale relied on her implicitly. 'She often wrote *long* letters to him in which she discussed very wisely political, economic and social problems. She was a very wise woman.'

Though he was even further removed from New Harmony than Robert Dale Owen, William Maclure preserved an influence there that lasted through the 1830s and beyond. His sister and brother, Anna and Alexander Maclure, were liberal and conscientious in giving access to the books and material he had left in their care. Whatever the reservations felt by New Harmony's immediate neighbours as a result of the community experience, scientists were drawn to the town as to a seat of learning.

In 1832 one of the most renowned and scholarly amateurs of the time, Prince Maximilian of Neuwied, spent the winter at New Harmony; he was accompanied by a suite of experts, including a taxidermist and an artist, Karl Bodmer, whose skill rivalled Lesueur's. Prince Max must have had a special interest in the Rappite history of the town since Neuwied was the site of a Moravian colony. He had begun his scientific explorations in Brazil and already had a volume describing its natural history and ethnology to his credit. Now he seized upon Say and Lesueur—'le bon Lesueur'—for companions and delved happily about the countryside. His observations were published at Coblentz in two sumptuously illustrated volumes in 1838–43 as *Reise durch Nord Amerika.*

Perhaps the oddest visitor was C. A. Rafinesque, a wildly disorganized Italian genius. He lived in a magpie's nest of specimens which he dragged half across America ending at Lexington in Kentucky. Rafinesque's passion was to discover new species, a feat which he accomplished to his own satisfaction but the despair of his scientific colleagues because he depended on a system of subdivision so minute as to be almost imperceptible.

The journal kept by the Scottish geologist, Sir Charles Lyell, gives a clear impression of what the town was like when he visited it in 1846.

Some large buildings, in the German style of architecture stand conspicuous ... the principal edifice being now appropriated as a public museum, in which I found a good geological collection, both fossils and minerals ... Lectures on chemistry and geology are given here in the winter. Many families of superior intelligence, English, Swiss, and German have settled in the place and there is a marked simplicity in their manner of living which reminded us of Germany. They are very sociable and there were many private parties, where there was music and dancing, and a public assembly once a week ... where quadrilles and waltzes were danced, the band consisting of amateur musicians.

We found also among the residents, a brother of William Maclure, the geologist, who placed his excellent library and carriage at our disposal. He lends his books freely among the citizens, and they are much read. We were glad to hear many of the recent publications, some of the most expensively illustrated works, discussed and criticized in society here. We were also charmed to meet with many children, happy and merry, yet perfectly obedient; and once more to see what, after the experience of the last two or three months, struck us as a singular phenomenon in the New World, a shy child.

The Institution of Mutual Instruction failed because the townspeople could not afford to go on paying fees. It was replaced by an establishment rather like a Mechanics Institute where working men could go, free of charge, to rest, read, and educate themselves. In the late 1830s William Maclure had taken it under his care. He gave its members, as a meeting-place, a wing of the great second church of the Rappites which stood on his land, and placed an order with a London bookseller for $1,000-worth of books to form the nucleus of their library.

Advancing years had not diminished his desire to bring 'positive knowledge' within the reach of everyone. But the loss of a considerable part of his fortune as a result of his connection with Robert Owen, together with the death of his most trusted assistants, Marie Fretageot and Thomas Say, obliged him to abandon plans to transfer the educational experiment from Indiana to somewhere in Europe. In spite of this Maclure was, on the whole, content in his old age. Mexico suited him; he particularly enjoyed the way the climate and vegetation changed as he went to and from the high plateau. He pondered often and without trepidation the subject of his approaching death. He wanted someone to collect his bones so that his skeleton might be displayed for the edification of students at the Academy at Philadelphia. When at last he did die—in 1840 at the age of 77, just as he was about to make a long delayed visit to New Harmony—the list of his belongings was impressive. They included some 30 buildings at New Harmony and 10,000 acres of land in the vicinity, more than 1,000,000 reals in Spanish securities, a house in Alicante, two convents, 41,000 francs in French securities, notes and mortgages on properties in America and Europe, over 100 boxes of prints and minerals, and nearly 2,000 plates of engravings and illustrations, including those for Michaux's great work on trees, the *Sylva.*

Anna and Alexander Maclure inherited their elder brother's material fortune. His spiritual legacy passed to the third son of his former associate at New Harmony, David Dale Owen, who in his turn developed and passed it on. For though it was through Maclure's example that he devoted his life to geology, it was David Dale Owen himself who became one of the first scholars learned in this new branch of knowledge who put it to practical use on a vast scale. Whether they actually met is not known for David Dale, with his youngest brother, Richard, did not arrive in New Harmony until the spring of 1828 after the break between their father and Maclure. But it is recorded that he was immediately drawn into scientific activities then proceeding; taking over, for example, the regular meteorological observations begun by Gerard Troost.

It was the moment when, at the age of 20, he was poised to choose between two vocations, being endowed with sufficient talent to excel in either. At Hofwyl where he and Richard had followed their older brothers in 1823, he had studied chemistry, and discovered a natural ability for drawing. In 1826 financial problems arising from the purchase of Harmony obliged Robert Owen to remove his sons from school sooner than was intended. They went to join Mrs Owen and her three daughters in the lodgings in Glasgow. There David Dale, Richard, and their sisters took the opportunity to attend the famous lectures at the Andersonian Institute of Dr Andrew Ure who was a pioneer in the application of science to industry, and whose classes for working men had begun in 1809. David Dale's interest kindled; he not only eagerly absorbed scientific knowledge, but observed the way to communicate it simply and effectively.

Yet when he was at Harmony in 1828 and the question arose as to what was to become of him, he expressed a desire to concentrate on painting. He was sharply discouraged by, among others, Frances Wright, who told his father that his abilities ought to be directed to something *useful.*

Necessity reinforced her advice, and on his return to New Harmony in 1834 David Dale cast about for a means to apply his scientific knowledge with a view to making money. He fixed first on a venture into castor oil for which there was a market at New Orleans. When he shortly turned seriously to geology the business was attached to his brother's store.

His passion for scientific enquiry threatened to engulf him. The kitchen of the small Rappite house where he took up residence was rapidly transformed into a laboratory overflowing with bones, rocks, plants, dead animals, and apparatus for his experiments which, always messy, were sometimes positively dangerous. Anna and Alexander Maclure took pity on him and gave him the use of the great stone granary which stood behind the house they occupied. It was so massively constructed that it was sometimes taken as a fort into which the Harmonists intended to retire if attacked by Indians. In fact it was typical of the barns all German settlers raised as the first and most essential building on new land. Now its mortar was crumbling and its walls white with the salt used over the years in pickling pork.

With it the Maclures gave David Dale the use of the scientific instruments their brother William had ordered to be shipped to Harmony in 1826. He found himself master of globes made in France, a balance, weights, and a microscope, an orrery, an adult skeleton complete with brass springs and joints, and 'a small tin house for electrical conflagration'. On moving into the granary David Dale began collecting mineralogical and geological specimens. Alexander Maclure told William that there was no museum or laboratory like it west of the Alleghenies.

He began to fit himself for a professional career as a geologist. It was why he went to medical school at Cincinnati in 1835 where he studied anatomy and physiology the better to understand palaeontology. Back at New Harmony he wrote an *Outline of Geology* which begged its readers to accept that the subject was not one of curious enquiry but of vast practical utility. He soon had an opportunity to prove his ability: in 1837 he was invited to produce a preliminary survey of Indiana. The need for such exact knowledge was only just dawning upon the State and Federal authorities. His report was impressive and illustrated with a series of his own precise and vivid drawings. In 1839 he was appointed principal Government agent to survey land about to be opened to settlement. His task was to find and record mineral resources before trees were felled and the fields laid out.

The area in question measured 11,000 square miles on either side of the Mississippi in Wisconsin and Iowa. Making his headquarters at St Louis, Missouri, David Dale collected $3,000 worth of supplies and camping equipment, engaged 139 sub-agents and their assistants, formed them into 24 working groups and issued these with simple mineralogical tests and skeleton maps. The steamboat which took them to the site was a travelling geological school for hardly any of them had an idea of what they were supposed to do. David Dale's letters home were illustrated with drawings of his men in stove pipe hats and what appear to be their

Sunday suits, perched on wagons or lounging beside camp fires, and full of tales of Indians—not threatening but inquisitive, and puzzled.

In due course David Dale Owen was directed to survey land in Minnesota, Michigan, Arkansas, and Kentucky. The task was immense and physically demanding; it lasted twenty years. It brought work and money to New Harmony which became the Western headquarters of the survey. Besides overhauling wagons and renovating camping equipment, sacks and boxes had to be made to contain the samples of coal, iron and lead ore, and sometimes silver, which were the prizes for which David Dale and his assistants were searching.

The children of New Harmony therefore grew up with the sight of the long procession of wagons and pack mules departing in the spring, returning laden with surprises. As Maclure had always wished, scientific knowledge became an integral part of their lives—and a cheerful one, for there were excursions when the children went hunting for fossils, and picnics on top of Indian mounds. When David Dale moved into the Maclures' old house which Father Rapp had built, its large and graceful rooms were hung with drawings, and an ichthyosaurus stood in the hall. Beside the wonderful array of specimens in the granary museum there were many private collections, some specialized—one house was lined with glass jars containing rats, mice, and every sort of snake. The Workingmen's Institute had a wealth of books and journals, while the loose engravings and prints brought to the town by Maclure for use in the schools were still scattered about.

Like his father and his eldest brother, David Dale Owen was a romantic, and this came out in the design of the new laboratory which was built next to the old one in 1859. It was a small but sturdy castle in the Scots baronial style, with a tower, turrets, arches, and a lantern window; steps and a courtyard. Battlements and an encircling moat were not provided at the time but are there in spirit. The treasure defended then was natural history, celebrated in ornaments like the trilobite carved on the door and the great fish aloft forming the weather vane.

David Dale Owen was a likeable man; modest, unassuming, but as capable as George Rapp and Robert Owen of inspiring other people to see what he saw. In those days doubt had not yet entered into the field of science; it seemed to lead forward to discoveries that would benefit the human race, never disturb or destroy it. This positive, optimistic, and healing concept promoted what was truly called the 'afterglow' in New Harmony. It lasted some twenty years after the collapse of the Owen community and restored a unity of purpose which had not been seen since the departure of the Harmony Society. Building upon foundations laid by William Maclure and his Philadelphia colleagues, David Dale Owen, his family and friends—who were also his neighbours—came as near as possible to the ideal proposed by John Speakman to Thomas Say in 1822. This *was* a secular community of rational beings whose individual interest depended on the prosperity of the whole, who though not rich had a school for themselves and their children, and who had taken a knowledge of nature as their pole star, the grand concept towards which all their exertions were directed.

CHAPTER 16

THE DEBATABLE LAND

As Mary Jane had foreseen, Robert Dale Owen relished his role as a representative of the people, the prestige it commanded being much to his taste. He confessed that he stood out among the plain-speaking farmers who, together with the occasional sharp-witted lawyer, made up the Indiana Legislature. Indeed his education and experience were far in advance of theirs; he had been to one of the best schools in Europe, had mingled with leaders of opinion on both sides of the Atlantic. As Editor of the *Free Enquirer* he had fought the politicians with their own weapons. He was, besides, an asset to his Democratic colleagues when campaigning on the stump, tireless in riding from one small clearing to another, speaking fluently and persuasively. With the memory of his father's discomfiture at the hands of the Parliamentary Select Committee of 1816 always in his mind, he was diligent and particular in getting up the points of whatever case he was called upon to argue. His courtesy and command of procedure made him an ideal chairman of committees.

But as a politician he was a totally different person from the ardent reformer who had lived in the mind of Frances Wright and through her had been associated with many of the most radical thinkers in the United States. His conduct as a legislator was cautious to a fault, and subservient to the orders of his party's leaders. For example, although he privately deplored the unequal position of married women under the law, it was more than a decade before he became involved in any substantial effort to legislate in favour of change. The ardour of the true reformer had waned with the removal of the two most powerful influences upon him—his father and Frances Wright. He was left with the need to tone down his dangerous reputation if he was to survive as a politician, and his opponents were aware of this. Extracts from his leaders in the *Free Enquirer* and—if they were really desperate—from *Moral Physiology*, were used by them in election campaigns.

As the inhabitants of Posey County, Indiana obviously recognized, since they re-elected him, Robert Dale Owen was genuinely concerned to represent their interests. But it was his misfortune that this ambition put him at odds with his former associates, especially over the problem of Negro slavery. Twice before the Civil War Robert Dale opposed the abolitionists, who promptly called him traitor.

His chief preoccupation as a member of the House of Representatives, to which he was elected in 1842, was as a champion of the need for the United States to extend her boundaries to their natural limits; on the west, the Pacific Ocean; to the south, the Rio Grande. This led him to support the annexation of Texas from Mexico, a move which he was naïve enough to believe could take place without provoking war. When it broke out its ferocity appalled him.

In 1844, in pursuit of the same objective he was one of the first Congressmen to urge a change in the status of the Oregon Territory which lay across the northern frontier with Canada. Though its sovereignty was divided between the United States and Great Britain, in practice it had long been a fief of the Hudson's Bay Company. As the question was aired in Congress relations between Washington and London became increasingly strained, until there was a definite risk of hostilities.

It was the moment when Robert Owen chose to appear once more in the Federal capital and, through his son, the Congressman, offer his services as a mediator in the dispute. Dutifully Robert Dale opened doors for his father who, once he was face to face with influential persons, abandoned Oregon in favour of his old obsession—the quadrilangular villages. 'Owen went over the same preamble that I had heard from him 27 years ago in London, which he afterwards crowded upon me year after year here', John Quincy Adams complained, 'and from which I have hoped for the last fifteen years that this country was forever delivered.'

It was fifteen years since Robert Owen had been in the United States and more than ten since he had seen his family. During that time his only constant source of income was the £300 a year his sons sent him from the estate at Harmony; he had been obliged to redeem their promise following the collapse of the Labour Exchange which had involved him in considerable debt. In spite of this the years betwen 1829 when he left Indiana, and 1844 when he returned for a prolonged visit were those of his greatest effectiveness among the English working class.

He became an object of veneration for groups of disciples scattered throughout the industrial towns, who addressed him as their Social Father. He was High Priest of what he now described as the religion of socialism. As he went about the country he preached against the 'crimes' of religion, property, and marriage, and bravely defended himself in the face of hostility and sometimes physical abuse from outraged church-goers. Owen's manner on the platform during these ordeals was unwavering; a small, spare man looking younger than his years, dressed always in black, he spoke quietly if interminably, and was unyielding in the face of questions; reasoned argument altogether failed to break his flow. According to Friedrich Engels who may have encountered him at this period, he was 'of almost sublime and child like simplicity and at the same time one of the few born leaders of men'.

In contrast to his manner, his language was dramatic, marked by the millennial fervour that increased with time. His vision of happiness in another world eventually cut him off from the vast majority of the people who came to hear him. As they became aware of their ability to help themselves, chiliastic dreams which had long comforted—and according to some historians, made docile—the underprivileged, began to fade away. In England, in the late 1830s, and the 1840s, the straight road forward was by means of the political agitation of the Chartists, among whom were some of Owen's most loyal supporters, who regretfully abandoned him when they saw that he was wholly uninterested in their movement. They and their associates chose a road that led to pragmatic socialism, while the Owenites embraced an ethical position that called for the observance of a special way of life.

Owen's dedication to his vision and the need to impress its urgency on others involved him in much hardship as he grew old. He sacrificed comfort, financial security and domestic happiness in a prodigious effort at communication. To put his ideas into practice was still beyond him, as the sole example of a community formed in England according to his system demonstrated. In 1844 that arrogance which had played so large a part in destroying the chances of success beside the Wabash, forced his own disciples to remove him from his position as Governor of Harmony Hall in Hampshire. Begun in 1839, it was plagued by difficulties already experienced at New Harmony—lack of planning, inadequate finance, overcrowding, and as bankruptcy loomed, a serious shortage of provisions. Owen did not wait to see its demise but in the autumn of 1844 departed for America.

The ideas of the eccentric French communitarian philosopher, Charles Fourier, were preoccupying American intellectuals at the time. They were busy forming phalanxes—small groups of 'cultivated' people who retired to the country to live the simple life. Owen claimed that he had taught Fourier all he knew, and visited some of the communities so inspired, among them Hopedale and Brook Farm. As Quincy Adams's comment suggests, he was still soliciting funds for his own model village. According to Hopedale's founder, the former Universalist minister, Adin Ballou, Owen 'flatters himself he shall be able by some means to induce capitalists or perhaps Congress to furnish the capital for this object'. A sum of $1,000,000 was mentioned.

Ralph Waldo Emerson was full of praise for 'the most amiable, sanguine, and candid of men'. According to Emerson, Owen had not the least doubt that he had hit on the plan of right and perfect socialism, or that mankind would adopt it; 'he made the best impression by his rare benevolence . . . and preached his doctrine of labor and reward with the fidelity and devotion of a saint in the slow ears of his generation'.

Emerson decided that Owen and his fellow philosophers overlooked one fact—life.

They treat man as a plastic thing, or something that may be put up or down, ripened or retarded, molded, polished, made into solid or fluid or gas at the will of the leader; . . .
Yet in a day of small, sour, and fierce schemes, one is admonished and cheered by a project of such friendly aims and of such bold and generous proportions; there is an intellectual courage and strength in it which is superior and commanding; it certifies the presence of so much truth in the theory, and in so far is destined to be fact.

Regarding the Oregon affair, Owen behaved as he had done on previous occasions when granted audience by those in positions of power—he read consent to his proposals into the simple fact of their receiving him. He was so far encouraged by the attitude of official Washington that he broke his sojourn in the United States for an urgent return to London. The Foreign Secretary, Lord Aberdeen, received him only to tell him that he brought no information new to Her Majesty's Government. The Prime Minister, Sir Robert Peel, altogether refused to admit him to his presence, stating in a letter that 'no public advantage would arise from Mr Owen's authorized interference'.

Owen was 74 when he returned to England in 1845, but he had thirteen more years to live. During those years numbers of his disciples fell away, though small and devoted groups remained in towns like Birmingham, Manchester, and Stockport. He kept in touch with them, and proclaimed his unvarying message to the world by means of publications whose titles reveal their content. *Robert Owen's Journal, explanatory of the means to well place, well employ, and well educate the Population of the World*; *The Rational Quarterly Review*; *The New Existence of Man upon the Earth*; and lastly, the

Millenial (*sic*) *Gazette*. According to Frank Podmore's biography these no longer recorded the varying fortunes of great Socialist experiments, 'their columns were filled with repetitions of Owen's message in various forms, leading articles, addresses to Government, letters to prominent statesmen and with reports of Owen's previous publications . . . In short his mind was feeding on itself.'

But it had one more turn to take which some writers treat as an aberration it would be kinder to ignore, and which was regarded by his free-thinking disciples at the time as nothing less than apostasy. It was, rather, the natural consequence of everything that went before, and puts beyond doubt Owen's sincerity; his earnest belief that he was a special instrument to bring about the millennium.

Not long after his return from the United States in 1845 Owen, who had been without a settled home for many years, went to live at a hotel near Piccadilly kept by a Mr William Cox. He was treated most kindly there, almost as a member of the family; Cox even took charge of his remittance from New Harmony which was worryingly delayed at times. He doled out small sums in an effort to make it go round. William Cox was one of the first people in England to be caught up in the enthusiasm that originated in the United States for something whose nature—whether science or religion—was as yet undecided. It was at Cox's Hotel, Jermyn Street, that Owen encountered spiritualism. It was presented to him in the form of a famous medium, a Mrs Hayden, a forerunner of the army that was shortly to invade England. His interest was the more readily aroused since she sold him a book on the subject by his friend, Adin Ballou, who was a believer in the supernatural. As Robert Owen interpreted it, spiritualism might have been specially designed to strengthen and encourage his own particular mission.

From the communications which have been made to me through the aid of this American medium, from the father of our present Sovereign [the Duke of Kent] [Thomas] Jefferson, [Benjamin] Franklin, and Grace Fletcher, I am informed that these new manifestations, or revelations, from the spiritual, or more truly the refined material world, are made for the purpose of changing the present false, disunited, and miserable state of human existence, for a true, united, and happy state, to arise from a new universal education, or formation of character, from birth, to be based on truth, and conducted in accordance with the established laws of human nature.

Grace Fletcher had died in 1817 at the age of 21. Though she knew Robert Owen as an acquaintance of her mother, Elizabeth Fletcher, the celebrated bluestocking, hostess, and pillar of the Unitarian Church in

Edinburgh, she had never been a disciple of his, as he claimed. Her family were outraged by his invoking her name and begged him to desist.

He shortly formed a close relationship with a spirit whom he addressed as the Crowned Angel of the Seventh Sphere, with whom he sustained a touchingly courteous dialogue. He struggled to reconcile these new manifestations, which seemed to him to come from God, with his lifelong aversion to established religion, and his own vocation. In particular, he referred to that aspect of Calvinism which had always distressed him, to counter which he had summoned a desperate optimism and clung to it in the face of all reality. 'I would if I could believe in the Atonement of Christ', he told the Crowned Angel,

but without other evidence the whole scheme of the Redemption appears to me inconsistent with the power and other attributes of God, to diminish His wisdom, goodness, and power. Of the character of Jesus Christ and his mission on Earth as a superior medium I have the highest opinion but that he was the son of God it was only as all good spirits, angels are His son. If I am in error regarding the Atonement [he went on politely] I should be most happy to be [corrected?] by means which I can comprehend.

When Robert Owen's children in Indiana learned of these activities they were distressed. Writing to his old friend, Nicholas Trist, Robert Dale remarked,

I regret, as you do, and as every judicious friend must, the strange infatuation that has overtaken my good father. His weak point always was to believe in every body and every thing that favoured, or professed to favour his peculiar views. While on other points his judgement is commonly excellent, on this he has been, all his life, liable to be grossly deceived.

In June 1853 when he wrote this letter, Robert Dale was on the point of leaving New Harmony for Europe where he called on his father at Cox's Hotel. He was on his way to take up the appointment of Chargé d'Affaires at Naples which post had been offered him as a mark of favour for his support of the successful Presidential candidate, and as a consolation for the loss of the prize he most coveted, nomination to the Senate. His acceptance of Naples seemed to many of his former associates as much an offence as his tolerating slavery. It must have enraged Frances d'Arusmont, for the regime to which he was accredited was the most corrupt in Europe. The gilded fantasies of Rapp's old antagonist, the Duke of Württemberg, were as nothing beside the ostentation of Ferdinand II of the Two Sicilies, nicknamed King Bomba.

Robert Dale was not in a position to refuse the offer. Beside the Senate, the House of Representatives was closed to him. He had served two

terms as Congressman and would have liked a third but a rival seized the
party's nomination, pleading Dale Owen's aloofness and favouritism
towards his own family when distributing patronage. He made the best
of it to Trist, describing Naples as 'the very post which of all others, I
desired . . . of all minor posts it is the favourite'. Mary Jane and some of
his children, and their cousins from New Harmony, joined him there
during his term of office which lasted from 1853 to 1858.

King Bomba's brother, Prince Luigi, dabbled in spiritualism and
invited Robert Dale to his seances. These were enlivened by the arrival in
1856, with a party of Polish aristocrats from Florence, of the most famous
and controversial medium of the day—the young, red haired, con-
sumptive genius, the electrifying Daniel Dunglass Home. Robert Dale
Owen was familiar with him because Home's first landfall in Europe
from America was in England, at Cox's Hotel, Jermyn Street. According
to D. D. Home's own account, his mediumistic powers were in abeyance
at the time of his visit to Naples; yet raps and apparitions did not fail to
manifest themselves in Prince Luigi's salon. Home identified the source
as Robert Dale Owen who believed him.

In those days spiritualism was a broad church, embracing phrenology
and mesmerism. As Mrs Townsend had discovered as far back as 1822
when she visited Braxfield House, the entire Owen family was absorbed
in defining character from the shape of people's heads—phrenology was
all the rage. In 1842 at New Harmony, a Doctor Buchanan gave a series of
lectures which Robert Dale attended, that combined phrenology with
some attempt at hypnotism. The demonstration that accompanied the
Doctor's exposition of 'neurology', as he termed his subject, had something in common with a medium's practice, in that emotional reactions
were produced before an audience in a volunteer whose head was
manipulated by the lecturer. These 'experiments' so excited Robert Dale
that he published a glowing account in the local paper of the new field to
be opened by the science of neurology.

Though he represented himself as keeping an open mind about the
meaning and possible effect of spiritualism, privately he acknowledged
that he had experienced a revelation; at last the call had come for him to
serve mankind. Henceforth it would be his duty to seek out and soberly
evaluate psychic phenomena. He shortly had an opportunity to confide
in his father. Towards the end of 1856 Robert Owen wrote to his eldest
son, asking him as Trustee of his grandfather's estate in Scotland, to
advance him £500, either as a gift or a loan. The elder Owen wanted this
to finance the publication of his autobiography, *The Life of Robert Owen*

written by Himself, and also to enable him to commission a diorama of his ideal village.

Robert Dale's answer gave compelling reasons as to why he must refuse to sanction payment from the Dale Trust. He was shortly to be replaced at Naples and since he proposed to devote himself to spiritualism he suspected that his political career was altogether at an end. His own income from New Harmony was no more than £200 a year, while his brothers and sister there existed on half that amount. If it was a question of their father's health and comfort none of them would hesitate to contribute. But it was not. It was to gratify the old obsession which Robert Dale now examined in the light of his own new purpose, and rejected. If his researches into spiritualism convinced him of its reality, Robert Dale told his father, he expected much more prompt and radical changes in the moral and social condition of mankind from its dissemination, in a rational form, than from Robert Owen's other means of social progress. 'I think that society has already received, chiefly through your own exertions, as much or even more of the doctrine of socialism than it can be made, at present, to understand, or it is at all prepared to adopt.' To give the public the means of communicating with another world, Robert Dale wrote, was a purpose 'as benevolent as that which prompted my grandfather [David Dale] to devote thousands to charitable objects and you to spend thousands more to combat error and establish truth'.

The money had, however, to be paid. It was found that Robert Owen had committed himself too far for the *Life* to be abandoned. He would end in prison, he said, if the debt to the printer was not discharged. He was continually paying out money he could not afford so that his message might be put before the people as often and in as many forms as possible. He was extremely old, weak, and knowingly near death but entirely undaunted. His behaviour disturbed his children who, far removed from him in the United States, could not hope to restrain what they regarded as his irresponsibility. In October 1858, aged 87, and with failing sight, he embarked upon a last adventure.

The National Assocation for the Promotion of Social Science was holding its annual meeting at Liverpool. Owen was determined to address it, and so he did, though on the day he took two hours to be dressed and was carried to the hall in a sedan chair. His old friend, Lord Brougham, was presiding. He made it possible for Owen to begin his speech which followed the familiar theme. When the old man faltered, Brougham, with a tact and skill that was long remembered, brought the proceedings to an end, congratulated Owen, and had him gently removed to his hotel where he became unconscious.

After two weeks he surprisingly recovered. Instinct, a quality which he had deliberately excluded from his own ideal system, took control of him, mind and body, so that he was inspired to undertake a long and arduous journey. By train and coach he travelled to the place where he had been born in the previous century and which he had not seen for nearly eighty years—Newtown in mid-Wales.

The name he gave at the Bear Hotel was fictitious, but the townspeople soon realized that the sick old man issuing invitations for the Magistrates and other civic leaders to call on him to discuss 'arrangements' that would make Newtown the happiest place on earth, was none other than Robert Owen. His eldest son, who was already in London, was sent for because those who watched by him were anxious lest he should die with only strangers to attend him, though as one of them said, 'everybody was kind to him and he was kind to everybody'. On 17 November 1858, in the presence of Robert Dale, he died; his last words being 'Relief has come.'

He was given a Christian burial, a fact which outraged the freethinkers among his remaining supporters. In defence of this the Rector of Newtown, The Revd John Edward, who performed the service, explained that he had been unaware of Owen's anti-sectarian views, never having read a syllable of his writings. From what Owen said in his presence before he died, the Rector judged him to be 'in religion a pantheist rather than a sceptic, an innovator in the constitution of society rather than a disbeliever in God'. According to Mr Edward, Owen expected the Second Coming.

Salvation also beckoned to Robert Dale Owen, who through spiritualism had returned to belief in a Christian God. His passionate desire to become as much of a leader and benefactor of mankind as his father seemed to him to be, was doomed to bitter disappointment.

But things went well at first. After winding up his father's affairs in England Robert Dale returned to New Harmony with members of his family. Once again Mary Jane was called upon to support him in a course which, though less controversial than the views he had expressed in *Moral Physiology*, he knew would attract ridicule. It would lessen the respect of him for some of his friends, he told her, and alienate others. Nevertheless it was his duty. He saw the force he was investigating as nothing less than a lever to promote the moral advancement of mankind. 'The grade of belief in immortality and another world is too feeble in the minds of the masses seriously to influence their conduct or determine their actions. They want a more living belief than they can daily realize.'

Mary Jane adopted her husband's faith, as did their daughter Rosamond, and some of her Owen cousins, the children of William Owen and Jane Fauntleroy who had accompanied them to Europe. The special nature of the town in which they lived was thereby prolonged; as Harmony had been in the beginning it remained, a watchtower on the frontier of what Robert Dale Owen, in one of his books about spiritualism, called the Debatable Land, between this world and the next.

Though he went to some trouble publicly to stress the scientific nature of his interest in the subject, spiritualism did not appeal to the scientific member of the family, David Dale Owen. He and his younger brother, Richard, remained loyal to the Independent faith of their grandfather which their mother had taught them. But David Dale had little time to ponder the change that came over Harmony after his family's return from Europe, or to enjoy his fine new laboratory. He died in 1860 when he was only 52. In the opinion of his friends he committed suicide by overwork. His second brother predeceased him by many years. Life, which was not conspicuously fair to William Owen, was also short. He died in 1842 after a long illness and when he was not quite forty. Richard lived on until 1890 dying as a result of a bizarre but appropriate accident, given the special nature of Harmony; calling for a drink of water he was handed embalming fluid by mistake and died in agony.

With the outbreak of the Civil War in 1860 there was an upsurge of interest and belief in spiritualism. By then Robert Dale Owen had published his first book on the subject, *Footfalls on the Boundary of Another World*. It was widely read and respected for its scholarly research, and made him one of the leading authorities in that field.

At the same time he received much public attention as a result of a letter he addressed to the President, Abraham Lincoln. His motive for writing it was the same as that which permitted him to undertake special war work—buying arms for the northern forces. Robert Dale was shocked into the belief that everything possible must be done to save the Union which the war between North and South threatened to destroy. He therefore set aside his misgivings on the subject of Negro slavery and, though he never went so far as to advocate civil rights, urged Lincoln to set all of them free immediately. The letter which was released to the newspapers at the same time as he wrote it, came days before the Emancipation Proclamation and earned him a place in history.

Once the Civil War was over Robert Dale became immersed in spiritualism again. He passed the time corresponding with like minded people, investigating incidents and writing books and articles. After the death of Mary Jane in 1871, from fever at New Harmony, he was less frequently there though he continued to depend on the slender income from the land. In spite of fees from literary work he was mysteriously short of money.

In 1874 disaster overtook him. He had been commissioned to write a series of articles for the *Atlantic Monthly*, one of which contained an unequivocal endorsement of the celebrated medium, Katie King. Doubts had been expressed about her authenticity. Robert Dale attended one of her seances and stated that he was satisfied she could not have faked what he saw, it was a physical impossibility. 'Therefore Katie, not being an inhabitant of this world, was a denizen of another, made visible to us, for the time, by some process which has been called materialization', he wrote. But as the article went to press he received irrefutable evidence that she was a fraud. It was too late to revise his statement and he publicly admitted that he had been deceived.

Spiritualists were devastated, while unbelievers mocked. Robert Dale fell ill and into a delirium. His family always maintained that he had been attacked by a chill brought on by overwork; they had him temporarily confined in a lunatic asylum.

He gave way there to ideas that were rooted in the past, that had disturbed him long before he became involved with spiritualism, or had even seen New Harmony. In the words of George Jacob Holyoake, the English freethinker who was for a time close to Robert Owen, and was well acquainted with Robert Dale, his delusions had nothing to do with the reason why he was chronically short of money—his habit of presenting gold rings to female spirits. His mind had gone back to his Scottish childhood and the lineage of which he was so proud. 'Towards the end of his days he fancied himself the Marquis [*sic*] of Breadalbane, and proposed coming over to Scotland to take possession of his estates', Holyoake said. 'He had a great scheme for recasting the art of war by raising armies of gentlemen only, and proposed himself to go to the then raging East and settle things there on a very superior plan. He believed himself in possession of extraordinary powers of riding and fighting.' He was from his youth upward, a man of absolute moral courage, Holyoake said; a lesser person would have kept quiet about Katie King in the hope the public would forget.

He never recovered from the shock. He died in 1877 and the obituaries agreed with Holyoake. That in politics Robert Dale Owen was not so much a force as an ornament, and he never fulfilled the promise of his youth by becoming a leader of men.

THE EYE OF FAITH

THREE times imagination or, as Father Rapp described it, the 'eye of hope' created settlements out of nothing in the forest. Of these only the second, Harmony on the Wabash, experienced change when the Rappites gave way to new people and new ideas. At Economy in Pennsylvania, the last town that they built, long after their first leaders had disappeared, faith preserved an attitude, as if in amber.

The special nature of the Society's government exhausted Frederick Rapp. In 1834, after suffering from a long-standing chest infection, he died, though only 60. The obituary in *Nile's Register* remarked: 'He was a very strong minded and intelligent man, and we believe a most scrupulously honest one. he was the chief actor or agent for the Harmonists, whose peculiar habits have been often described and to whom his loss will, probably, be irreparable.'

It was nothing of the sort. At the age of 77 George Rapp assumed the temporal as well as the spiritual power, appointing agents to act as he desired. He avoided death for 13 years until he was 90 in 1847, and seemed surprised at its approach. As one of the elders who watched by him reported, 'Father Rapp's strong faith in the literal fulfilment of the promise concerning the personal coming of Jesus Christ, and the gathering of the whole of Israel, remained unshaken to his last moments, as was shown by his last words, when he felt the strong grip of the hand of approaching death, saying, "If I did not so fully believe that the Lord has designed me to place our society before his presence in the land of Canaan I would consider this my last."

In 1874 his successors as leaders of the Harmony Society sent Jonathan Lenz to wind up their connection with the town beside the Wabash. He bought the huge church which had not been finished at their departure in 1824, had all but the east wing pulled down, and gave it and the land to the town. The bricks from the part that was demolished were used to build a wall around the open grassy space where more than 200 of the Rappites lie in unmarked graves. The cemetery is there today, on the edge of town, not far from the river, on slightly elevated ground. The Wabash flows low down between its banks, hidden from sight behind a fringe of trees. It is not much visited and gives passage only to an occasional shallow-bottomed boat. It is not forgotten; it represents a threat to Harmony. If a levee is not built, one day it may flood and obliterate the town.

ABBREVIATIONS

APS   American Philosophical Society
BL   British Library
Co-op Union   Library of the Co-operative Union, Manchester
NHWI   New Harmony Workingmen's Institute

NOTES

1. A Place Prepared by God

Page 6. Pietism. Drummond, A. L., *German Protestantism since Luther*, p. 79. Pinson, K. S., *Pietism as a factor in the rise of German nationalism*, pp. 13 ff.

Page 6. the village of Iptingen. Arndt, K. J. R., George Rapp's Harmony Society, 1785–1847, p.i ff.

Page 6. Karl Eugen. Fauchier-Mangan, A., *Les petites cours d'Allemagne au 18ième siècle*, p. 200.

Page 7. the Duke was condemned. Kabale und Liebe, II ii.

Page 7. belief fled from the cold church. Leibbrandt, G. *Die Auswanderung aus Schwaben nach Russland*, p. 29.

Page 7. 'I surrendered my will'. Arndt., op. cit., p. 18–19.

Page 8. 'Philosophy had come'. Williams, Aaron, *The Harmony Society at Economy, Pennsylvania*, p. 11.

Page 9. 'of all the preachers they heard'. Ibid., p. 38.

Page 9. Rapp's answers on this occasion. Arndt, op. cit., p. 24.

Page 10. 'I am a prophet'. Ibid., p. 30.

Page 10. Boehme's inspiration. Drummond, op. cit., p. 53.

Page 10. Boehme's book describing Eden. Aurora, oder die Morgenröte im Aufgang.

Page 11. a belief traditional in Swabia. Leibbrandt, op. cit., p. 54.

Page 11. 'der Räpple'. Römer, C., *Kirchliche Geschichte Württembergs*, p. 519.

Page 12. Rapp warned not to preach. Arndt, op. cit., p. 49.

Page 12. Hard work and fruitful harvests. Ibid., p. 48.

Page 13. Frederick Rapp's letters. Arndt, K. J. R., *Harmony on the Connoquenessing*. This is part of an as yet unfinished series giving an English version of thousands of documents from the Harmony Society's archive. They are being transcribed, translated and published by Professor Arndt who has spent a lifetime deciphering the old German script and Swabian dialect in which most of them are written. The present narrative draws heavily on his work; references are to his translation.

Page 13. he wrote to Napoleon. Arndt, George Rapp's Harmony Society, p. 458.

Page 13. millennialists' attitude. Leibbrandt, op. cit., p. 60.

Page 15. Count Zinzendorf. Gollin, G. L., *Moravians in Two Worlds*, pp. 10 ff.

Page 15. Jefferson wrote to Gallatin. Arndt, G. R.'s Harmony Society, p. 65.

Page 16. 'with all my strength I wrestled'. Arndt, Harmony on the Connoquenessing, p. 8.

Page 16. the petition to Congress. Arndt, G. R.'s Harmony Society, p. 84.

Page 16. *a hostile observer.* Sealsfield, C., *The Americans as They Are*, p. 60.

Page 17. *the articles of the Harmony Society.* Arndt, *G. R.'s Harmony Society*, p. 72.

Page 18. *Heckewelder's description of the Wabash.* Sprengel, M. C., ed., *Reisejournal ... von Bethlehem in Pensilvanien, nach dem Posten St. Vincent am Wabashfluss.*

Page 18. *the death of Johannes.* Williams. op. cit., p. 31.

Page 19. *'The* Harmonie *will cast out filth'.* Arndt, *G. R.'s Harmony Society*, p. 102.

Page 19. *Melish's book.* Melish, J., *Travels in the United States of America in the years 1806, 7, 9, 10 and 11.*

Page 21. *description of* Harmonie. Ibid., p. 64–83.

2. Western Waters

Page 23. *their enemies.* e.g. Jacob Schick. See Arndt, *A Documentary History of the Indiana Decade of the Harmony Society 1814-1824*, ii, p. 224–6.

Page 24. *a premonition about the Wabash.* Ibid., i, p. 2.

Page 24. *the opinion of seasoned travellers.* e.g. Volney, C. F., *Tableau du sol et du climat des États-Unis*, p. 366; Michaux, A., in Thwaites, R. G., *Early Western Travels*, iii, p. 67.

Page 24. *their trunks like towers.* Ibid., xii, p. 213.

Page 24. *Description of Vincennes.* Volney, op. cit., p. 368–75.

Page 24. *Rapp buys land.* Arndt, *Indiana Decade*, i, p. 7.

Page 25. *vapour rising from the rivers.* Volney, op. cit.

Page 25. *Frederick to get a steam engine.* Arndt, *Indiana Decade*, i, p. 77.

Page 27. *'the torment of doing business'.* Andressohn, J., 'Twenty Additional Rappite Documents', J. L. Baker to Frederick Rapp, 7 July 1813, in *Indiana Magazine of History*, No. 44, 1948.

Page 27. *Frederick's demands.* Arndt, *Indiana Decade*, vol. i, p. 27. Note: The Langenbacher family was known as Baker or Becker in the US.

Page 28. *overgrown with nettles.* Ibid., p. 18; Flower, G., *History of the English Settlement in Edwards County, Illinois*, p. 61.

Page 29. *'I must learn more than ever before'.* Arndt, *Indiana Decade*, p. 77.

Page 31. *they paid in ... skins of animals.* Woods, J., 'Two Years Residence in the Settlement on English Prairie', in Thwaites, op. cit., p. 210.

Page 31. *'settlers all precautious now.'* Arndt, *Indiana Decade*, p. 131.

Page 32. *Frederick's journey down the Ohio.* Ibid., p. 85.

Page 32. *sale of old* Harmonie. Ibid., p. 226, 127–n.

Page 32. *'to make fertile fields and gardens'.* Ibid., p. 171.

Page 33. *'the Sound should not only be solemn'.* Arndt, *Indiana Decade*, i, p. 391.

Page 34. *description of* Harmonie. in Lindley, H., *Indiana as seen by early Travelers*, accounts by Hulme, Hebert, and others.

Page 33. *'it is surely a joy to be here'.* Ibid., p. 109.

Page 33. *the 1820 census.* Hopple, D. A., *New Harmony and the 1820 Census.*

Page 34. *style of building at* Harmonie. Blair D., 'Harmonist Construction' in *Indiana Historical Publications*, Vol. 23. 1964.

Page 34. *an ancient and mysterious air.* Schneck, J., *The Rappites.*

Page 35. *'Error, superstition and religious mania'.* Arndt, *Indiana Decade*, ii, p. 224.

Page 35. *the exodus due to religious* 'schwärmerei'. Leibbrandt., op. cit., p. 88.

Page 36. *room for 100 families.* Arndt, *Indiana Decade*, ii, p. 237.

Page 36. *Rapp's sister writing from Iptingen.* Ibid., p. 356.

Page 37. *the Americans to break them.* Ibid., p. 708.

Page 37. *trading conditions difficult.* e.g. Ibid., i, p. 696–8.

Page 37. *a secret hoard.* Arndt, George Rapp's Harmony Society, p. 574–6.

Page 38. *150 people seen reaping a field.* Lindley, op. cit., p. 515.

Page 38. *withheld access to water mill.* Arndt, *Indiana Decade*, ii, p. 294, 413–14, 440–1.

Page 38. *'even quakers talk like soldiers'* Fordham, E. P., *Personal Narrative*, p. 171.

Page 38. *the militia officers confused.* Arndt, *Indiana Decade*, ii, p. 446.

Page 38. *a suspicion that Rapp influenced the vote.* Ibid., p. 440.

3. A Call to Cancel Domesday Book

Page 40. *The* Philanthropist *published.* No. XX (1815).

Page 40. *they had joined a new joint stock company.* BL, Place Papers, Add. 35, 153, fo. 68 n. For transferable shares see, Ibid., Bentham Papers; Add. 33, 546. fo. 237.

Page 40. *William Allen.* Ibid., Add. 35, 152, fo. 15; Gilpin, C., *The Life of William Allen*, pp. 180, 182, 208.

Page 40. *Allen relied on Mill.* BL, Place Papers; Add. 35, 152, fo. 15.

Page 41. *Allen and Bentham took shares in New Lanark.* Ibid., Add. 35, 153. fo. 68, and see Owen, Robert, *The New Existence of Man upon the Earth*, Pt V, Allen to Owen. 8 Jan. 1814.

Page 41. *Robert Owen's career.* See, for example, Podmore, F., *Robert Owen*, Cole, G. D. H., *The Life of Robert Owen.*

Page 41. *Dale's alleged neglect of the New Lanark work people.* Owen, Robert, *A New View of Society: or, Essays on the Principle of the Formation of Human Character, and the Application of the Principle to Practice.* For doubts expressed at the time on the validity of Owen's claims about improvements see the *Examiner*, 4 Aug. and 1 Sept. 1816, and BL, Place Papers, Add. 35, 152. fo. 214.

Page 41. *'a systematic plan'* Sidmouth Papers, Robert Owen to Viscount Sidmouth, 1 Sept. 1813.

Page 41. *he kept Sidmouth constantly informed.* BL, Lieven Papers, Add. 47, 277, fo. 52.

Page 41. believing himself to have been specially chosen. See, for example, Sidmouth Papers,'Lady Sidmouth's Tour of Scotland'; Mrs Mary Townsend to Lord Sidmouth, 12 and 13 Oct. 1821.

Page 41. the name of Harmonie *before the public.* The Times, 9 Apr. and 29 May 1817.

Page 42. Birkbeck's career. Flower, op. cit., pp. 20 ff. Thomson, G. S., *A Pioneer Family* (The Birkbecks).

Page 42. Imlay's description of the prairies. Imlay, Gilbert, *A Topographical Description of the Western Territory of North America*, 1792.

Page 43. 'tall and pale like vegetables'. Birkbeck, Morris, *Notes on a Journey from the Coast of Virginia to the Territory of Illinois*, 4th edn., p. 116.

Page 43. concentration of capital. Ibid., pp. 130 ff.

Page 43. Birkbeck's plans for settlers on the prairie. Ibid., p. 134. Library of Congress, Madison Papers, Birkbeck to Madison, 18 Sept. 1817.

Page 43. comment by the Edinburgh Review. *Edinburgh Review*, June–Sept. 1818, vol. xxx.

Page 44. Cobbett's denunciation. Cobbett's Weekly Political Register, 6 and 13 Feb. 1819, 7 July 1821.

Page 44. Cobbett's opinion of the Rappites. Ibid., 6 Feb. 1819.

Page 45. 'the utopian and visionary schemes!' Evans, Thomas, *Christian Policy in Full Practice among the people of Harmony . . . by a Spencean Philanthropist*, p. 15.

Page 45. English letters and journals describe Harmonie. See, for example, John Woods, in Thwaites, op. cit., x, p. 210; Hebert, William, 'A Visit to the Colony of Harmony, in Indiana, in the United States of America', in Lindley, op. cit.; Blaney, William Newnham, 'An Excursion through the United States and Canada', Ibid.; Hulme, Thomas, 'Journal of a Tour in the Western Countries of America', in Thwaites. op. cit., vol. x.

Page 45. George Courtauld's career. Coleman, D. C., *Courtauld's An Economic and Social History*, pp. 33, 42, 51 ff. Courtauld, Stephen, *The Huguenot Family of Courtauld.*

Page 46. 'the dissolution should be provided for'. Courtauld, George, *Address to those who may be disposed to remove to the United States of America. On the advantages of Equitable Associations of capital and labour in the formation of Agricultural Establishments in the interior country*, 1820, pp. 22 ff.

Page 46. Rapp a true religious leader. Flower, op. cit., p. 283.

Page 46. 'reserve . . . induces . . . suspicions'. George Courtauld, op. cit., p. 18.

Page 46. took the pamphlet to Robert Owen. Stephen Courtauld. op. cit., ii, p. 139.

Page 46. the other shareholders remonstrated. Gilpin, op. cit., i, p. 244.

Page 47. Owen's plan which he discussed with Place. BL, Place Papers, Add. 35, 152, fo. 222.

Page 47. 'by way of punishment for infringement of the rules' Reports, Committees, vi, 1823, *Select Committee on the Employment of the Poor in Ireland*, Owen's evidence, p. 90.

Page 48. '*the eye of the community*'. Ibid., p. 94.

Page 48. Harmonie *beautifully laid out.* George Courtauld, op. cit., p. 11.

Page 48. *Courtauld's account republished.* In, for example, *Glasgow Journal*, 3 Nov. 1819.

Page 48. *His latest piece of propaganda.* Owen, Robert, *Three Letters to David Ricardo.*

Page 48. '*the Society at Indiana . . . is . . . increasing in wealth*'. Ibid., p. 30.

Page 49. '*innumerable communities of paupers*'. *Political Register*, 2 Aug. 1817.

Page 49. '*let us alone Mr Owen*'. Hone's *Reformist Register*, 23 and 30 Aug. 1817.

Page 49. *Wooler accused the government.* *Black Dwarf*, 20 Aug. 1817.

Page 50. *Vansittart ready to ask for £20,000.* *The Economist*, No. 14, p. 220.

Page 50. *Owen indulged in the discounting of bills.* Brotherton Library, Leeds, John Marshall's Tour Book, 26 Sept. 1807.

Page 50. *Place, who kept a watching brief on Owen.* BL,Add. 27,791, fo. 262: 'A detailed account of the proceedings of Mr Owen would be as curious as useful. It would form a remarkable item in an account of the manners and customs of the people. I may perhaps someday set about such a work.'

Page 50. '*his villages would answer as a mere mercantile speculation*'. Place Papers, Add. 35, 153. fo. 68, Place to Hodgskin, 9 Sept. 1819.

Page 50. *Owen writes to George Rapp.* Flower, op. cit., p. 372-3.

Page 52. *two emissaries sent home.* Arndt, *Indiana Decade*, pp. 340, 347,352.

Page 52. *the book of record burnt.* Arndt, *George Rapp's Harmony Society*, p. 491.

Page 53. *the court case went against them.* Arndt, *Indiana Decade*, ii, p. 119.

Page 53. *They could not expect justice from local people.* Arndt, *Harmony on the Wabash in Transition*, pp. 647, 701.

Page 53. *prospectus for the sale of* Harmonie. Arndt, *Indiana Decade*, ii, p. 871.

Page 54. *Richard Flower at New Lanark.* White, M., ed.,*A Sketch of Chester Harding, Artist*, p. 87.

Page 54. '*the famous Mr Owen*'. Arndt, *Harmony on the Wabash in Transition*, p. 262.

Page 55. *John Quincy Adams's view of Robert Owen.* Adams, C. F., ed., *Memoirs of John Quincy Adams*, iii, pp. 551-2; xii, pp. 116, 117.

Page 55. *Peter Drinkwater's Reputation.* Chaloner, W. H., 'Robert Owen, Peter Drinkwater and the early factory system in Manchester' in *Bulletin of the John Rylands Library*. No. 37, (Sept. 1954).

4. 'A speculative, scheming, mischievous man...'

Page 59. 'Here was a village ready built'. Owen, R. D., *Threading My Way*, p. 210.

Page 59. the price was less than one third. Podmore, op. cit., p. 220.

Page 59. The Rappites' income. Owen, R. D., op. cit., p. 211.

Page 59. 'the share will be saleable'. National Library of Wales, Galpin corr., Hamilton to Owen, 5 Dec. 1820.

Page 60. Owen disapproved of emigration. Owen, R., *Three Letters to David Ricardo*, p. 10.

Page 60. an outlet for the working people. e.g. BL, Place Papers, Add. 37, 949, fo. 64. 35, 153, fo. 68.

Page 60. the Combination Acts to be repealed. Hansard, New Series, vol. 11, col. 811, 21 May 1824.

Page 60. 'the present proprietors'. Marshall, op. cit., 26 Sept. 1800.

Page 60. Independents strong at New Lanark. Ibid., Macnab, H. G., *The New Views of Mr Owen of Lanark Impartially Examined*, p. 135.

Page 60. Universal vice and drunkenness. Compare Henry Houldsworth's opinion of the Scots work people. His experience resembled that of Owen in that he ran a cotton mill in Manchester before moving to Glasgow in 1800. According to Houldsworth, 'we had, when I first went to Scotland a decent, respectable sober set of Scotchmen who, although not very industrious, or anxious to make great exertions, were superior to the class of people we have now'. *Select Committee on Artizans and Machinery*, v (1824), p. 385.

Page 61. Owen compared himself to Crusoe. Revue Encyclopédique, Owen interview with Jullien de Paris, Oct. 1822.

Page 61. 'the contest of myself against the world.' Columbia University, Cuba Papers, Robert Owen to R. D. Owen, Dec. 1856.

Page 61. a prospectus for the sale of the mills. SRO, Campbell of Jura Papers, Robert Owen to John Campbell, 8 Oct. 1812. See also *A Statement regarding the New Lanark Establishment*, John Moir, Edinburgh, 1812.

Page 61. Southey found the hill steep. Southey, R., *Journal of a Tour in Scotland*, 1819, p. 260.

Page 61. barricaded against trespassers. e.g. SRO, UP Innes Mack, CS 235 L 14/9, *Lanark Twist Co.* v. *Edmonston*, 1810.

Page 62. 'nice and valuable machinery'. Owen, R., *A Statement*, p. 20.

Page 62. the work people's evidence. Select Committee on the State of Children employed in the Manufactories of the UK, 1816, p. 167; Factories Enquiry Commission 1833, First Report, A.1., pp. 74, 96.

Page 63. Owen's autobiography, Owen, R., *The Life of Robert Owen written by Himself* [referred to below as *Life*].

Page 63. 'the most revolting system'. Pears, T. C., ed., *New Harmony An Adventure in Happiness*, p. 51.

Page 63. Brought up in Calvinism. Author's note: When Owen was born at Newtown in mid-Wales in 1771, Calvinistic Methodism had already made its appearance and was distinct from the faith that Whitefield and Wesley were preaching in England. According to *Life*, p. 3, the attempt by Methodists to convert Owen when he was eight or nine marked the beginning of his alienation from sectarian religion.

Page 63. 'thus was I forced'. Owen, R., *Life*, p. 17.

Page 63. Prompted him to intervene disastrously. In, for example, the campaign for a Ten Hours Bill. See Ward, J. T., 'Owen as Factory Reformer', in Butt, J., ed., *Robert Owen Prince of Cotton Spinners*, pp. 99–131.

Page 64. 'He had a vacant place in his mind'. Thompson, E. P., *The Making of the English Working Class*, p. 783.

Page 64. Owen dismissed as Manager. Signet Library, Edinburgh, Session Papers, 631: 17, Robert Owen's petition, 29 June 1815.

Page 64. affronted by Owen's financial activities. Robertson, A. J., 'Robert Owen and the Campbell Debt 1810–1822', in *Business History*, xi, No. 1 1969. SRO, Jura Papers: 'Memorial and queries for opinion of counsel for Archibald Campbell of Jura 2 Dec. 1816'. Butt, op. cit., 'Robert Owen as a Business man'.

Page 64. 'new arrangements' at the mills. SRO, GD 64/1/247, Owen to Jura, 29 July 1812, and Alex. Campbell of Hallyards to John Campbell 116, 17 Aug. 1812.

Page 64. Mrs Owen borrowed money. Signet Library Session Papers 631: 17, R. Humphreys' evidence.

Page 64. Stuart's dinner party. Bodleian Library, Abinger Papers, William Godwin's diary, 8 Jan. 1813.

Page 64. Godwin took Owen. Ibid., e.g. Jan.–May 1813, Apr.–May 1814.

Page 64. Hazlitt pounced. Hazlitt, W., *Works*, p. 121.

Page 65. Place and Mill edited the Essays. BL, Place Papers, Add. 27, 791, fo. 262; Add. 35, 152, fo. 218.

Page 65. 'he nodded to me'. Ibid., Add. 35, 153. fo. 14.

Page 65. 'all my respect for Owen'. Ibid., Add. 37, 949, fo. 50.

Page 65. 'now I have to complain' Ibid., Add. 35, 152, fo. 218.

Page 66. the silent monitor. Owen, R., *Life*, pp. 80, 136.

Page 66. military police. Macnab, op. cit., p. 126.

Page 66. a curfew and random searches. Brown, J., *Remarks on the plans and publications of Robert Owen Esq. of New Lanark*, 1817, pp. 43 ff. See also Owen, R., *The New Existence of Man upon the Earth*, Pt. V, 'Original Regulations and Rules for the inhabitants of New Lanark made by Robert Owen in 1800'.

Page 66. 'the most barefaced and impudent thing'. BL, Place Papers, Add. 37, 949, fo. 50.

Page 67. great excitement as to the effect of Lancaster's system. Society of Friends' Library, John Thomson MSS, 'William Allen's account of the founding of

Lancaster's schools'. BL, Place Papers, Add. 27, 823, 'History of Joseph Lancaster's Schools'.

Page 67. Lancastrian schools opened in England and Scotland. Ibid., and see Society of Friends' Library, 'William Allen's account'.

Page 67. a joint stock company formed. BL, Place Papers, Add. 35, 153, fo. 68. Owen, R., *New Existence*, Pt. V, Allen to Owen, Jan. 1814.

Page 67. a school organized according to Lancaster's system. British and Foreign School Society Report, May 1817, and see Sidmouth Papers, Sir William Congreve to Lord Sidmouth, 5 Jan. 1817:'[Owen's] institute is only one year old and that at present confined to a sort of Lancastrian school for the rising generation mixed up with Balls, Concerts, Marching and Counter-marching and Cotton Spinning in a very odd kind of medley.'

Page 67. the Bible as an aid to learning. Society of Friends' Library, 'William Allen's account'.

Page 68. confused state of the New Lanark books. Society of Friends' Library, William Allen's diary for 1815 (one volume only).

Page 69. instruction in the factory work they would have to perform. Select Committee on the . . . Poor in Ireland, 1823, p. 102 n. Owen complained most bitterly—*Life*, p. 131—of the refusal by Sturges Bourne's Committee on the Poor Laws to hear him in 1816. The 1823 Committee on Ireland covered precisely the same ground but Owen made no reference to his evidence before it.

Page 69. 'I hate and am sick at heart'. Marshall, Mrs J., ed., *The Life and Letters of Mary Shelley*, i, p. 147.

Page 69. Hazlitt gave a glimpse of him. Hazlitt, *Works*, vi, p. 66.

Page 70. 'He takes the politeness of great men'. BL, Place papers, Add. 35, 152, fo. 77.

Page 70. Mrs Townsend's visit to New Lanark. Sidmouth Papers, 'Lady Sidmouth's Tour of Scotland', Oct. 1821.

Page 71. Irish reaction to Owen's plan. Owen, R., *Proceedings at the several Public Meetings held in Dublin by Robert Owen Esq. 1823.* Anon., *A Letter . . . on the delusive nature of the system proposed by Robert Owen for the amelioration of the condition of the People in Ireland*, 1823.

Page 72. the Committee pressed Owen. Select Committee on the . . . Poor in Ireland, Introduction, pp. 90 ff.

Page 73. 'Having the immediate direction of those individuals'. Ibid., p. 89.

Page 73. Owen lost his case. National Library of Wales, Galpin corr., G. Mudie to Owen, 29 Aug. 1848.

Page 73. Sir W. de Crespigny on Owen's scheme. Hansard, New Series, vol. xi, col. 900, 26 May 1824.

5. The Halfway House

Page 74. typhoid fever at New Lanark. Aiton, op. cit., p. 40 n. The death in May 1824, of John Walker, Owen's closest colleague among the New Lanark shareholders, may have contributed to his decision to depart.

Page 74. attempt to ban the Bible. SRO, Register of the Presbytery of Lanark, 14 Aug. 1823. Gilpin, op. cit., ii, pp. 362, 366.

Page 74. 'a man of great pretentions'. Owen, R., *Life*, p. 95.

Page 74. reports were circulating. e.g. the Presbytery of Lanark's remarks; Aiton's book which was published in the summer of 1824, as were M'Gavin's criticisms.

Page 74. Owen's dismissal of seven workers. Aiton, op. cit., p. 36, *Glasgow Chronicle*, 17 Jan. 1824.

Page 75. unrest in the cotton industry. Select Committee on the Combination Laws. 1825, p. 330; *Annual Register*, 1824.

Page 75. hard put to pay the rent. Purdue University Robert Dale Owen's Journal, 1824 (unpublished).

Page 75. a halfway house. White, op. cit., p. 59.

Page 75. Owen's project resembled that of the Moravians. Adams, op. cit., iii, p. 551.

Page 75. Coke of Norfolk and Owen. Stirling, A. M. W. *Lady Elizabeth Spencer-Stanhope*, ii, p. 14.

Page 76. John Dunn Hunter's career. Drinnon, R., *White Savage: The Case of John Dunn Hunter.*

Page 76. Hunter at Owen's meetings. e.g. *Morning Post*, 30 July 1823.

Page 76. Hazlitt on Hunter. Hazlitt, W., *Works*, iv, p. 198.

Page 77. the latter wrote in his journal. Snedeker, C. D., ed., *The Diaries of Donald Macdonald. 1824-1826.*

Page 77. 'now I command Soldiers'. Sidmouth Papers, 'Lady Sidmouth's Tour of Scotland'.

Page 77. Macdonald's career. Snedeker, op. cit., Introduction.

Page 78. Owen's activities in New York. Ibid., pp. 175 ff.

Page 78. Griscom's career. Griscom, J. H., *Memoir of John Griscom.*

Page 79. Allen's journeys on the Continent. Gilpin, op. cit., i, pp. 270 ff.

Page 79. Griscom at Hofwyl and New Lanark. Griscom, J., *A Year in Europe*, i, p. 382, and ii, p. 373.

Page 80. 'a community something like the Harmonists.' New Harmony Workingmen's Institute, Series I, Speakman to Say, 1823(?)

Page 80. 'Nor is it the least of our hopes'. Transactions of the American Philosophical Society, vol. 43, Pt. 1, Philipps, M. E., 'The Academy of Natural Sciences of Philadelphia'.

Page 80. Maclure's work on geology. Maclure, W., *Observations on the Geology of the United States, Explanatory of a Geological Map*, 1810.

Page 81. Owen and the Academicians. Macdonald's Diary, p. 34. William Owen's Diary, pp. 206, 207.

Page 81. 'children are passive compounds'. Owen, Robert, *A New View of Society (Dent, 1927), pp. 22-3.*

Page 82. 'a system kept in play by absolute power'. Southey, R., op. cit., p. 265.

Page 82. *as his eldest son remarked.* Library of Congress, MSS Division, Trist Papers, Robert Dale Owen to Trist, 10 June 1853.

Page 83. *Marie Fretageot.* See Bestor, A., *Backwoods Utopias*, pp. 108, 153–8; Idem, *Education and Reform at New Harmony: Correspondence of William Maclure and Marie Duclos Fretageot 1820-1833.*

Page 83. *Owen on Pestalozzi and de Fellenberg.* Owen, R., *Life*, p. 177.

Page 83. *'children must be taken'.* Quoted in Bestor, *Education and reform*, p. 312.

Page 84. *'he said he had come to promote plans.'* William Owen's Diary, p. 43.

Page 84. *journey to Pittsburgh.* Ibid., p. 47, Macdonald's Diary, p. 220.

Page 85. *The Rapps anxious.* Arndt, *Harmony on the Wabash in Transition*, pp. 299, 313.

Page 85. *Flower's glimpse of old* Harmonie. Flower, op. cit., p. 34.

Page 85. *Rapp's reaction to Robert Owen.* William Owen's Diary, p. 53.

Page 86. *the model ressembled Christianopolis.* Professor Arndt in conversation with the author.

Page 86. *debate on Owen's use of millenial language.* See, for example, Harrison, J. F. C., *Robert Owen and the Owenites in Britain and America*, pp. 92, 134.

Page 86. *he knew talk of the millennium would rouse his audience.* M'Gavin. op. cit., p. 691, Owen, R., *An Address delivered to the Inhabitants of New Lanark on January 1, 1816, at the opening of the Institution established for the Formation of Human Character.*

Page 87. *this . . . was Owen's genius.* BL, Place Papers, Add. 35, 144, fo. 429.

Page 87. *'the Society found New Harmony unhealthy'.* Macdonald's Diary, p. 231.

Page 88. *the arrival at* Harmonie. Ibid., pp. 243–5.

6. An Invitation to New Harmony

Page 89. *William's account of* Harmonie. William Owen's Diary, pp. 72.

Page 89. *village appeared v. small.* Macdonald's Diary, p. 246.

Page 89. *a dusky colour.* Ibid., p. 245.

Page 89. *Owen showed them how.* Owen, W., op. cit., p. 76.

Page 90. *the subject of gossip.* e.g. Robinson, Henry Crabb, *Diary*, vi, p. 249.

Page 90. *Birkbeck/Flower dispute.* Houghton Library, Harvard, F. Wright Coll, Camilla Wright to Julia Garnett, 10 Jan. 1826. Thwaites, R. G., *Early Western Travels 1748-1846*, xi, 1, p. 272–6.

Page 91. *Birkbeck's account of the prairie.* Birkbeck, M., op. cit., pp. 112 ff.

Page 91. *goods purchased from* Harmonie. Flower, op. cit., p. 278.

Page 92. *advantages of mutual association.* Macdonald, op. cit., p. 253.

Page 92. *a debate about religion.* Ibid., p. 257–8.

Page 93. *the State of the Union message.* Ibid., p. 259.

Page 93. *memorandum of agreement.* Arndt, *Harmony . . . in Transition*, p. 378.

Page 94. the National Intelligencer *praised.* Bestor, *Backwoods Utopias*, p. 111.

Page 95. Owen's meeting with Mrs Smith. Smith, M. B., *Fifty Years of Washington Society*, pp. 179, 196, 223.

Page 95. privileged to speak. Owen, Robert, *Discourses on a New System of Society as delivered in the Hall of Representatives in the presence of the President, the President elect, Members of Congress etc. 1825.*

Page 96. a profit making scheme. BL, Place papers, Add. 35, 153, fo. 68. *The Co-operative Magazine*, Jan. 1826, p. 31.

Page 97. Intelligencer publishes a debate. Bestor, op. cit., p. 112.

7. 'I shall have wonders to relate'

Page 98. 'our time was passed'. Macdonald's Diary, p. 289.

Page 98. William Owen told Pelham. Lindley, op. cit., p. 416.

Page 99. William at Vincennes. Co-op Union, Manchester, Robert Owen Papers, WO to RO, 7 Feb. 1825.

Page 99. activities at Harmony. William Owen's Diary, pp. 89, 106.

Page 99. 'I find the weather dull'. Ibid., p. 129.

Page 100. American females dislike working outdoors. Macdonald's Diary, p. 291.

Page 100. The Misses Wright arrive. William Owen's Diary, p. 128.

Page 101. Bentham's interest in Frances Wright. University College, London, Bentham Papers, Lafayette to Bentham, 14 Sept. 1821.

Page 101. Wright sisters' upbringing. Waterman, William R., *Frances Wright*; Eckhardt, C. M., *Fanny Wright: Rebel in America.*

Page 101. She tried to persuade Lafayette to adopt her. Library of Congress. Lafayette Papers, Lafayette to C. Wilkes, 8 Nov. 1827.

Page 101. the Carbonari conspiracy. Waterman, op. cit., p. 68.

Page 101. 'I dare say you marvel'. Ibid., p. 74.

Page 103. Birkbeck and Flower received at La Grange. Flower, op. cit., p. 364.

Page 103. Departure of the Rappites. Macdonald's Diary, p. 293.

Page 104. A Universalist Minister. Note: As the name implies the Universalists held that salvation was available to everyone. As such the belief would commend itself to Robert Owen.

Page 104. Constitution of the Preliminary Society. Reproduced in Lockwood, G., *The New Harmony Movement*, pp. 84–91.

Page 104. 'every log cabin swarming with children'. Fordham, E. P., *Personal Narrative of travels in Virginia etc. 1817-1819*, p. 120.

Page 104. a limit fixed to subsistence. Pears, op. cit., p. 13.

Page 104. one new member wrote. Ibid.

Page 105. Owen's letter to William Allen. Co-op Union, Manchester, Robert Owen Papers, RO to WA. 21 Apr. 1825.

Page 106. *Allen helped the Separatists.* Gilpin, op. cit., i, p. 312.

Page 106. *Owen pleaded the climate.* Pears, op. cit., p. 15.

Page 106. *Thomas Pears.* Note. The letters of Thomas and Sarah Pears, edited by a descendant as *New Harmony. An Adventure in Happiness*, contain much detail about the course of events at this stage.

Page 108. *William Pelham's account of events.* Pelham's letters are reproduced in Lindley, H., ed., *Indiana as seen by early travelers*, pp. 360 ff. They supplement and corroborate the Pears's account.

Page 109. *Robert Owen's attitude to slavery. Robert Owen's opening speech . . . also his Memorial to the Repoublic of Mexico . . . and a Narrative of the Proceedings*, p. 185 ff.

Page 110. *Harmony in August 1825.* Co-operative *Magazine*, Feb. 1826, Letter by Charles Clarke, and Co-op Union, Manchester, Robert Owen Papers, WO to RO, 14 Oct. 1825.

Page 111. *adverse reports reach Economy.* Arndt, *Harmony . . . in Transition*, pp. 563, 705.

Page 111. *Reason for Harmonists leaving.* Macdonald's Diary, pp. 263–4.

Page 111. *'Respecting the responsibility of Mr Owen'.* Arndt, op. cit., p. 645.

8. *A Family Forsaken*

Page 115. *'acting a friendly . . . part'.* Elliott, Josephine, M., ed., *To Holland and New Harmony Robert Dale Owen's Travel Journal. 1825-1826*, p. 214.

Page 115. *a rage of speculation. Annual Register*, 1825.

Page 115. *Owen discouraged orders when the price was high.* BL, Bentham Papers, Add. 33, 545, fo. 338.

Page 115. *'the times have been tremendous'.* Ibid., Add. 33, 546, fo. 237.

Page 116. *efforts to dismiss Owen.* Gilpin, op. cit., ii, pp. 362, 366.

Page 116. *'indifference bordering on contempt.* NHWI, Maclure–Fretageot corr., Mac. to MF., 15 July 1825.

Page 116. *Owen paid the Rapps the original sum.* Arndt, *Harmonie on the Wabash in transition*, p. 645.

Page 116. *Owen told the Select Committee. Select Committee on . . . Ireland*, 1823, p. 97.

Page 116. *His shares not realized until 1828.* BL, Bentham Papers, Add. 33, 546, fo. 237.

Page 116. *Address to the London Co-op Society. The Times*, 27 Sept. 1825.

Page 117. *Ann Caroline's illness.* Elliott. op. cit., p. 222.

Page 117. *'Notwithstanding you think'.* Ibid., p. 278 n.

Page 117. *'benevolent individuals, committees etc.'* Aiton, op. cit., p. 13.

Page 118. *'so as not to be annoyed by it'.* Owen, Robert, *Life*, p. 136.

Page 118. *the partners dismissed Owen.* Co-op Union, Manchester, Robert Owen Papers, J. Wright to RO, 10 Dec. 1825.

Page 118. *'he thinks he is spoiled.'* Ibid., WO to RO, 7 Feb. 1825.

Page 118. *Robert Dale's illness.* Owen, R. D., *Threading My Way*, p. 98. Podmore, op. cit., p. 94.

Page 118. *'the well born Scot'.* Leopold, Richard, *Robert Dale Owen.*

Page 119. *Robert Dale's education.* Library of Congress, MSS Division, Trist Papers, RDO to NT, 13 Aug. 1829.

Page 119. *a tour of manufacturing establishments.* Owen, R. D., *Threading My Way*, p. 101.

Page 119. *Owen's mauling. Select Committee on the state of children employed in the manufactories of the UK*, 1816, iii, pp. 36, 86–9.

Page 119. *'this oppressor of childhood.'* Owen, R. D., *Threading My Way*, p. 104.

Page 119 *Owen on his children's education.* Owen, R., *Life*, p. 179.

Page 120. *less committed witnesses.* e.g. 'Letters from Hofwyl by a Parent', in *Saturday Magazine*, 20 Dec. 1834.

Page 120. *Robert Dale's love of riding.* Elliott, op. cit., p. 92; Robert Dale Owen's Journal, 1824, unpublished.

Page 120. *the schools at New Lanark.* Owen, R. D., *An Outline of the System of Education at New Lanark.*

Page 121 *the Pestalozzian ethos grafted on to the Lancastrian system.* NHWI, Maclure–Fretageot corr., Mac. to MF, 30 Jan. 1824.

Page 121. *Dr Philip Price.* NHWI, Series I, Price to Marie Fretageot, 7 Sept. 1824.

Page 121. *In love with Margaret.* Elliott, op. cit., p. 272–3 n. Owen, R. E., *Threading My Way*, p. 187.

Page 122. *Joseph Applegarth.* Note. This spelling in preference to Applegath. The R is clear in, for example, the name as written by Mrs Townsend in her account of her visit to New Lanark in 1821. Sidmouth Papers. 'Lady Sidmouth's Tour of Scotland'.

Page 122. *Whitwell's career. Gentleman's Magazine*, 1840. ii, p. 107.

Page 122. *Stedman Whitwell planning Orbiston.* Houghton Library, Harvard, BMS Am 1949, RDO to John Neal. 26 July 1824.

Page 122. *Miss Whitwell. Cooperative magazine*, Dec. 1826, p. 375.

Page 122. *'My father criticized'.* Elliott, op. cit., p. 233.

Page 123. *William let fly.* Co-op Union, Manchester, Robert Owen Papers. W. Owen to R. Owen. 16 Dec. 1825.

Page 124. *contrary to Madame's understanding.* NHWI, Maclure–Fretageot corr. Mac. to MF 31 Jan. 1825. MF to Mac. 11 Feb. 1825.

Page 124. *the school of industry at Alicante.* Gil Novales, *William Maclure in Spain*, p. 82 ff. NHWI, Series V, Maclure's Notebook, Vol. 26.

Page 124. *Maclure's tour of Ireland, Scotland.* Ibid., Journal 30, 31 July 1824.

9. The Philanthropist

Page 126. *foxes looked out of the windows.* Quoted in Merrill, G. P., *The First 100 Years of American Geology*, p. 33.

Page 126. *a Gallic focus.* Mims, S. L., ed., *Voyage aux États-Unis de L'amérique*, p. XXII ff.

Page 126. *various reconnaisances were made.* e.g. Collot, V. A., *A Journey in North America.*

Page 126. *written by a fellow émigré of Talleyrand.* Volney, C. F., *Tableau du sol et du climat des États-Unis.*

Page 126. *Volney known to Maclure.* American Philosophical Society, Letters of S. G. Morton; Maclure to Morton 27 Dec. 1836.

Page 127. *'La tête vide'.* Chinard, G., *Volney et l'Amérique*, p. 50.

Page 127. *Maclure's life and career.* Morton, S. G., *Memoir of William Maclure*, 1841; Hardy, J. D., Jensen, J. H., Wolfe, M., eds., *The Maclure Collection of French Revolutionary Materials*; Gil Novales, A., *William Maclure in Spain*; Armytage, W. H. G., 'William Maclure, 1763–1840. A British Interpretation', in *Indiana Magazine of History*, Mar. 1951.

Page 127. *Maclure's business in textiles, e.g. his acquaintance with the Glasgow cotton master, Henry Monteith.* NHWI, Series V, Maclure's Journal, 21 July 1824.

Page 127. *les idéologues.* Gusdorf, George, *Les sciences humaines et la Pensée occidentale* VIII. *La Conscience révolutionnaire Les Idéologues*, p. 80.

Page 127. *Maclure's connection with Maine de Biran, Cabanis, etc.* NHWI, Maclure–Fretageot corr., Mac. to MF, 1 June 1821.

Page 127. *'I adopted rock hunting'.* American Journal of Science and Arts, vii, p. 256.

Page 127. *'as ignorant as a pig'.* NHWI, Maclure–Fretageot corr., Mac. to MF 25 Sept. 1826.

Page 128. *Lancastrian education in France.* Gilpin, op. cit., pp. 235, 240, 255.

Page 128. *Pestalozzi addressed him.* Pestalozzi, H., *'Sämtliche Briefe'.* v, pp. 233, 259, vii, p. 190.

Page 128. *Joseph Neef.* Hackensmith, C. W., *Biography of Joseph Neef. Educator in the Ohio Valley.*

Page 130. *Thomas Say.* Dictionary of American Biography; Academy of Natural Sciences; Coll. 455 and 13; Weiss, T., and Zeigler, G., 'Thomas Say. Early American Naturalist'.

Page 131. *Gerard Troost.* Dictionary of American Biography; Academy of Natural Sciences, Coll. 372.

Page 131. *Charles Alexandre Lesueur.* Ord. G., *Memoir of C. A. Lesueur*, in Coll. 136 A, Academy of Natural Sciences; Hamy, E. T., *Les Voyages du Naturaliste Ch. Alex. Lesueur dans l'Amérique du nord (1815-1837).*

Page 132. *Lesueur's drawings.* Guiffrey, J., *Dessins de Ch.-A. Lesueur, exécutés aux États-Unis de 1816 à 1837.*

Page 132. *the correspondence preserved at New Harmony.* NHWI, Maclure–Fretageot corr; Note: Many of the letters are reproduced in their entirety in Bestor, A., *Education and Reform at New Harmony*, which gives an invaluable account of events from 1826 to 1828.

Page 133. *'I should wish to see the women take their … share'.* NHWI, Maclure–Fretageot corr., Mac. to MF, 18 Jan. 1824.

Page 133. *the tone impressed some people.* e.g. Gil Novales, op. cit., p. 44.

Page 133. *Mrs Trollope implies.* Trollope, F., *Domestic Manners of the Americans*, i, pp. 12, 13.

Page 133. *Achille not Marie's son.* NHWI, Hodge–Fretageot Papers, MF to Mac. 12 May 1821, 'on leaving France my intention is to leave in [Phiquepal's] hand a paper in which I will recommend him to give any [no?] kind of religion to Achille not in my name but as being charged by the boy's parents who are Quakers', and see, Ibid., Series I. Zede to Maclure, 10 Dec. 1833.

Page 133. *Joseph Fretageot.* Ibid., Series I, J. Fretageot to his wife, 15 Nov. 1821, 12 Mar. 1823.

Page 135. *'40 heads and only several pairs of hands'.* Arndt, K. J. R., *Harmonie on the Wabash in Transition*, p. 770.

Page 135. *voyage of the* Philanthropist. Elliott, op. cit., pp. 237–264; Duclos, V. C., *Diary and recollections*, in Lindley op. cit., p. 537.

10. Lord Proprietor

Page 137. *Owen's slogan, the Boatload of Knowledge.* Lindley, op. cit., p. 405.

Page 137. *Owen a wonderful man.* Ibid., p. 409.

Page 138. *Owen to proceed to the Community of Equality.* Pears, op. cit., p. 50, 56 ff.

Page 138. *Constitution of the Preliminary Society.* Lockwood, op. cit., p. 84–91.

Page 138. *Financial collapse in England.* Annual Register 1826, Co-op Union, Manchester, Robert Owen Papers, J. Wright to R. O. 10 Dec. 1825.

Page 138. *Constitution of Community of Equality.* Lockwood, op. cit., pp. 104–11.

Page 139. *the military police.* Macnab, H. G., op. cit., p. 127.

Page 140. *'speaking falsehoods all our lives'.* Pears, op. cit., p. 60.

Page 140. *according to Whitwell.* Co-operative Magazine, ii, Jan. 1827.

Page 141. *'the worm i' the bud'.* Ibid.

Page 141. *not calculated for hewing down timber.* Pears, op. cit., p. 72.

Page 142. *'the obstinate prejudices'.* Bestor, *Education and Reform at New Harmony*, p. 330.

Page 142. *the nucleus.* Pears, op. cit., p. 76 ff.

Page 142. *the memorandum of these arrangements.* NHWI, Hodge–Fretageot Papers, *Short Account of all the transactions between Robert Owen and William Maclure.*

Page 143. *The original system of running villages. The Economist*, Number 25, 14 July 1821.

Page 143. '*The System I like*'. Pears, op. cit., p. 65, 77–9.

Page 144. *Neef's proposal.* Brown, P., *Twelve Months in New Harmony*, p. 108.

Page 144. *Paul Brown*. Lockwood, op. cit., pp. 137–9, 147; Harrison, op. cit., p. 76; Bestor, *Backwoods Utopias*, p. 189 n.

Page 144. *Owen . . . a trading man.* Brown, op. cit., p. 15.

Page 145. *Harmonists' agent urged Rapp to dispose of bonds.* Arndt, *Harmonie on the Wabash in Transition*, p. 778.

Page 145. *Maclure not responsible for Owen's actions.* NHWI, Hodge–Fretageot Papers, *Short account of transactions between Robert Owen and William Maclure.*

Page 145. *Maclure's course of independent action.* Ibid.

Page 146. '*let every herring hang*'. *New Harmony Gazette*, 17 May 1826.

Page 146. *a period of working very hard.* BL, Place Papers, Add 35, 152 fo. 222; *Co-operative Magazine*, No. 1. Jan. 1826, p. 31.

Page 146. '*Owen is growing unpopular*'. Pears, op. cit., p. 81.

Page 147. *described tasks as a* corvée. Lindley, op. cit., p. 433.

Page 148. *a feudal barony.* Brown, op. cit., p. 109.

Page 148. *Owen's account of the benevolent old man. Revue Encyclopédique*, Vol. 18, 1823; p. 5, Jullien de Paris' visit to New Lanark, Oct. 1822.

Page 148. '*Harmonyphobia*'. NHWI, Hodge–Fretageot Papers, Applegarth to Maclure, 4 Aug. 1826.

Page 148. '*a Rib of talent*'. Ibid. Maclure–Fretageot corr., Mac. to MF, 20 June 1826.

11. *The Declaration of Mental Independence*

Page 150. *The Trinity of evils.* Oration containing a Declaration of Mental Independence. *New Harmony Gazette*, 12 July 1826.

Page 152. *Baptists, Quakers, etc.* Lindley, op. cit., pp. 373, 377.

Page 152. '*he is bigoted against bigotry*'. Pears, op. cit., p. 80.

Page 152. *The benefits of marriage on the frontier.* Rohrbough, M. J., *The Trans-Appalachian Frontier*, p. 34.

Page 153. *tension in the family.* Owen, R. D., *Threading my Way*, p. 64.

Page 153. *as Francis Place remarked.* BL, Place papers, Add. 35, 144, fo. 429.

Page 153. '*I did all I could*'. Ibid., Mac to ?, 20 Sept. 1826.

Page 154. *Lucy pregnant by Thomas Say.* Ibid., Hodge–Fretageot papers, MF to Mac. 7 July 1826.

Page 154. *the freedom Mr O took with them.* Ibid., Maclure–Fretageot corr., Mac to MF., 21 Aug. 1826.

Page 154. *good land in Ohio.* Ibid., 21 July 1826.

Page 155. 'Owen is not my partner'. Ibid., 21 Aug. 1826.

Page 155. Phiquepal's school. Academy of Natural Sciences, Coll. 464.

Page 156. 'if I ever got out'. Lockwood, op. cit., p. 246.

Page 156. Owen refused permission for crops to be gathered. NHWI. Hodge-Fretageot Papers; Applegarth to Maclure. 13 Aug. 1826.

Page 156. Discourses on education. New Harmony Gazette, 23 and 30 Aug. 1826.

Page 156. 'He rants'. NHWI, Maclure–Fretageot corr., Mac. to MF., 30 Aug. 1826.

Page 158. the covenant. Brown, op. cit., p. 60 ff.

Page 158. Owen's monopoly at the store. Select Committee on . . . Ireland, p. 90 ff.

Page 158. wages paid once a month. Aiton, op. cit., p. 42 note. Questioned by Aiton, Owen agreed that of the monthly wage bill at New Lanark in 1824 of £3,000, only £1,000 was regularly paid in cash. The rest was in tokens for the store.

Page 159. Owen in need of money. NHWI, Maclure–Fretageot corr., Mac. to MF, 28-Nov. 1826.

Page 161. Owen's attack on Education Society and Neef's response. Brown, op. cit., p. 80; New Harmony Gazette, 22 Nov. 1826.

Page 161. Maclure's account of dealings with Owen. NHWI, Hodge–Fretageot Papers, *Short Account of all the transactions between Robert Owen and William Maclure.*

Page 161. Owen's account of events at New Harmony. Owen, R., *Address delivered by Robert Owen at a Public Meeting held at the Franklin Institute . . . Philadelphia . . . June 25 1827.*

Page 162. 'that mist . . . refracted objects'. NHWI, Hodge–Fretageot Papers, Mac. to MF, 7 Jan. 1827.

12. *A tall, thin, talking woman*

Page 163. Selling and buying. Brown, op. cit., p. 86.

Page 163. a projected funeral. Ibid.

Page 163. an editorial. New Harmony Gazette, 28 Mar. 1827.

Page 164. a general cupidity. Owen, R. D., *Threading My Way*, p. 264.

Page 165. 'if you knew the horrors'. Houghton Library, Harvard, F. Wright coll., FW to JG, 8 June 1825.

Page 166. 'when I first visited Harmonie'. Ibid.

Page 167. The Garnett correspondence. Letters held by the Houghton Library, Harvard, by and to the Garnett sisters and their mother. Julia Garnett became Madame Pertz, the main body is therefore referred to as the Garnett-Pertz Collection. The Frances Wright Collection is separate. What information it contains about Nashoba was reproduced virtually uncut in the *Harvard Library Bulletin*, Vol. 23, 1975, 'The Nashoba Plan'.

Page 167. Lafayette confided. Yale University Library, Benjamin Franklin Coll., LF to JG, 3 Sept. [?] 1825.

Page 167. Lafayette on George Flower. Ibid., 16 Mar. 1826.

Page 168. 'She could pass all the wretchedness in Paris.' Gilbert, Amos, *Memoir of Frances Wright*, p. 23.

Page 168. 'a tall, thin, talking woman'. Williams, S., ed., *Journal of Washington Irving*, p. 42.

Page 168. Jefferson told her. Library of Congress, Jefferson Papers, TJ to FW, 7 Aug. 1825.

Page 168. Madison warned her. Ibid., Madison Papers; JM to FW, 1 Sept. 1825.

Page 168. 'Rejoice with me'. Houghton Library, F. Wright Coll., CW to J & HG, 8 June 1825.

Page 169. a life of constraint. Ibid.

Page 00. He could not undertake it without aid. Ibid., CW to JG, 10 Jan. 1826.

Page 170. Birkbeck's death. See Chapter 10, p. 9.

Page 170. Received 15 slaves. Houghton Library, F. Wright Coll., FW to JG, 11 Mar. 1826.

Page 171. 'Remember dear loves'. Ibid.

Page 171. 'Miss Wright would be a great help'. NHWI, Hodge–Fretageot Papers, Mac. to MF, 19 Dec. 1826.

Page 171. 'her talents and influence'. Houghton Library. F. Wright Coll., CW to JG, 20 Aug. 1826.

Page 172. Maclure astonished. NHWI, Hodge–Fretageot Papers, Mac. to MF, 19 Dec. 1826.

Page 172. 'that positive good sense'. Ibid., Maclure–Fretageot corr., MF to Mac., 17 Jan. 1827.

Page 172. 'I must reply in person'. Houghton Library, F. Wright Coll., quoted by CW to JG, 8 Dec. 1826.

Page 173. Robert Owen and birth control. See, for example, Holyoake, G. *Sixty years of an Agitator's Life*, i, p. 127; Richard Carlile, *The Republican*, xi, 1825; BL, Place Coll., Vol. 68, p. 105.

Page 173. population would be regulated. Ibid., Place Papers, Add. 35, 152, fo. 222.

Page 174. 'It is the moral condition'. Houghton Library, Garnett Pertz coll., FW letter to Sismondi, copied by Julia Garnett.

Page 175. Sismondi regretted. Ibid., Sismondi to HG, 29 Apr. 1827.

Page 175. 'A New St Theresa. Ibid., Sismondi to JG, 9 Sept. 1827.

13. Co-operation has well nigh killed us all

Page 176. Co-operation has killed…' Quoted in Waterman, op. cit., p. 130.

Page 176. 'More congenial associates'. Owen, R. D., *Threading My Way*, p. 270.

Page 176. *Professor Mylne.* Murray, D. *Memoirs of the old College of Glasgow*, pp. 103, 401.

Page 176. *state of Nashoba.* Owen, R. D., op. cit., p. 271.

Page 177. *Camilla critical of Eliza.* Houghton Library, F. Wright coll., CW to JG, 8 Dec. 1826.

Page 177. *'I have left my Camilla'.* Ibid., FW to JG, 25 July 1827.

Page 177. *Mylne horrified.* Ibid., Garnett-Pertz coll., Mylne to JG, 12 Aug. 1827.

Page 178. *'Owen . . . has little limit'.* Ibid.

Page 178. *Frances's description of Richardson.* Ibid. F. Wright coll., FW to JG, 11 Mar. 1826.

Page 178. *Robert Dale on Richardson.* Owen, R. D., *Threading My Way*, p. 268.

Page 178. Nashoba Journal. Quoted in Waterman, op. cit., p. 115 ff.

Page 179. *Camilla to Wilkes.* Houghton Library, Garnett-Pertz coll., quoted in Wilkes to JG, 15 Oct. 1827.

Page 180. *'such is the issue of the plans'.* Ibid.

Page 180. *'I . . . believe Frances incapable'.* Ibid., JG to Sismondi, n.d. (summer of 1827).

Page 180. *Margaret disappoints Robert Dale.* Owen, R. D. op. cit., p. 199.

Page 181. *'the more I see of the Old World'.* Chicago University Library, Bonaventure Lafayette coll., RDO to FW, 27 Aug. 1827.

Page 181. *Robert Dale on Mary Shelley.* Owen R. D. op. cit., pp. 288-9.

Page 182. *'Now then practise yourself'.* Bennett, B. T., ed., *The Letters of Mary Shelley*, ii, p. 16. MS to RDO, 9 Nov. 1827.

Page 183. *'dear, noble, single hearted Fanny.'* Houghton Library. Garnett-Pertz coll., FT to JG, 17 May 1827.

Page 183. *'My dearest Harriet'.* Ibid., 8 Oct. 1827.

Page 183. *'at which my heart sickened'.* Ibid., Garnett-Pertz coll., FT to HG, 7 Dec. 1828.

Page 183. *'the gates of the most rigid convent'.* Ibid., HG to JP, 12 Dec. 1827.

Page 184. *hit out all round.* Trollope, Frances, *Domestic Manners of the Americans*, i, p. 25 ff.

Page 184. *criticism of Maclure and Marie Fretageot.* Trollope, F., op. cit., i, pp. 12, 13.

Page 184. *Henry wrote home.* Trollope, Frances Eleanor, *Frances Trollope; Her Life and Literary Work*, i, p. 111.

Page 184. *Drawing of Nashoba.* Trollope, F., op. cit., facing p. 38.

Page 184. *'I was a very poor creature.'* Houghton Library, Garnett-Pertz coll., FT to HG, 7 Dec. 1828.

Page 185. *Camilla's marriage.* Payne-Gaposchkin, Dr C., *Harvard Library Bulletin*, xxiii, 1975, p. 448 n.

Page 185. Mrs Trollope on Whitby. Houghton Library, Garnett-Pertz coll., FT to JP, 20 May 1829.

Page 185. reasons advanced for Camilla's marriage. See, Heineman, H., *Mrs Trollope. The triumphant feminine in the 19th century*, p. 270, n. 36; Library of Congress, F. Wright coll., note by Sylva d'Arusmont.

Page 185. Camilla's reason for marriage, 'of a very peculiar nature', Houghton Library, F. Wright coll., CW to HG, 26 Apr. 1828.

Page 185. Wilkes had sight of document. Ibid., Garnett-Pertz coll., Wilkes to JP, 30 Sept. 1828.

Page 186. 'that there might be a child'. Gilbert, Amos, op. cit., p. 35.

Page 186. Explanatory Notes. Waterman, op. cit., pp. 125–8.

Page 187. Writs issued against Robert Owen. Posey County 'Deed Book', E.

Page 187. 'the tangled web' of Owen's affairs. Houghton Library, F. Wright coll., CW to HG, 20 Nov. 1828; NHWI, Maclure–Fretageot corr., Mac. to MF, 18 Feb. 1829, MF to Mac. 12 Mar. 1829; Branigin–Owen Papers, Bond of 29 Oct. 1828.

Page 188. Robert Owen leaves New Harmony. Houghton Library, F. Wright coll., CW to HG, 20 Nov. 1828.

Page 188. 'She thought it would be a poor appropriation of her talents.' Ibid.

14. *This presiding spirit of our forests*

Page 191. To New Harmony by Dearborn carriage. Ferrall, Simon, *A Ramble of 6,000 miles through the United States of America*, p. 85.

Page 192. his friends Erving and Rich. NHWI, Series I, G. Erving to Maclure, 1819, 1820. etc.; BL, Place papers, Add. 27, 858, fo. 94.

Page 192. Lesueur's belongings. Academy of Natural Sciences Philadelphia, Coll. IX and 136 C.

Page 192. Lesueur's career at New Harmony. Hamy, op. cit., pp. 44, 70.

Page 192. Barrabino's portrait. Academy of Natural Sciences, Coll. 136.

Page 193. Owen's career at New Harmony. Ferrall, op. cit., p. 100 ff.

Page 194. blinded by partiality. Ibid.; BL, Place papers, Add. 35, 153, fo. 220.

Page 194. 'He says he has sold his own ... shares'. Ibid., Maclure–Fretageot corr., Mac. to MF, 28 Jan. 1829.

Page 195. Rothschild and Baring 'direct' Owen to Mexico. Ibid., MF to Mac., 9 Jan. 1829.

Page 195. John Dunn Hunter in Mexico. BL, Place papers, Add. 27, 858, fo. 125; Drinnon, op. cit.

Page 195. Mexican minister to Robert Owen. Co-op Union, Manchester, Robert Owen Papers, Rocafuerte to R. Owen. 17 Oct. 1828.

Page 195. 'He was ... recommended to the Bishops'. NHWI, Maclure–Fretageot corr.; Mac. to MF, 28 Jan. 1829.

Page 196. Owen's mood in Mexico. Owen, Robert, *Robert Owen's Opening Speech
... also his Memorial to the Republic of Mexico and a Narrative of Proceedings therein. . .*

Page 197. No time to pay off mortgage. NHWI. Maclure–Fretageot corr.; MF to
Mac., 8 April 1829.

Page 197. Owen/Campbell debate. Trollope, F., op. cit. i, p. 205.

Page 197. a realignment at New Harmony. NHWI, Maclure–Fretageot corr.,
1828/29.

Page 198. Frances Wright as lecturer. Waterman, op. cit., p. 161; Ferrall, op. cit.,
p. 15.

*Page 198. Frances Wright's autobiography. Biography, Notes, and Political Letters of
Frances Wright d'Arusmont.*

Page 198. 'Our little place furnishes news'. NHWI, Maclure–Fretageot corr., MF to
Mac. 30 Jan. 1829.

Page 199. William left in charge. NHWI, Maclure–Fretageot corr., 28 Nov. 1829;
Indiana Historical Society, Owen–Dorsey Papers, RDO to Dorsey, 31 Jan. 1830.

Page 199. Maclure's loss $100,000. NHWI, Maclure–Fretageot corr., Mac. to MF,
12 Aug. 1829.

Page 200. Rappite buildings in decay. NHWI, Maclure–Fretageot corr., MF to
Mac., 11 Sept. 1 1829.

Page 202. Count Leon. Arndt, K. J. R., *George Rapp's Harmony Society*, pp. 468,
522, 529.

Page 202. Madame's change of plan on hearing of Leon. NHWI, Maclure–Fretageot
corr., MF to Mac., 8 Nov. 1831. Mac. to MF, 7 Jan. 1821.

Page 203. 'Europe will not suit you'. Ibid.

Page 203. cholera in Paris. Ibid., MF to Mac., 27 Mar. 1832.

Page 203. certain members of the Academy complained. e.g. George Ord and Reuben
Haines.

Page 204. Say's opinion of New Harmony. American Philosophical Society, Philadelphia, Letters of American Scientists to Charles Lucien Buonaparte; Say to
CLB, 6 Jan. 1828, Dec. 1828, 5 July 1830.

Page 205. Say's need for scientific books. NHWI, Maclure–Fretageot corr., Say's
postscript in Madame's letter, 12 Nov. 1829.

Page 205. 'I never will forgive Maclure.' American Philosophical Society, George
Ord to C. L. Buonaparte, 14 Oct. 1838.

Page 205. Lesueur's last days. Academy of Natural Sciences, Philadelphia,
Coll. 280, Biog. note.

15. Afterglow

Page 207. the old houses in decay. NHWI, Branigin–Owen corr., Robert Dale
Owen to Mary Jane Owen, 25 July 1833.

Page 207. 'that aristocratical spirit'. Library of Congress, Trist Papers, RDO to Nicholas Trist, 25 Apr. 1834.

Page 207. his obligation to repay $10,000. NHWI, Branigin–Owen corr., RDO to MJO, 9 Oct. 1832.

Page 208. Robert Dale's friendship with Nicholas Trist. Leopold, op. cit., p. 72.

Page 208. 'I fear she is not sincere.' Co-op union, Manchester, Robert Owen Papers, RDO to RO. 21 Feb. 1831.

Page 208. He had never been in love with her. Owen, R. D., op. cit., p. 266.

Page 209. re-settling the slaves in Haiti. Perkins, A., and Wolfson, T., *Frances Wright Free Enquirer*, p. 274.

Page 209. Camilla desolate. Houghton Library, F. Wright corr., CW to JP, 1 Nov. 1829.

Page 210. Grief would delay her in Paris. Co-op Union, Manchester, Robert Owen Papers, FW to RO, 26 Mar. 1831; Waterman, op. cit., p. 229 ff.

Page 210. Madame Fretageot's visit to Frances. NHWI, Maclure–Fretageot corr., MF to Mac., 25 Dec. 1831.

Page 210. Mary Jane Robinson. Leopold. op. cit., p. 107 ff.

Page 211. Observed her behaviour with children. Library of Congress, Trist Papers, RDO to NT, 25 Apr. 1834.

Page 211. A frank description of his bride. Ibid., RDO to NT, 12 Feb. 1832.

Page 212. essential to his sense of well being. NHWI, Branigin–Owen corr., RDO to MJO, 18 Aug. 1833.

Page 212. Lodgings in Glasgow. Burgerbibliothek Bern, David Dale Owen to E. de Fellenberg, Oct. 1826.

Page 212. Jane's responsibility. Co-op Union, Manchester, Robert Owen Papers, Jane Owen to Robert Owen, 10 Nov. 1828.

Page 212. illness of Mrs Owen, Anne and Mary Owen. NHWI, Branigin–Owen corr., RDO to MJO, 7 Sept. 1832.

Page 213. National Equitable Labour Exchange. Podmore, F., *Robert Owen*, p. 405 ff.

Page 213. The d'Arusmont children. Note. According to the Garnett-Pertz correspondence in the Houghton Library, Harvard, the *second* child died a few weeks after its birth in the spring of 1832. But in his *Manuel de nos affaires* in the Frances Wright collection in the Library of Congress, Phiquepal notes the birth of only one child, Sylva d'Arusmont on 25 Apr. 1832. The existence of a first child, born out of wedlock, which Marie Fretageot saw on her visit to Frances in December 1831, was not recorded, or referred to, by its parents.

Page 213. Mary Jane's education in France. NHWI, Branigin–Owen corr., RDO and MJO, June, July, August 1832.

Page 214. 'Harmony will suit you and me'. Ibid.

Page 214. 'I have made up my mind'. Ibid., MJO to RDO, 14 Aug. 1833.

Page 215. *Robert Dale on Margaret.* Ibid., RDO to MJO, 29 Sept. 1832.

Page 215. '*I can't put on manners*'. Ibid., MJO to RDO, 14 Aug. 1833.

Page 215. '*it is a noble estate.*' Library of Congress, Trist Papers, RDO to NT, 30 Mar. 1832.

Page 215. '*or if they would be* quite *satisfied anywhere*'. Ibid., RDO to MJO, 12 Sept. 1832.

Page 216. *Phiquepal's settlement with the Owens.* Library of Congress, F. Wright coll., *Manuel de nos affaires.*

Page 216. '*Frances's charm was broken*'. Brownson, O., op. cit., p. 120.

Page 216. '*the wreck of what she was*'. Ibid., p. 127.

Page 216. *Frances's later career.* Library of Congress, F. Wright coll., notes by Sylva d'Arusmont; Academy of Natural Sciences, Coll. 464.

Page 217. *Life at New Harmony and the Triple Wedding.* Leopold, op. cit., p. 129.

Page 217. *His new sisters-in-law.* Co-op Union, Manchester, Robert Owen Papers, RDO to RO, 15 May 1837.

Page 217. '*My wife and sister appreciated*'. Library of Congress, Trist Papers, RDO to NT. 30 Apr. 1834.

Page 218. *The whole town agog.* NHWI, Series I, Alex. Maclure to William Maclure, 29 Dec. 1834.

Page 219. *Public works at New Harmony.* Leopold, op. cit., p. 130 et seq.

Page 219. *Her daughter, Rosamond.* Owen, Rosamond Dale. *My Perilous Life in Palestine*, p. 41; Columbia University, Cuba Papers, Box 4, Notes by Rosamond Dale Owen.

Page 220. *Prince Max of Wied.* Lockwood, op. cit., p. 315.

Page 220. *Lyell's journal.* Lyell, Sir C., *A Second Visit to the United States of America*, ii, p. 271.

Page 221. *Maclure's life in Mexico.* American Philosophical Society, Letters to S. G. Morton; Mac. to Morton, 24 Nov. 1835.

Page 222. *David Dale Owen's career.* Hendrickson, W. B., *David Dale Owen.*

Page 222. *Frances told his father.* Co-op Union, Manchester, Robert Owen Papers, FW to RO, 10 Nov. 1831.

Page 223. *He fell heir to.* Hendrickson, op. cit., p. 20.

Page 224. *the children of New Harmony grew up.* Snedeker, Caroline Dale, *The Town of the Fearless.*

Page 224. *The new laboratory.* To be seen today at New Harmony.

Page 225. *The ideal community proposed by John Speakman.* NHWI, Series I, folder 11. Speakman to Say, 1823? See Chapter 5, p. 80.

16. *The Debatable Land*

Page 226. He confessed he stood out. Owen, R. D., 'Recallings from a Public Life', in *Scribner's Monthly*, xv, Dec. 1877.

Page 226. his father's discomforture. Owen, R. D. *Threading My Way*, p. 102.

Page 226. Robert Dale as politician. Leopold, op. cit., p. 142 ff.

Page 226. no substantial effort at reform. Ibid., p. 155.

Page 227. Robert Dale denied the abolitionists. Ibid., pp. 208–9, 272–3.

Page 227. the Oregon question. Ibid., p. 191 ff.

Page 227. 'Owen went over the same ... preamble'. Adams, J. Q., op. cit., xii, pp. 116–17.

Page 227. his only source of income. Podmore, op. cit., p. 615.

Page 227. The religion of socialism. Cyclopaedia of Religious Denominations, 1853, 'Socialism', by Robert Owen.

Page 228. Owen's manner on the platform. Grant, James, *Portraits of Public Characters; Robert Owen*.

Page 228. 'a born leader of men'. Engels, Friedrich, *Socialism: Utopian and Scientific*, p. 20.

Page 228. the Owenites. Taylor, B., *Eve and the New Jerusalem*; Harrison, J. F. C., op. cit.

Page 229. 'he flatters himself'. Quoted in Lockwood, op. cit., p. 308.

Page 229. 'the most amiable'. Emerson, R. W., quoted in Lockwood, op. cit., p. 310.

Page 229. British government replies to Owen. Podmore, op. cit., p. 587–8.

Page 230. 'His mind was feeding on itself'. Podmore, op. cit., p. 602.

Page 230. Cox took charge. Ibid., p. 615.

Page 230. Mrs Hayden. Ibid., p. 605.

Page 230. Owen's view of the manifestations. Ibid., p. 604.

Page 230. Grace Fletcher. Fletcher, E. Mrs, *Autobiography of Mrs Fletcher*, p. 110.

Page 231. 'I would if I could believe'. Robert Owen Memorial Museum, Newtown, Letters on Spiritualism.

Page 231. 'I regret, as you do'. Library of Congress, Trist Papers, RDO to NT, 10 June 1853.

Page 231. denied the nomination. Leopold, op. cit., p. 250.

Page 232. 'of all the minor posts the favourite'. Library of Congress, Trist Papers, RDO to NT, 10 June 1853.

Page 232. seances at Naples. NHWI, Branigin–Owen papers, Mary Jane Owen's journal; Columbia University, Cuba Papers, Rosamond Dale Owen's notes.

Page 232. Robert Dale's powers. Jenkins, E., *The Shadow and the Light. A defence of D. D. Home. The Medium*, p. 73.

Page 232. the Owens and phrenology. Sidmouth Papers, 'Lady Sidmouth's Tour of Scotland'; Owen, R. D., *Threading My Way*, p. 297 ff.

Page 232. Dr. Buchanan's demonstration. Owen, R. D., *Neurology; An Account of some experiments in Cerebral Physiology.*

Page 232. Robert Owen's request for £500. Columbia University, Cuba Papers, RO to RDO, Dec. 1856. Douglas, P. H., *Some new material on the lives of Robert Owen and Robert Dale Owen.*

Page 233. Owen at Liverpool. Podmore, op. cit., p. 625.

Page 234. Owen at Newtown. Holyoake, G., *Life and Last Days of Robert Owen*, Robert Owen Memorial Museum, Newtown, accounts by David Thomas and the Revd. John Edward.

Page 234. 'the grade of belief'. Columbia University, Cuba Papers, RDO to Mrs Dufour, n.d.; Columbia University, Cuba Papers, RO to RDO, Dec. 1856.

Page 235. their daughter became a spiritualist. Ibid., Rosamond Dale Owen's notes, and see her autobiography, *My Perilous Life in Palestine.*

Page 235. letter to Lincoln. Leopold, op. cit., p. 355.

Page 235. did not advocate civil rights. Ibid., pp. 272, 362.

Page 236. 'therefore Katie'. Ibid., p. 402.

Page 236. Robert Dale's delirium. Holyoake, *Sixty Years*, i, pp. 124, 125; Columbia University, Cuba Papers, Rosamond Dale Owen's notes.

Epilogue. The eye of faith.

Page 238. The eye of hope. See Chapter 2, p. 29.

Page 238. He was a strong minded man. Quoted in Arndt, *George Rapp's Harmony Society*, p. 554.

Page 238. Rapp's last words. Ibid., p. 599. Note: His successors upheld the strict and peculiar way of life that Father Rapp devised for the Society, but found new ways of adding to its wealth. As the nineteenth century advanced the Society acquired large holdings in land, railways, steel, and oil. When death had sharply reduced its members the question arose as to who would inherit. Numerous attempts in the courts to force a distribution of the Society's wealth among the heirs and relations of the original members failed. The great store amassed over more than a hundred years went in the end to three survivors.

SELECT BIBLIOGRAPHY

Adams, C. F., ed., *Memoirs of John Quincy Adams* (Lippincott and Co., 1874).

Aiton, The Revd. J., *Mr Owen's objections to Christianity and New View of Society and Education, refuted, by a plain Statement of Facts . . .*, 2nd edn. (Edinburgh, 1824).

Albjerg, V. L., *Richard Owen: Scotland, 1810, Indiana, 1890* (1946).

Andressohn, J. C., 'Twenty Additional Rappite Manuscripts', in *Indiana Magazine of History* (June 1949).

Annual Register, The (1824, 1825, 1826).

Anon., *A Letter . . . on the delusive nature of the System professed by Robert Owen for the amelioration of the condition of the People in Ireland* (Dublin, 1823).

Armytage, W. H. G., 'William Maclure. 1763–1840: A British Interpretation', in *Indiana Magazine of History* (Mar. 1951).

—— *Heavens below: Utopian experiments in England. 1560–1960* (Routledge and Kegan Paul, 1961).

Arndt, K. J. R., *George Rapp's Harmony Society, 1785-1847* (Fairleigh Dickinson UP, 1972).

—— *George Rapp's Successors and Material Heirs, 1847-1916* (Fairleigh Dickinson UP, 1971).

—— *George Rapp's Separatists. 1700-1803: Prelude to America* (Harmony Society Press. 1980).

—— *Harmony on the Connoquenessing* (Harmony Society Press, 1980).

—— *A Documentary History of the Indiana Decade of the Harmony Society, 1814-1824* (Harmony Society Press, 1982).

—— *Harmony on the Wabash in Transition, 1824-1826* (Harmony Society Press, 1982).

Barwell, Mrs., *Letters from Hofwyl* (Longman, Brown, Green and Longmans, 1842).

Beer, Max, *A History of British Socialism* (G. Bell and Sons, 1920).

Bennett, B. T., ed., *The Letters of Mary Shelley* (Johns Hopkins UP, 1983).

Bernard, Sir Thomas, 'Mr Dale's cottonmills at New Lanark' in *Report of the Society for Bettering the Condition of the Poor*, Vol. II (1800).

Bestor, A. E., *Backwoods Utopias: The Sectarian and Owenite Phases of Communitarian Socialism in America, 1662-1829* (Univ. of Pa. Press, 1950).

Bestor, A. E., ed., *Education and Reform at New Harmony: Correspondence of William Maclure and Marie Duclos Fretageot, 1820-1833* (Indiana Historical Society Publications, Vol. XV, No. 3, 1948).

Birkbeck, Morris, *Notes on a Journey through France . . . in July, August and September, 1814* (William Philipps, 1814).

—— *Notes on a Journey in America, from the Coast of Virginia to the Territory of Illinois. With proposals for the establishment of a colony of English*, 4th edn. (James Ridgway, 1818).

—— *Letters from Illinois*, 2nd edn. (Taylor and Hessey, 1818).

Birbeck, Morris, *Extracts from a Supplementary Letter from the Illinois; an Address to British Emigrants; and a Reply to the Remarks of William Cobbett Esq.* (James Ridgway, 1819).

Blaney, W. N., 'An Excursion through the United States and Canada', printed in Lindley, Harlow, ed., *Indiana as Seen by Early Travelers* (Indiana Historical Collections, Vol. III, 1916).

Blatchly, C., *An Essay on Common Wealths*, 1822[?].

Boewe, C., *Prairie Albion* (Southern Illinois University Press, 1962).

Bole, J. A., *The Harmony Society: A Chapter in German-American Cultural History* (Philadelphia, 1904).

British and Foreign School Society, *Report* (1815).

Brown, J., *Remarks on the plans and publications of Robert Owen Esq., of New Lanark* (1817).

Brown, Paul, *Twelve Months in New Harmony* (Reprinted by Porcupine Press Inc., 1972).

Brownson, Orestes, *The Convert: or Leaves from My Experience* (Edward Dunigan & Bros., 1853).

Buchanan, B., *James Buchanan and his descendants* (Printed for private circulation, 1923).

Butt, J., ed., *Robert Owen. Prince of Cotton Spinners* (David and Charles, 1971).

Chaloner, W. H., 'Robert Owen, Peter Drinkwater, and the early factory system', in *Bulletin of the John Rylands Library*, No. 37 (Sept. 1954).

Checkland, S. G., *Scottish Banking: A History. 1695-1973* (Collins, 1975).

Chinard, Gilbert, *Volney et l'Amérique* (Johns Hopkins Univ. Press, 1923).

Cobbett, William, *A Year's Residence in the United States of America* (1819).

Cole, G. D. H., *The Life of Robert Owen*, 2nd edn. (Macmillan, 1930).

Coleman D. C., *Courtauld's: An Economic and Social History* (Clarendon Press, 1969).

Collot, G. H. V., *A Journey in North America* (Paris, 1826).

Combe, Abram, *The Sphere of Joint Stock Companies* (1825).

Courtauld, George, *Address to those who may be disposed to remove to the United States of America. On the advantages of Equitable Associations of capital and labour* ... (1820).

Courtauld, S. L., *The Huguenot Family of Courtauld* (Privately printed, 1966).

Cyclopaedia of Religious Denominations (J. J. Griffin, 1853).

Dejung, E., and others, eds., *Sämtliche Briefe. Herausgegeben vom Pestalozzianum und von der Zentralbibliothek in Zurich* (1946–).

Dictionary of American Biography.

Dictionary of National Biography.

Drinnon, R., *White Savage: The Case of John Dunn Hunter* (Schocken Books, 1972).

Drummond, A. L., *German Protestantism since Luther* (Epworth Press, 1951).

Duclos, V., 'Diary and Recollections', in Lindley, H., ed., *Indiana as Seen by Early Travelers* (Indiana Historical Coll., Vol. III, 1916).

Duss, J. A., *The Harmonists: A Personal History* (Harrisburg, 1943).

Eckhardt, C. M., *Fanny Wright: Rebel in America* (Harvard UP, 1984).

Elliott, J. M., ed., *To Holland and to New Harmony: Robert Dale Owen's Travel Journal. 1825-1826* (Indiana Historical Society Publications, Vol. 23, No. 4).

Engels, F., *Socialism: Utopian and Scientific* (Allen and Unwin, 1920).

Erickson, C., ed., *Emigration from Europe. 1814-1914* (Adam and Charles Black, 1976).

Fauchier-Mangan, A., *Les petites cours d'Allemagne aux dix-huitième siècle* (Flammarion, 1947).

Ferrall, Simon, *A Ramble of Six Thousand Miles Through the United States of America* (London, 1832).

Fisher, G. P., *Life of Benjamin Silliman. M.D. LL.D.* (Sampson, Low, Son and Marston, 1866).

Fleming, G. A., *A Day at New Lanark* (1839).

Fletcher, Mrs E., *Autobiography of Mrs Fletcher of Edinburgh. Compiled and arranged by the survivors of her family* (Private circulation, 1874).

Flower, G., *History of the English Settlement in Edwards County, Illinois* (Chicago Historical Society, 1882).

Fordham, E. P., *Personal Narrative of Travels in Virginia, Maryland ... etc.* (Cleveland, 1906).

Gilbert, A., *Memoir of Frances Wright: The Pioneer Woman in the cause of human rights* (Cincinnati, Published for the author, 1855).

Gil Novales, A., *William Maclure in Spain* (Iniciativas de Cultura, 1981).

Gilpin, C., ed., *Life of William Allen, with Selections from his correspondence* (London, 1846).

Gollin, G. L., *Moravians in Two Worlds* (Columbia Univ. Press, 1967).

Grant, J., *Portraits of Public Characters (Robert Owen)* (Saunders and Otley, 1841).

Griscom, John, *A Year in Europe* (Collins, 1823).

Griscom, J. H., *Memoir of John Griscom* (Robert Carter, 1859).

Guillois, A., *La Salon de Mme Helvétius. Cabanis et les Idéologues* (Paris, 1896).

Gusdorf, G., *Les Sciences humaines et la Pensée occidentale: La Conscience révolutionnaire: Les Idéologues* (Payot, 1978).

Gutek, G. L., *Joseph Neef: the Americanisation of Pestalozzianism* (Univ. of Ala. Press, 1978).

Hamy, E. T., *Les voyages du naturaliste Charles Alexandre Lesueur dans l'Amérique du nord. 1815-1837* (Société des Américanistes de Paris, 1904).

Hansard (New Series, Volume 11).

Hardy, J. D., Jensen, J. H., and Wolfe, M., *The Maclure Collection of French Revolutionary Materials* (Univ. of Pa. Press, 1966).

Harrison, J. F. C., *Robert Owen and the Owenites in Britain and America* (Routledge and Kegan Paul, 1969).

Hebert, W., 'A Visit to the Colony of Harmony, in Indiana, in the United States of America', printed in Lindley, *Indiana as Seen by Early Travelers* (Indiana Historical Coll., Vol. III, 1916).

Heineman, H., *Mrs Trollope: The triumphant feminine in the 19th century* (Ohio UP, 1979).

Hendrickson, W. B., *David Dale Owen: Pioneeer Geologist of the Middle West* (Indiana Historical Coll., Vol. 28, 1943).

Hiatt, J. W., ed., *Diary of William Owen from November 10, 1824 to April 20, 1825* (Indiana Historical Society Publications, Vol. IV, 1906).

Holyoake, G. J., *Life and Last Days of Robert Owen of New Lanark ...* (London, 1859).

Holyoake, G. J., *Sixty Years of an Agitator's Life* (T. Fisher Unwin, 1893).

Hopple, D., 'New Harmony and the 1820 Census'.

Hulme, T., 'Journal of a Tour in the Western Countries of America', Printed in Lindley, ed., *Indiana as Seen by Early Travelers*.

Imlay, G., *A Topographical Description of the Western Territory of North America* (1792).

Jenkins, E., *The Shadow and the Light: A defence of D. D. Home, The Medium* (Hamish Hamilton, 1982).

Knox, R. A., *Enthusiasm* (Clarendon Press, 1950).

Latrobe, B. H., *The Virginia Journals of Benjamin Henry Latrobe. 1795-1798* (Yale UP, 1977).

Leibbrandt, G., *Die Auswanderung aus Schwaben nach Russland. 1816-1823* (Stuttgart, 1926).

Leopold, R., *Robert Dale Owen: A Biography* (Harvard UP, 1940).

Lindley, H., ed., *Indiana as Seen by Early Travelers* (Indiana Historical Coll., Vol. III, 1916).

Lockwood, G., *The New Harmony Movement* (D. Appleton, 1905).

Lyell, C., *A Second Visit to the United States of America* (John Murray, 1849).

Maclure, W., *Opinions on Various Subjects, Dedicated to the Industrious Producers* (New Harmony, 1831).

—— *Observations on the Geology of the United States, Explanatory of a Geological Map* (American Philosophical Society, 1809).

Macnab, H. G., *The New Views of Mr Owen of Lanark impartially examined, as rational Means of ultimately promoting the productive Industry, Comfort, Moral Improvement, and Happiness of the Labouring Classes of Society ... also Observations on the New Lanark School...* (London, 1819).

Marshall, Mrs J., ed., *The Life and Letters of Mary Wollstonecraft Shelley* (R. Bentley and Son, 1889).

Melish, J., *Travels in the United States of America in the years 1806, 7, 9, 10 and 11* (Belfast, 1818).

Merrill, G. P., *The First 100 Years of American Geology* (Yale UP, 1924).

M'Gavin, W., *The fundamental principles of the New Lanark System exposed* (Glasgow, 1824).

Morton, S. G., *Memoir of William Maclure* (American Journal of Science, Vol. XLVII, 1844).

Murray, D., *Memoirs of the old College of Glasgow* (Glasgow UP, 1927).

Noyes, J. H., *History of American Socialism* (Lippincott, 1870).

Ogg, F. A., *The Old North West* (Yale UP, 1919).

Owen, Robert, Note: Only those works referred to in the text are listed here; some of the titles have been abbreviated. For a comprehensive bibliography of works by and about Owen see Harrison, J. F. C., *Robert Owen and the Owenites in Britain and America* (Routledge and Kegan Paul, 1969).

—— *A Statement Regarding the New Lanark Establishment* (John Moir, Edinburgh, 1812).

—— *A New View of Society: or, Essays on the Principle of the Formation of Human Character, and the Application of the Principle to Practice* (Everyman's series, 1927).

—— *An Address delivered to the Inhabitants of New Lanark on January 1, 1816, at the opening of the Institution for the Formation of Human Character*, printed in Volume 1A of the *Life* (see below).

—— *Mr Owen's Proposed arrangement for the Distressed Working Classes shown to be consistent with sound principles of Political Economy in three letters addressed to David Ricardo. M.P.* (Longman, Hurst, Rees, Orme and Brown, 1819).

—— *Report of the Proceedings at the several Meetings held in Dublin by Robert Owen Esq. on the 18th March...* (Dublin, 1823).

—— *Discourses on a New System of Society as delivered in the Hall of Representatives in the presence of the President, the President elect, Members of Congress etc....* (1825).

—— *Oration containing a Declaration of Mental Independence delivered at New Harmony, Indiana* (New Harmony, 1826).

—— *Address delivered by Robert Owen at a Public Meeting at the Franklin Institute in Philadelphia... June 25th 1827* (Philadelphia, 1827).

—— *Robert Owen's opening speech, and his Reply to the Revd. Alex. Campbell... also Mr Owen's Memorial to the Republic of Mexico ... and a Narrative of the Proceedings* (Cincinnati, 1829).

—— *The Book of the New Moral World...* (London, 1836).

—— *The New Existence of Man upon the Earth...* (London, Parts 1–5, 1854; 6–8, 1855).

—— *Life of Robert Owen. Written by Himself. With Selections from His Writings and Correspondence.* Vol. I. (Effingham Wilson, 1857).

—— *A Supplementary Appendix to the First Volume of the Life of Robert Owen, Containing a Series of Reports, Addresses, Memorials, and other Documents Referred to In That Volume*, Vol. 1A (1858).

Owen, Robert Dale, Note: Only the works mentioned in the text are listed here. A comprehensive bibliography will be found in Richard Leopold's *Robert Dale Owen: A Biography* (Harvard UP, 1940).

—— *An Outline of the System of Education at New Lanark* (Glasgow, 1824).

—— *Moral Physiology: or, a Brief and Plain Treatise on the Population Question* (New York, 1830).

—— *Pocohontas: A Historical Drama in Five Acts: with an Introductory Essay and Notes by a Citizen of the West* (New York, 1837).

—— *Footfalls on the Boundary of Another World* (Philadelphia, 1860).

—— *The Wrong of Slavery, the Right of Emancipation and the future of the African Race in the United States* (Philadelphia, 1864).

—— *The Debatable Land between This World and The Next* (New York, 1872).

—— *Threading My Way: Twenty Seven Years of Autobiography* (Trubner & Co., 1874).

Packard, F. A., *The Life of Robert Owen* (Philadelphia, 1866).

Parkman, F., *France and England in North America. La Salle and the Discovery of the Great West* (Little, Brown, 1881).

Parliamentary Papers, 'Report of the Select Committee on the State of Children employed in the Manufactories of the United Kingdom', Vol. III (1816).

—— 'Report of the Select Committee on the Employment of the Poor in Ireland', Vol. VI (1823).

—— 'Report of the Select Committee on Artizans and Machinery', Vol. V (1824).

—— 'Factories Enquiry Commission. First Report of the Central Board on the Employment of Children' (1833).

Payne-Gaposchkin, C., 'The Nashoba Plan' in *Harvard Library Bulletin*. Vol. 23 (1975).

Pears, T. C., *New Harmony, an Adventure in Happiness: The Papers of Thomas and Sarah Pears* (Indiana Historical Society Publications, Vol. XI, 1933).

Pelham, W., 'Letters of William Pelham, written in 1825 and 1826', in Lindley, ed., *Indiana as Seen by Early Travelers* (Indiana Historical Coll., Vol. III, 1916).

Perkins, A., and Wolfson, T., *Frances Wright. Free Enquirer: Study of a Temperament* (Reprinted by Porcupine Press Inc., 1972).

Phillips, M. E., 'The Academy of Natural Sciences of Philadelphia'. In *Transactions of the American Philosophical Society*, Vol. 43, Part 1.

Pinson, K. S., *Pietism as a factor in the rise of German Nationalism* (Columbia UP, 1924).

Podmore, F., *Robert Owen: A Biography* (George Allen and Unwin, 1923).

Pollard, S., *The Genesis of Modern Management* (Edward Arnold, 1965).

Pollard, S., and Salt, J., eds., *Robert Owen: Prophet of the Poor: essays in honour of the two hundredth anniversary of his birth* (Macmillan, 1971).

Robertson, A. J., 'Robert Owen and the Campbell Debt. 1810–1822'. In *Business History*, Vol. 11, no. 1 (1969).

Rohrbough, M. J., *The Trans-Appalachian Frontier* (OUP, 1978).

Römer, C., *Kirchlicher Geschichte Württembergs* (Verlag der Evangelischen Bücherstiftung, 1865).

Rondthaler, E., *Life of John Heckewelder* (Philadelphia, 1847).

Royal Lancastrian Institute for the Education of the Poor, 'Report of the Committee', 1812.

Schneck [or Schnack], J., and Owen, R., *The History of New Harmony* (New Harmony, 1890).

Sealsfield, C., *The Americans as They Are* (London, 1828).

Shapiro, S., *Capital and the Cotton Industry in the Industrial Revolution* (Cornell UP, 1967).

Sherman, J., *Memoir of William Allen. F.R.S.* (Gilpin, 1851).

Smith, M. B., *Fifty Years of Washington Society* (T. Fisher Unwin, 1906).

Smout, T. C., *A History of the Scottish People. 1560-1830* (Collins, 1969).

Snedeker, C. D., *The Diaries of Donald Macdonald. 1824-1826* (Indiana Historical Society Publications, Vol. XIV, 1942).

—— *The Town of the Fearless* (Doubleday, Doran & Co. 1931).

Spencean Philanthropist, A. [Thomas Evans], *Christian Policy in Full Practice among the People of Harmony* ... (London, 1818).

Southey, R., *Journal of a Tour in Scotland* (John Murray, 1929).

Sprengel, M. C., ed., *Reisejournal von Bethlehem in Pennsylvanien, nach dem Posten St. Vincent am Wabashfluss* [Heckewelder's Journal] (1794).

Stewart, G., *Curiosities of Glasgow Citizenship* (James Maclehose, 1881).

Stewart, W. A. C., and McCann J., *The Educational Innovators. 1750-1880* (Macmillan, 1967).

Stirling, A. M. W., *Letter Book of Lady Elizabeth Spencer Stanhope* (John Lane, 1913).

Taylor, B., *Eve and the New Jerusalem* (Virago, 1983).

Thomas, D., 'Travels through the Western Country in the Summer of 1816' in Lindley, ed., *Indiana as Seen by Early Travelers*.

Thompson, E. P., *The Making of the English Working Class* (Gollancz, 1965).

Thomson, G. S., *A Pioneer Family* [the Birkbecks] (Cape, 1953).

Thwaites, R. G., *Early Western Travels. 1748-1846* (The Arthur H. Clark Co., 1905).

Trollope, Mrs F., *Domestic Manners of the Americans* (Whitaker, Treacher, and Co., 1832).

Trollope, F. E., *Frances Trollope: Her Life and Literary Work* (R. Bentley and Sons, 1895).

Unwin, G., *Samuel Oldknow and the Awkwrights* (Manchester UP, 1924).

Vail, R. W. G., 'The American Sketchbooks of a French Naturalist 1816-1837', in *Proceedings of the American Antiquarian Society*, New Series, Vol. 48 (1938).

Volney, C. F., *View of the Climate and Soil of the United States* (J. Johnson, 1804).

Waller, A., and Glover, G., eds., *The Collected Works of William Hazlitt* (Dent, 1902).

Washburn, E. G., *Sketch of Edward Coles* (Chicago Historical Society, 1882).

Waterman, W. R., *Frances Wright* (Columbia UP, 1924).

Weiss, H., and Ziegler, G., *Thomas Say: Early American Naturalist* (Charles C. Thomas, 1931).

White, M. D., ed., *A Sketch of Chester Harding, Artist* (Boston, 1890).

Williams, A., *The Harmony Society, at Economy, Pennsylvania* (1866).

Williams, S., ed., *Journal of Washington Irving 1823-1824* (Harvard UP, 1931).

Wilson, W. E., *The Angel and the Serpent: The Story of New Harmony* (Indiana University Press, 1964).

Winsor, J., *The Westward Movement* (Houghton, Mifflin, 1897).

Woods, J., 'Two years' Residence in the Settlement on the English Prairie', in *Early Western Travels*, Vol. X.

Wright, Frances afterwards called d'Arusmont, *Altdorf, a Tragedy* (M. Carey & Son, Philadelphia, 1819).

—— *Views of Society and manners in America . . .* (Longman, Hurst, Rees, Orme and Brown, 1821).

—— *A Few Days in Athens* (Longman & Co., 1822).

—— *Biography, notes and political letters of Frances Wright D'Arusmont* (J. Mylls, Dundee, 1844).

—— *England the Civilizer.*

UNPUBLISHED SOURCES

United States

Source	Location
Branigin–Owen Papers	New Harmony, Indiana, Workingmen's Institute
Correspondence of William Maclure and Marie Duclos Fretageot	Ibid.
Maclure's Journals	Ibid.
Hodge–Fretageot Papers	Ibid.
Miscellaneous Papers	Ibid.
Frances Wright Collection	Houghton Library, Harvard
Garnett–Pertz Correspondence	Ibid.
Bonaventure Lafayette Collection	University of Chicago Library
Frances Wright Collection	Manuscript Division, Library of Congress
Madison Papers	Ibid.
Jefferson Papers	Ibid.
Trist Papers	Ibid.
Letters of S. G. Morton	American Philosophical Society
Letters of American scientists to Charles Lucien Buonaparte	Ibid.
Papers concerning Maclure, Lesueur, Say, and Phiquepal	Academy of Natural Sciences, Philadelphia
Robert Dale Owen's Journal for 1824	Purdue University, Indiana
Cuba Papers	Columbia University, New York
Frances Wright Collection	Ibid.

Britain

Source	Location
Place Papers	British Library
Bentham Papers	Ibid.
Liverpool Papers	Ibid.
Lieven Papers	Ibid.
Bentham Papers	University College, University of London
Sidmouth Papers	Devon County Record Office
Campbell of Jura Muniments	HM Register House, Edinburgh
Lanark Twist Co. v. *Edmonston*	Ibid.
Register of the Presbytery of Lanark	Ibid.
Letters of David Dale	Ibid.

Britain

Source	Location
R. Humphreys v. *Robert Owen*	Court of Session Papers, Signet Library, Edinburgh
John Marshall's Tour Book	Brotherton Library, Leeds
Galpin Correspondence	National Library of Wales
Robert Owen Papers	Co-operative Union, Manchester
Robert Owen Papers	Robert Owen Memorial Museum, Newtown, Wales
Correspondence and diary of William Allen	Society of Friends' Library, London
William Godwin's Diary: Abinger Papers	Bodleian Library, Oxford
Robert Owen Papers	Nuffield College Library, Oxford
Owen–Fellenberg correspondence	Burgerbibliothek, Bern, Switzerland

INDEX